MAKE A WAY SOMEHOW

The John Ben Snow Prize

This prize is given annually by the Press for an original manuscript of non-fiction dealing with some aspect of New York State.

1978   *Warrior in Two Camps*
        William H. Armstrong

1979   *Black Education in New York State*
        Carleton Mabee

1980   *Landmarks of Otsego County*
        Diantha Dow Schull

1981   *Joseph Brant, 1743–1807*
        Isabel Thompson Kelsay

1982   *Upstate Travels*
        Roger Haydon

1983   *Gustav Stickley, the Craftsman*
        Mary Ann Smith

1984   *Images of Rural Life*
        DeWitt Historical Society of Tompkins County

        Marietta Holley
        Kate H. Winter

1985   *Upstate Literature*
        Frank Bergmann, editor et al.

1986   *Proud Patriot*
        Don R. Gerlach

1987   *Old-Time Music Makers of New York State*
        Simon J. Bronner

1988   No prize given

1989   *Landmarks of Oswego County*
        Judith Wellman

1990   *Clear Pond*
        Roger Mitchell

1991   *Women's Humor in the Age of Gentility*
        Linda A. Morris

1992   *Make a Way Somehow*
        Kathryn Grover

Make a Way Somehow

*African-American Life in
A Northern Community
1790–1965*

Kathryn Grover

SYRACUSE UNIVERSITY PRESS

Research for this book was funded by the New York State Council on the Arts, the Geneva Historical Society, and the Strong Museum.

This book is published with the assistance of a grant from the John Ben Snow Foundation.

The paper used in this publication meets the minimum requirements of American National Standard for Information Sciences—Permanence of Paper for Printed Library Materials, ANSI Z39.48-1984. ∞™

Library of Congress Cataloging-in-Publication Data

Grover, Kathryn, 1953–
    Make a way somehow : African-American life in a northern
community, 1790–1965 / Kathryn Grover. — 1st ed.
        p.   cm.
    Includes bibliographical references and index.
    ISBN 0-8156-2626-6 (cloth). — ISBN 0-8156-2627-4
    1. Afro-Americans—New York (State)—Geneva—History.   2. Geneva
(N.Y.)—Race relations.   I. Title.
F129.G3G76   1994
974.7'86—dc20   94-9827

Manufactured in the United States of America

For my parents,
who taught me to look at the other side.

KATHRYN GROVER is an independent researcher, writer, and editor in American history. She lives in New Bedford, Massachusetts.

Contents

Figures

Acknowledgments

This book tries to describe the life and experience of a group of people of African descent, most of them long passed and some of them still living. For every person I feel I have come to know in Geneva in the course of researching and writing it, there are hundreds I have not. This book offers an interpretation of only part of the experience of those I did come to know, the part that has made it into the historical record, the part that could, or would, be talked about.

Acknowledgments are never sufficient thanks for anyone, and I cannot imagine ever knowing how to thank the people who made this work possible in different ways. I would not have been brought to the subject were it not for Dorothy Ebersole, former education director, and Michael F. Wajda, former executive director, of the Geneva Historical Society. I will always be grateful to Dorothy for creating the connection between me and the society and for her constant encouragement. Michael's faith in me helped me believe that I could make something of the topic. His own belief in the project and his fund-raising and community skills developed the support we needed to create an exhibition on Geneva's African Americans and a short illustrated catalog to accompany it.

The research itself was funded by the New York State Council on the Arts, the Geneva Historical Society, and the Strong Museum, whose administration granted me a six-month research leave in 1989 and 1990. I am grateful also to the Strong for allowing me time after I returned to work to complete the manuscript and begin to revise it.

Librarians and archivists at these institutions and others were most helpful, particularly after I ceased to be affiliated with one. I must thank Carol Sandler and Carolyn Bloch at the Strong Museum, Scarlett Stevens at the Episcopal Diocese in Rochester, Charlotte Hedje at Hobart and William Smith Colleges, Stefan Bielinski at the New York State Museum, Steven Walker at the Ontario County Records Center and Archives, Andy Simons at the Amistad Research Center, Gould Coleman at Cornell University's Olin Library, Karl Kabelac at the University of Rochester's Department of Rare Books and Special Collections, and, finally, Eva Sirken, formerly at the University of Rochester Library, whose finding skills are marvelous. Also, Dr. Lois Porter of the New York State Agricultural Child Care Program, Craig Williams at the New York State Museum, Wilma Townsend at Ontario County Historical Society, Georgia Barnhill at American Antiquarian Society, Matt Mulcahy at the Smithsonian Institution's National Museum of American History, Kay Ambry at the Cornell Migrant Program in Alton, New York, Dr. Jim Kimball at the State University of New York at Geneseo, and, particularly, Marjory Allen Perez, Wayne County historian, provided invaluable help.

Many institutions supplied critical information and documents to the research—Albany Institute of History and Art; Amistad Research Center, Tulane University; Church of St. Luke and St. Simon Cyrene, Rochester; Dewitt Historical Society, Ithaca; First Baptist Church, Geneva; Geneva Free Library; George Arents Research Library, Syracuse University; Hobart and William Smith Colleges; Lavery Library, St. John Fisher College, Rochester; New York State Archives; Tioga County Historical Society; Trinity Episcopal Church, Geneva; University of Rochester Library; and Waterloo Historical Society. Thanks also to Mr. and Mrs. H. Merrill Roenke for permitting me access to the documents from the VanTuyl kidnapping of 1857.

I feel fortunate to have friends to thank for their unfailing assistance and generosity, in particular Judy Emerson and Steve Mickle. Because I am uncomfortable with the combination of statistics and computers, they set up and taught me to use a database program to record the presence of and details about individual African Americans in Geneva. I could not have done the research without the database, or without their support in countless other practical and spiritual respects. Steve's own remarkable and unique use of statistics never fails to amaze many. Eleanore Clise, Megan Ferrara, and Steve O'Malley at the Geneva Historical Society constantly took time to help me out amid all their other work. Steve and Megan mailed me Geneva newspaper clippings of startling irrelevance just to make me laugh, and I appreciate more than I can say the time we spent

talking in Geneva bars. Jack Finzar, a volunteer at Geneva Historical Society, traced post–1925 families through city directories and
helped compile census statistics; he also sang and taped the songs
Art Kenney taught him years ago and interviewed one of the barbershop singers he and Art harmonized with. The interest of these
particular Genevans in their town is so complete as to include virtually everything that ever happened there, everyone who ever
lived there. Because they love the place they live in without qualification, they and people like them make it possible to write genuine
community history, and they make work like mine more real, more
pleasurable, and more meaningful. Their good humor and kindness
are impossible to repay.

I want also to thank Oksana Carpenter and Jean Warner, on
staff at the Strong Museum, for helping me in critical ways. Strong
Museum photographer Don Strand not only did all the reproduction
photography for this book and the exhibition, but he also lugged
and set up his equipment and copy stand at cold and remote loca-
tions to shoot pages from deed books and censuses, which he could
not have found very exciting. Still, his work is wonderful, and his
outlook often rescued me from despair. And I am grateful to Nancy
Russell at Geneva High School, who allowed me to use two of her
students, Yvette Collins and Chris Singleton, to record data from the
manuscript censuses; it was then that I began to appreciate the complexities of our current efforts to incorporate this research into the
public school curricula.

Finally, my greatest debt is to the African-American people of
Geneva, New York. I cannot begin to characterize the depth of their
vitality, commitment, and good faith. Even people whom I never
had time to interview, such as Lucile Mallard, were inestimably kind
to me. Despite the fact that I have been interviewing people almost
all of my life, it has never been easy for me, and interviewing people
whose experience is so different from my own was especially hard. I
will always be grateful for the candor, thoughtfulness, and gracious-
ness of those who permitted me to talk to them, especially Dorothy
Cooke, Charles Kenney, Trudy Spencer, John Kenney, Rosa Blue,
Robby Robinson, Jim and Beth Henderson, and Frances Craven,
who helped me repeatedly despite her serious illness. They were
circumspect, reflective, sincere, and affecting, and I cannot express
what their help has meant to me. Apart from that, the present-day
Kenneys and the past Whitakers were, for me, inspiring examples of
family love, love of an extent and character I had never really seen

before. I have always been theoretically conscious of the fact that I cannot truly know anyone through historical research, but the concrete and mysterious wonder of these families made this idea real for me and heightened my feelings of respect for, and humility toward, Geneva's long-vanished African-American people. This respect marks a boundary between them and me that no amount of historical effort could remove. And this book, in a sense, is as much about what we don't know as it is about what we do. That we know so little about Harriet Bias or Margaret Douglass or Sam Thornton enhances the enigma of Art Kenney, an enigma this book tries to make sensible even as it fails to comprehend it fully.

Kathryn Grover

New Bedford, Massachusetts
January 1994

MAKE A WAY SOMEHOW

Prologue

On 16 March 1871, the Ontario Debating Club took the stage at Association Hall in Geneva, New York, for a public debate against a group of men from nearby Penn Yan. The auditorium, according to the local *Geneva Gazette*, was "crowded with auditors, including those of both races and sexes," who had come to hear the clubs argue the question "that the works of nature are more pleasing to the human eye than the works of art."[1]

The Ontario Debating Club was an African-American men's club, which accounts for the *Gazette's* particular characterization of the audience assembled for the March event. Since January, these men had gathered weekly for practice debates at Geneva's west branch district school on High Street, a segregated institution in the middle of a largely segregated neighborhood (fig. 1). They each paid fifty-two cents a week in dues; each week, fifteen cents of the total went to one of their members, the chairmaker and porter Albert E. Arnold, who opened the schoolhouse and furnished lamps for the meetings. Sometimes, the men asked their wives and other African-American women to judge their "evening discussions" on such assertions as "the condition of the colored man is no better than it was previous to the war," "the African has suffered more wrongs at the hands of the white man than the indian," and "colored schools are a disgrace to all concerned in them."

But when the debaters met in Association Hall, their judges were white men, and the newspaper shows that they argued a different and far less volatile question. It was one thing to elect to debate the merits of segregated schools in the confines of their

1

1. The west branch district school on High Street, Geneva, New York, about 1870. Built in 1853 as one of three district schools, the High Street school stood on a lot purchased from the African-American porter Roswell Jeffrey. It served a largely African-American neighborhood and remained segregated until 1873. *Courtesy Geneva Historical Society.*

principal neighborhood. It was another to argue the question before an audience at Association Hall. For in the early 1870s, African Americans were scarcely 3 percent of Geneva's population, and the fact of segregated schools was the sorest point of their postwar lives in the village. They had struggled and failed to find a place for black youth (then even less than 3 percent of the local school population) in the Classical and Union School, the only local equivalent of a high school. Local school district officials repeatedly turned a deaf ear to African-American pleas that new constitutional amendments invalidating racial discrimination be respected. They continued instead to heed a decades-old state law permitting segregated schools "where the presence of colored children is offensive to a majority of the people in the district."[2]

Because whites were the overwhelming majority in Geneva, they must also have composed most of the audience at Association Hall on that March evening. The judges included Charles D. Vail, principal of the Classical and Union School, and Edgar Parker, the editor of the *Gazette,* which bitterly opposed school integration. Before such an assemblage, Geneva's African Americans clearly judged that to debate the relative merits of nature and art would be more politic than to air the "disgrace" that colored schools represented. As their numbers dwindled and their opportunities narrowed after the Civil War, such a public display of their discontent was not advised.

Yet, in the shelter of the High Street School, African-American men could argue far less remote questions. To these men, persistent discrimination and inequity made it hardly questionable that blacks suffered greater harm at the hands of whites than did Indians. And the struggle to integrate village schools cast new and real doubt on the notion that the war had improved the colored man's situation. These were not hypothetical issues argued only on the basis of accepted fact and ethical principles. To Geneva's African Americans, they were real, local conflicts.

But they were conflicts whose intensity was muted, both by official neglect and by the conscious efforts of Geneva's African Americans to pick carefully the sites at which such issues would be aired or, sometimes, to skirt them altogether. Before the Civil War, when African Americans approached 10 percent of the village's total population and reform activity flooded the region, Geneva's blacks behaved differently. They organized their own school and at least three churches. They repeatedly played host to early August emancipation day celebrations attended by thousands throughout the region. They were delegates to national and state colored people's conventions, suffrage association meetings, and Liberty party conclaves. They raised money to support antislavery lecturers and the area's African-American newspapers. Their activism was so notable that, in 1849, the usually vitriolic Samuel Ringgold Ward, an African-American clergyman and editor of the Syracuse newspaper *Impartial Citizen,* wrote, "I know of no community of colored persons, in a more rapid and healthy state of improvement than those of Geneva."[3]

Still, the larger community in which these people then lived was patently inhospitable. In the same year that Ward made his visit, African-American activist Henry Bibb pronounced Geneva "the most aristocratic, pro-slavery hole I have visited" on his tour of Upstate towns with black populations.[4] Indeed, antislavery and suffrage work was a small pocket of reform in a village whose broader sentiments opposed racial equality. And after the disheartening 1850s,

the number of African Americans in Geneva declined steadily; transience, always a fact of their collective existence, became more visible as the population slipped away. Political activity among those
who remained fell slowly into decades-long quiescence.

Such men as Richard Harrison and James Bias, both Ontario Debating Club members in 1871, were among perhaps hundreds of African Americans who came to Geneva and left it within weeks,
months, or years as the face of local opportunity and opinion
showed its distinct features. Harrison is recorded as a Genevan in
only one census. And Bias, who married Albert Arnold's daughter
Harriet, left his family and the village behind after 1876. Although
population mobility may have been no more characteristic of blacks
than of whites in the same working-class circumstances, Geneva's
white population grew steadily until the 1930s. Yet the natural increase of the settled African-American population was never sufficient to offset the numerical, social, and psychic losses of continual
outmigration.[5]

Particularly in view of the ever-smaller share of village population they occupied, the persistence of some African-American families is no less remarkable than the transience of a great many others.
An African-American population did take root in Geneva; it did, for
a time, increase; it did foster an intricate and extensive network of
kin throughout central and western New York that compensated for
the small numbers and the constricted social and economic lives of
African Americans who lived and worked in Geneva itself. The Ontario Debating Club also included such men as John Bland, whose
ancestors were brought as slaves to Geneva around 1800 and whose
grandfather and uncle were the largest African-American property
owners in the village. Members of the Bland family remained in Geneva through the 1920s. The Arnold family lived in the village from
about 1840 to 1937. And the daughters of club member Benjamin
Franklin Cleggett, a fashionable barber who came to Geneva from
Rochester in the 1850s, lived in their family home on William Street
until the last of them died in 1960.

Such persistence suggests that Geneva, even if it was long and
accurately perceived to be an "artistocratic, pro-slavery hole," was
manageable for some African Americans. Overt discrimination was
ever present, and whites limited black access to almost every form of
opportunity—occupational skill and achievement, property, capital,
education. Yet even as the balance of power rested soundly with the
white majority, the balance of having to know the ways of the ma-

jority shifted principally to African Americans and other minorities. For blacks in particular, the inculcation and management of a stock of knowledge about whites became a practical and necessary life skill. African Americans knew how white Geneva worked, how whites typified—indeed, constructed—them. They accumulated and refined this knowledge, guarded its distribution carefully, revealed it in highly selective ways, and used it to carve a reasonably secure, if not especially or always comfortable, spot for themselves in local society. The fact that overt racial conflict was rare in Geneva just as likely suggests how sophisticated their understanding of local society was as it does their supposed passive accommodation to it.

They could develop, articulate, and use this body of understandings largely because intimate knowledge of the African-American people in their midst was precisely what whites lacked. "The Free Colored People of the United States occupy an unfortunate and exceptional position," the Unitarian clergyman James Freeman Clarke wrote in the *Christian Examiner* in 1859. "They stand among us, yet not of us. We know less of them than we know of the people of France and Italy."[6] With both wonder and dismay, countless African-American lecturers and activists, from Frederick Douglass to Mary Church Terrell, remarked upon this dumbfounding ignorance, a feature of racial relations expressed repeatedly in the tone and tendency of the accounts white Genevans left of African-American townspeople. Village newspapers rarely discussed local African-American life, and photographs recorded the presence and activities of African Americans almost as if by accident. They hold brooms and shovels in images of white stores and neighborhoods; they sit at the edges of photographs of white parades and white children; they hold the reins of the well-groomed horses of Geneva's elite (fig. 2). Multiple prints of some photographs of African-American Genevans sometimes carry entirely different names, suggesting that the identity even of more visible people was unclear to whites (fig. 3). "In many of our towns the number of colored people is much larger than most people living in those towns seemed to be aware of," the African-American clergyman Jermain Wesley Loguen wrote of the area around Syracuse in 1849. "Being wretchedly poor, and feeling themselves to be despised, they keep as much out of sight as they may."[7]

This invisibility and the lapse of knowledge associated with it obstruct modern-day analysis of African-Americans' past. Censuses scarcely take account of African Americans before 1850, when they

2. "Burton's Hotel, Exchange Street," about 1888–1894. The African-American porter at Burton's is not identified on the back of this stereoview. *Courtesy Geneva Historical Society.*

recorded the names of only heads of households: in 1840, 52 of the 311 African Americans in Geneva were householders, which means that only 17 percent of the total black population are known to us by name. After 1850, censuses chronically undercounted African Americans, and they cannot capture the extent of population turnover of African Americans moving from the East and South to the West, from farm to village, and from city to city in search of greater opportunity in other places.[8] It is therefore impossible even to speculate about how most African Americans who encountered Geneva perceived the village social system.

3. At least three prints of this image exist, each bearing a different identification. The print in the Geneva Historical Society's collection comes from the pages of an 1850s scrapbook and was identified on the reverse as Anthony Jupiter (1793–1872), "the old Negro janitor of Geneva Medical College." Two prints in the Hobart and William Smith colleges' archives are marked Martin Davis (1798 to c. 1865), who is in several other sources cited as the medical college's janitor; the other is marked "Sammy Dog-in-the Well," identified as Davis's assistant. *Courtesy Geneva Historical Society.*

The problem is compounded by African-American nomenclature, a particular legacy of slavery. Early records of African Americans typically record only first names: in Geneva, only one of the twenty-six slaves whom Virginians Gavin Lawson and John Nicholas registered with the Ontario County clerk in 1803 and 1804 was recorded with a surname. And the fact of enslavement prompted many to take several or wholly different names. Charles Peyton Lucas and Albert Arnold, both fugitive slaves, changed their names in flight before they settled in Geneva; and the reward notices that white slaveholders placed in newspapers sometimes warned that fugitives might use other names.[9]

Many others changed their names or took new ones upon being manumitted. In Geneva, only one African American may have borne the surname of his most recent owner. Frank Dorsey, recorded in the 1855 state census to be in the home of Daniel D. Chapin, was probably one of the forty slaves whom Daniel Dorsey brought from Maryland to Lyons, New York, just north of Geneva, in 1797; Chapin's wife was Daniel Dorsey's daughter. The surnames of all other African Americans freed in or around Geneva before 1820 were not shared by slaveholding families in the village or its environs, although such African-American surnames as Kenney, Lucas, Lee, and Bland were also the names of Virginia slaveowners to whom members of these families might once have belonged.[10]

Name changes are not problems for researchers only. They contributed to a psychic problem among African Americans themselves, an absence of rootedness that has formed a constant lament in African-American literature, an uneasy sense of amorphous ancestry that mitigated against one's ability to establish a sense of location in American culture and that enhanced one's feelings of marginality.

But marginality had an underside of peculiar advantage. The social position African Americans occupied, the condition Clarke perceived of being "among us, yet not of us," the sense that, as Richard Wright put it nearly a century later, "Negroes had never been allowed to catch the full spirit of Western civilization, that they lived somehow in it but not of it"[11]—was the source of both weakness and strength. Among whites, Frederick Douglass once alleged, it kept alive the sense that African Americans were "a characterless and purposeless people." Wright charged that "blacks were so *close* to the very civilization which sought to keep them out" that they could not help but share the "strivings" and crave the rewards it promised most people yet denied them.[12] Yet this proximity offered an opportunity for their close study of white power, and the seeming absence of character and purpose in their expression protected this study by making sustained observation possible. Photographs often capture this proximity as well as the marginality of blacks in local society. But marginality was the product of deliberate seclusion as well as of collective oversight. Most whites not only did not need or want to know blacks; they were systematically prevented from knowing them.[13] Blacks were not only kept at the edges of white society; they removed themselves from view. African Americans sought integration in school, factory, and church largely because it represented the only access to the promises that American society made to everyone. But when segregation became a means of control for whites and foreclosed opportunity for blacks, African Americans relied upon a set of attitudes, behaviors, and rules inaccessible to whites that offered the only avenue to security, the only means of control in a predominantly white world.

This book attempts to describe how African Americans understood the social, political, and economic system that Geneva presented, how they understood white views of the role that race played in controlling that system, and how they designed their lives with respect to these perceived realities. It uses the manuscripts, published works, deeds, wills, and genealogies of African Americans who lived in or around Geneva, black newspapers published from Boston to Rochester, and the published proceedings of African-American political meetings to analyze how African Americans managed the stereotypes that whites used both to distance themselves from and to structure their interaction with the racial minority.[14] For the modern period—when, ironically, traditional records are vastly less revealing—thirty interviews with African Americans who have considered Geneva home during at least part of their lives compose the primary data.

Sources written by whites have been used here to identify the "hot spots," for both blacks and whites, in the culture of the village and in American society generally. Without the Democrat-controlled *Geneva Gazette*, without its fervent hostility to integrated schools, without its occasional nod to the events that mattered to the village's black population, it would not be possible to sense how meaningful the question "that colored schools are a disgrace to all concerned in them" was to the Ontario Debating Club. The newspaper's tongue-in-cheek accounts of emancipation celebrations are often the only extant evidence that such events took place in Geneva, and its editors' commitment at least to the rudiments of journalism make it possible to appreciate how significant these celebrations must have been in the lives of the village's African Americans.

To some African Americans, the network of tradition and circumstance that Geneva presented seemed to be a "given reality," a structure whose "blinding objectivity" made it appear concrete, immovable, immutable.[15] Many who viewed the city in this way felt bound to reject it, to turn their backs on it, to leave it. But others— those who stayed—saw local society as less institutional, more personal, more fluid. To them, it was not a structure but a system. They worked around it, or they worked it around. Some accommodated themselves to it, particularly in the dismal decades between the Civil War and World War II when no northern town or city offered a comfortable place for African Americans. But before the Civil War, in its decade of aftermath, and after World War II, others saw Geneva as a system that could be influenced, changed in small ways, even loved. At these times, their numbers, their leadership, and their attitudes sometimes combined to press for more than small changes. This book is about those African Americans who came and stayed. And to the extent that it is possible, it looks at Geneva as they must have perceived it, that others might see the potential for knowing their own places more wholly.

Arrivals and Departures

Geneva sits on the northwest corner of Seneca Lake, the deepest of New York State's chain of Finger Lakes. It is 618 feet at its deepest point, and its surface has been known to freeze completely only four times since the area was settled. Seneca Lake is supposed to be the only inland body of water north of the Mason-Dixon Line that is open to navigation in all months of the year. When the Erie Canal system was viable, as it was for well more than a century, Seneca was the most trafficked lake in the state, not only because it is so deep but also because it is so long. It stretches thirty-six miles from the Ontario Plain at the north to within about twenty miles of the Susquehanna River, the natural route to the markets of Philadelphia and the Chesapeake Bay. The village also sat on the path of the two main state roads running west from Albany, what today are New York Route 5 and U.S. Route 20, and in the middle of what was once the nation's breadbasket, a long-fertile stretch of land that is still actively farmed (fig. 4).

Geneva's siting not only accounts for much of its later commercial and industrial prosperity; it also explains its population profile and its cultural attachment to the tidewater region. The village's developer was Charles Williamson, land sales agent for the Pulteney Associates, British investors who owned a large tract of land in the Genesee region. Blown off course on his trip to America, Williamson ended up in Baltimore and developed a network of acquaintance with wealthy men. On his trips to survey the area in 1792 and 1796, Williamson was taken with Seneca Lake and the bluff that rose along its northwestern edge. As the East Coast cities of New York,

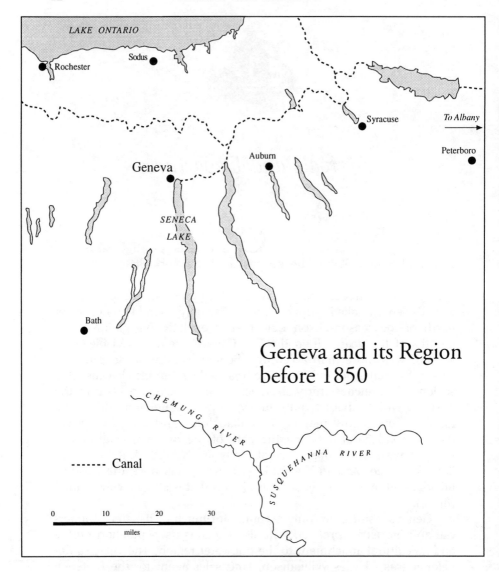

Geneva and its Region before 1850

Philadelphia, and Baltimore competed for commercial hegemony, Williamson and others viewed the Susquehanna River and Seneca Lake as the main route between the raw goods of western New York and the markets and finished products of Baltimore. Geneva, that part of Seneca Township that Williamson had designed and plotted in 1793, for a time served as headquarters for the land sales office of Pulteney Associates. Williamson set lot sizes and prices per acre specifically to attract those who would compose "a genteel society" and repeatedly sought to secure settlers from Maryland, Virginia, and Delaware.[1] Like other towns in which Williamson had a particular interest, such as Bath and Sodus, Geneva accordingly attracted a large number of southerners, a migration that colored the village's character immediately and permanently and made it a different kind of place than Auburn to the east or Canandaigua to the west, both of which more closely resembled New England in demographics and culture.

Most of Geneva's first African-American settlers were southern slaves brought to a northern climate in forced migrations from nearly exhausted plantation lands. Because Williamson encouraged southern slaveowners to graft the plantation system onto vast tracts of Genesee Country land, the nature of African-American work and life perhaps differed little, at least in its first decade, from what they had grown accustomed to in the South. But the North was a different place, politically and economically. Aside from the fact that the plantation order and the labor system that supported it were not feasible in the North, the natural rights philosophy that the successful Revolution seemed to validate affected northern ideas about race. By 1799, New York and other northern states had passed laws freeing enslaved African Americans either immediately or gradually. And in the next decade, the state incorporated a manumission society to encourage owners to release their slaves voluntarily, to protect these newly freed people, and to prevent their being kidnapped and sold back into slavery in places where such commerce remained legal. Indeed, until the 1830s, some whites and some blacks viewed an integrated society as not only possible but also desirable. Geneva's African-American population first began to thrive in this political climate, even as the sympathies of the community at large came to reject integration in any form.

1790–1820: Slaves and Early Freemen

Like other settlements in the Genesee Country, Geneva was settled first by people from the hill country of western New England

and eastern New York, the migration that streamed into the Mo-hawk Valley and beyond as soon as the Revolutionary campaigns against the indigenous Seneca Indians had removed the threat of hostility and competing claims to territory.[2] Geneva's first African-American settlers, two slaves who belonged to the Scottish-born physician Alexander Coventry, were part of this westward-moving group. One of them, Cuff, was also the first to bear a West African day name as his name; there were African-Americans with the sur-name Cuffe in Geneva into the twentieth century, and the names of such other black Genevans as James Suzey and Pompey Smash (also known as Henry Douglass) may be adaptations of other day names (fig. 5).[3]

The certain progenitors of the association between African Americans and the estate known as Rose Hill on the northeastern shore of Seneca Lake (technically in Fayette Township), Cuff and his wife, Bett, migrated with Coventry in 1792 from the Hudson Valley village of Claverack. The Hudson Valley was the stronghold of New York's slave system; indeed, the fact that New York had a higher proportion of slaves in its population—15 percent—than any other northern colony in 1746 is largely because of the prevalence of slave-holding in the valley and in New York City. The Dutch patroons and other enterprising men who settled there formed a coalition in 1785 that thwarted an attempt to abolish slavery in New York State, an action Massachusetts and Vermont had already taken. According to historian Phyllis Field, abolition was defeated by delegates from commercial farming areas who tended to belong to the Dutch Re-formed Church, were "educated, cosmopolitan, and non-Clinto-nians," and who shared a "property interest in slaves." Black abolitionist Samuel Ward would later call these men "the very low-est of all the early settlers of America. . . . These very same Dutch, as you find them now in the States of New York, New Jersey, and Pennsylvania, outAmerican all Americans, save those of Connecti-cut, in their maltreatment of the free Negro."[4]

Coventry was Scottish, not Dutch, and probably Presbyterian; his relations with his hired and enslaved people appear to have been rather straightforward. When Cuff learned of Coventry's intention to move, he declared his own intention to remain in Claverack un-less his owner would also purchase Bett, who belonged to a neigh-boring farmer. Cuff told Coventry that several men would buy him, and he refused to be sold to a previous owner who wanted to buy him back. Early in 1792, Coventry bought the "negro Wench named

5. Henry Douglass, known as "Pompey Smash," about 1880. Born into slavery at Rose Hill in 1812, Douglass's other name was almost surely his slave name. Pompey, like many other slave names, was a classical allusion; Smash may derive from "Quashee," the name given a west African male born on Sunday, although the term "smash" has also been used to describe carrying baggage. Douglass was a driver, cartman, and farm overseer in neighboring Waterloo. *Courtesy Terwilliger Museum of the Waterloo Library and Historical Society.*

Bett, also her youngest two children, the elder named Ann, and the youngest Jean, together with all their and her wearing apparel, and half their bedding" for fifty-two pounds and ten shillings, or about $130. In June, Coventry, his family, and his slaves and workers set out for Geneva.

As he had done in Claverack, Cuff performed farm and building chores for Coventry on his Seneca Lake property. Coventry also per-mitted him to keep some of the profits from crops he raised, wood he cut, ashes he collected from woodlot burning, and pelts from foxes and other animals he shot. On 3 November, Coventry wrote in his journal, "Sent Cuff over the Lake for the flour, and he stayed all day. I spoke pretty sharp to him: he said he was getting his pay from Jackson for his ashes. He got 2 yards of red broadcloth, at 30/- pr. yard. He took it so hard that I scolded him, he said he wanted another master. I told him to find a master for himself and wife, and I would sell them." But Cuff stayed with Coventry. On 19 June 1793, Cuff's wife died, Coventry suspected of tuberculosis, and when Co-ventry removed to Utica in 1796, Cuff probably went with him.[5]

Before 1800, a few other African Americans had been brought to the village. Local historian George S. Conover has stated that Thomas Powell, an English innkeeper who settled in Geneva at Wil-liamson's invitation, bought slaves from the Pulteney Estate for $330.68 in 1797; in the 1800 census, two free blacks and two slaves were listed at Powell's Geneva Hotel.[6] Philip Gillam, who was born in about 1755 and is said to have served with his owner James Rees in the Revolution, may have migrated with Rees from Philadelphia in 1798. Gillam lived in Geneva until his death in 1859, and his de-scendants lived in the city until 1931.[7] Like Powell, Rees had settled in the village at Charles Williamson's behest. So, perhaps, did John Woods, a mechanic whom Williamson employed to build the Ge-neva Hotel. By 1800, three of Seneca Township's eight free African Americans lived in Woods's household. Although his origins and the circumstances of his later life are obscure, Woods was the first to sell Geneva village land to African Americans.[8]

The migration of southern slaves to the Geneva region was in-spired both by Williamson and by the Maryland planter Peregrine Fitzhugh, whose sedge-infested lands drove him north to Lake On-tario's Sodus Bay between 1796 and 1800. Fitzhugh lived in Geneva while his thirty to forty slaves cleared the Sodus land, where he relocated before 1803. Six of the twenty slaves recorded as living in Seneca Township in 1800 belonged to another Maryland planter, Henry Brothers, and three years later their numbers were vastly in-creased by the migration of three related Virginia families—those of Gavin Lawson and his sons-in-law, Robert Selden Rose and John Nicholas. Fitzhugh's cousin, Colonel John Fitzhugh, helped accom-plish the movement of the families' slaves, some, perhaps most, of whom formed the stable nucleus of Geneva's black population over the next century. Similar migrations by other of Williamson's southern associates were the genesis of black settlement in rural Steuben, Seneca, and Wayne counties.[9]

George W. Nicholas, one of John Nicholas's grandsons, recorded the only surviving account of his family's northward trek in 1873 as he listened to his uncle Gavin Lawson Nicholas recount the story one Sunday afternoon at White Springs Farm. The Nicholas estate was on the west side of Seneca Lake, directly opposite the estate Robert Rose had bought from Coventry and renamed Rose Hill. The elder Nicholas was eight at the time of the move. George Nicholas took the story down "as near as possible in my uncle's words," and in 1901 he copied it over with parenthetical explanations of his own.

We left Hampstead (the name of the plantation in Stafford County Va) on Sunday October 21st 1803 . . . There were two stage coaches with four horses each, a driver and a postillion riding one of the leaders, a "coachee" with four horses, driver and postillion. The two stages were made at Hampstead by their own workmen (slaves) from timber cut on the place, the hubs of the wheels from locust trees near the house and after their arrival at Geneva, they were sold to Levi Stevens and ran on stage line from Albany to Geneva.

In the first stage were Mrs. Jane L. Rose (my grandmother) and (her sons) Gavin Lawson Rose, John N. Rose and Henry Rose in the arms of his colored nurse, Phillis Kenny (afterward Phillis Douglas and died on the Carter Road).

In the other stage were Mrs. Lawson (mother of Mrs. Nicholas and Mrs. Rose) Aunt Peggy (Miss Margaret Rose, a sister of Mrs. Lawson) and their maid Susannah Dunkinson (colored).

In the "coachee" were Mrs. Anne Nicholas (my grandmother) her children, Ann (afterwards Mrs. Abm. Dox) Susan (afterward Mrs. Orin Clark) Jane, George and Robert C. in arms of his colored nurse Alice Bowman; Judge Nicholas, Mr. Rose (my two grandfathers) George H. Norton (a nephew of Judge Nicholas and afterward father of Rev. John N. Norton and Rev. George H. Norton) were on horse back with two led horses.

Mr. Gavin Lawson (my great grandfather) and Gavin Lawson Nicholas (who gave me these details) were in a phaeton with two horses and a driver.

Four 4 horse wagons for the colored people and their baggage came with about seventy five colored people directly north over the Alleghanies [sic] in charge of Col. John Fitzhugh.

The men and the women, who were able, walked; the invalid women and small children rode in the wagons. They went about half a mile together, then the whites turned to the right, and the blacks to the left and did not meet again until they met in Geneva about the middle of November. The whites came by Albany, the blacks directly north thru Pennsylvania. They had had parties here for two years previously raising crops and making preparations.[10]

The slaves' version of this journey has not survived, if it was ever recorded. In 1881, Garrett Kenney, one of only two former Rose-Nicholas family slaves then still living, gave a lecture on the migration at the High Street School. The address was announced in, but not covered by, the local newspapers, and no copy of the talk survives. In an account of a similar move that he and other slaves of Virginia planter William Helm made to Sodus Bay in 1797, the black abolitionist Austin Steward recalled the pain of separation "from our old home and fellow-slaves, from our relatives and the old State of Virginia." Steward wrote in his 1857 autobiography, "To-day, they are in the old familiar cabin surrounded by their family, relatives and friends; tomorrow, they may be scattered, parted forever."[11] But like Coventry, John Nicholas appears to have tried to keep families intact by buying spouses and children from other owners before he moved north.[12]

In towns such as Geneva and Sodus, there were more slaves than African-American free people in 1810; the balance was exactly opposite in every other Ontario County town where African Americans lived. Between 1794 and 1810, New York State's slave population had fallen from 21,324 to 15,107, but Ontario County's grew between these years as a result of the migration of southern families. By 1810, with fifty-eight slaves, Seneca Township had the largest slave population and was the second largest town in the county; Bloomfield, the largest town, had no slaves among its 1810 residents.

These slaves took up residence at a time when state legislators were in the midst of debating, and ultimately altering, their legal status. Four years before Lawson, Rose, Nicholas, and their slaves settled around Geneva, the state had passed a law promising to free all female slaves born after 4 July 1799 after they had worked for their owners until they were twenty-five; all male slaves born after that date had to work until the age of twenty-eight, at which point they too would be freed automatically. In effect, all slaves in the state would become free people on 4 July 1827, an intention that state legislators reaffirmed in 1817. The 1799 law also validated slave marriages, allowed African Americans to hold property, and required masters to teach their slaves to read. An 1810 state law applied specifically to slaveowners in Ontario, Steuben, and Seneca counties who had emigrated from Maryland and Virginia in or after 1800. This legislation permitted them to hire their slaves out for seven-year terms "on condition that at the expiration of said period, the said slaves shall be free—the masters, however, to be liable to maintain all those who shall not be of sufficient ability to maintain themselves."[13]

The 1810 law stimulated a spate of manumissions that gave New York its first substantial population of free African-American people; between 1810 and 1820, Rose himself manumitted twenty-eight of his thirty-seven slaves. Some owners had freed slaves before 1810: perhaps motivated by more humanitarian considerations, Geneva merchant Timothy Allyn in 1799 freed Ginna, his "Negro girl now living in Geneva . . . in consideration of the good and faithful services" she had provided as well as "sundry other valuable causes and consideration moving me thereunto." Among these considerations might have been Allyn's reluctance to support Ginna as she grew older, as her manumission record contained the by-then standard language that she was younger than fifty years old and appeared able to support herself. In 1808 and 1809, John Nicholas freed his slaves John Duncan and "Mingo and wife Maria" with the same assertions.[14]

Moving north put African-American slaves in an entirely novel context in which the existence of antislavery feeling and of organizations formed in their interest made escape into freedom more tantalizing and less threatening than it was for their peers in the South. Between 1806 and 1826, slaveowners advertised in the *Geneva Gazette* for the return of twenty-three slaves, six of them women or girls, and these ads may represent only a fraction of the total number of slave escapes in these years. The notices offered rewards from one hundred dollars to six cents, the latter invariably for female slaves. In September 1826, Abraham Van Gelder of Seneca township offered only a penny for the return of his "black man servant named Harry, aged about 20 years, and would be free at 28." Van Gelder was evidently ignorant of the fact that state law would free Harry in less than a year.[15]

Clearly, not all slaves in the Geneva area lived harmoniously with their masters, as runaway notices in the *Gazette* and other early nineteenth-century newspapers attest. In 1814, after Austin Steward ran away, Helm placed advertisements in several area newspapers, including the *Gazette,* offering a forty-dollar reward for his retrieval. Steward's autobiography describes Helm's cruelty, intimated in the runaway notice itself, and several accounts attribute similar behavior to Robert Rose. One 1828 issue of the *Gazette* recalled that Rose had once shot and wounded "one of his slaves, of the name of Henry," for refusing to work on Sunday in Rose's brick kiln; and a biographical sketch of African-American porter Samuel Grant Lincoln, published in an 1893 county history, contains the family legend that Rose struck Lincoln's grandfather Peter, a Rose Hill slave, with his cane.[16]

Some who fled their masters were armed, probably not only to avoid capture but also to ensure permanent escape from an onerous life. When Charles, who "sometimes calls himself *Charles Condo,*" escaped from attorney Polydore B. Wisner in August 1807, he took with him "considerable clothing, and a gun." Condo, probably the same "black Charles" that Wisner indentured for eight years in 1808, ran away with printer Herman H. Bogert's slave Yaup, who called himself Jacob Murray. Bogert and Wisner, an attorney who had come to Geneva from Orange County in the lower Hudson Valley, suspected the two to have been "in company with some other runaway negroes, and will only travel in the night." In July 1816, Geneva hatter David Naglee advertised that his eighteen-year-old "Negro Boy" Philip Hardy had run away with clothes and a black leather wagon whip. The next year, a mulatto named Cephas, who had earlier been owned by Geneva attorney and farm tool manufacturer Thomas D. Burrall, escaped from William Smith in Waterloo with a French musket.[17]

Just as the runaway slave notices provide evidence of slaves' desperation, they also contain clues about the sources of their discontent. To aid in the capture of runaways, slaveowners usually described them—how tall they were, how old they appeared to be, what they wore when they escaped and what clothes they took with them, how black they were, how they walked and held their heads, whether they avoided people's eyes when spoken to.[18] They also described evidence of injury—inflicted by masters or precipitated by the hazardous work slaves were often consigned to do—that might have helped identify their wayward property. One notice published in the *Geneva Gazette* in 1807 sought the capture of a "black man" who had allegedly raped the wife of a Pennsylvania farmer and was suspected to have fled to the Genesee Country. "His left hand, which formally was scalded, has a smooth glossy appearance; and the little finger on that hand has contracted a stiffness, which prevents it from closing with the finger next to it," the notice stated. "The same accident has, in same measure diminished the size of that hand." Alexander Howard from Phelps, just north of Geneva, noted that his runaway slave Peter "has a scar over one of his eyes and also a large scar just below the ankle on the inside of one of his feet, which was occasioned by the cut of an axe." Austin Steward, Helm wrote in his 1814 notice, "has a large scar on the calf of one of his legs, occasioned by a wound, the skin and flesh having been torn by the hook of an ox chain." In addition to his own injury, Steward had also once stood in helpless witness as a "professed gentleman living in Bath" beat his sister senseless. Philip Hardy had "a scar on the back part of his head, where the hair is off." Maltreatment or no, the urge to escape was so great that women sometimes ran alone with young children, even infants.[19]

It is impossible to know who these runaways, and who many of those manumitted, were. But it is tempting to speculate. The escaped Charles Condo might have been Charles Condol and might have been brought to Geneva from Connecticut, New England's bastion of slaveholding interest. After his indenture was completed in 1816, he may have become the first in a long line of Condols in the village. Samuel Condol and his family, from Connecticut, were in Geneva by 1838; William Condol, possibly Samuel's brother, lived in Geneva with his large family by 1845.[20] Philip Hardy may have been part of the large and extended Hardy family, descendants of which live in Geneva today. Joseph Hardy, Sr., one of whose sons was named Philip, lived in Geneva as early as 1830; Beal Hardy, a free black who was probably married with one child, lived in Geneva in 1820. The "Henry" whom Rose mistreated was probably the elder Henry Douglass, manumitted in 1816.

There is no correlation between manumission and the tendency to stay in Geneva or to leave it; no particular sense of gratitude or loyalty seems to have continued to bind freed people to their one-time owners. John Nicholas manumitted a Robert Duncansen (or Dunkerson) in 1815 and a John Duncan (possibly also Duncansen) in 1808; Nicholas-Rose maid Susannah Dunkinson may have been wife or sister to these men. None of them are listed in Geneva censuses after 1820.[21] In 1811, Nicholas freed Alexander Graham and later

John Graham, both Geneva village property owners who disappeared from local censuses after 1830.

Other families, such as the Gillams, the Gatens, and the Kenneys, stayed in the village. Rose manumitted Tom and Godfrey Gaten in 1822; their descendants lived in the village until the 1890s. The Kenney family may have been a large one even before manumission, which may help to explain its persistence in Geneva to the present day. In 1815 and 1816, Rose manumitted Charles and John Kenney, Charles with his wife Aggy and children Jinny, Berlet, and Nancy. It is probable that John Kenney is the direct ancestor of the so-called "Castle Street" Kenneys and that the "Worthington Avenue" Kenneys descended from Garrett Kenney, for whom no manumission record survives. Garrett, John, Charles, and Phillis may have been siblings. But one cannot even speculate about the identity of many other formerly enslaved African Americans. Identified only by such first names as Mingo, Maria, Ginna, and Comfort, they may have been living as anonymous "free colored persons" in the homes of white people. They may have taken a spouse's name or an altogether new one. Or they may have left the village, either as freed or fugitive people, to seek kin or enlarged opportunity in other places.

1820–1860: Fugitives and Farm-to-Town Migrants

Centered on every principal land and water route going west, east, north, and south, Geneva transformed itself within twenty years of its initial settlement from a fur trading post into a transportation and commercial nexus. It was on the main path settlers took to the West; Williamson counted 570 sleds and families passing through the village in five weeks during the winter of 1797 and 1798.[22] Provoked largely by the perceived need to divert trade from Philadelphia, Baltimore, and Canadian markets to Albany and New York City, the Western Inland Navigation Company lobbied for nearly two decades to persuade the state to finance the improvements that created the Erie Canal. Geneva's entrepreneurs also succeeded in gaining state financing to develop the Seneca River into a feeder canal from the Erie to Seneca Lake. Officially opened in 1828, the Cayuga and Seneca Canal brought Erie barges into the village through an artificial channel that ran from the river through the marshlands along the northern rim of the lake. These marshes were widely regarded not only as useless but also as unhealthy, the source of the "Genesee Fever" that afflicted many early settlers, Williamson among them.

Laying the canal through this marshland along the shore transformed it into a utilitarian landscape. Canal barns were built along Geneva's waterfront "flat," or bottom, to house the mules and horses that had pulled the barges that far; steamboats then took over the job of towing these "lakers" from Geneva to the head of the lake at Watkins Glen or to the feeders that soon connected Seneca Lake to Keuka Lake and to the Chemung River. Warehouses for grain, goods, and lumber lined the shore, some extending out over the water on piers. By 1841, the flat also became the site of the tracks, rail yard, and depot of the Auburn and Rochester Railroad, one of the many lines that became part of the New York Central and Hudson River Railroad. Ten years later, the Erie Railroad reached the southern head of Seneca Lake, and a full fleet of steamboats, some large enough to carry fifteen hundred passengers with more than seventy canal boats in tow, ran between Watkins and other points on the lake to the Castle Street landing in Geneva (fig. 6).

Before the war, the flat was home to such small-scale manufactures as foundries, lumber and planing mills, and boat builders; but the prosperity of the village was built mostly on the business of moving finished goods and people from southern and eastern points west and moving agricultural and forest products east. The fruits of this commerce quickly became evident on the bluff above the commercial district. Fine Federal, Greek Revival, and Gothic Revival homes were constructed on both sides of South Main Street, despite Williamson's intention that the east or water side of the street should remain undeveloped to preserve a view of the lake. Geneva (later Hobart) College built its academy and theological school on the west side of South Main Street in 1825. And because of its southern population, Geneva became a center of Episcopalianism in upstate New York: Trinity Episcopal Church, begun in 1806, was the second largest Episcopal congregation in the region by the early 1830s and headquarters of the Western New York Diocese from 1839 to 1865. The spires of Hobart and Trinity Church enhanced the village's image as a stable, civilized, Episcopalian community.

Yet in contrast to the cultured aspect of South Main Street, the flat was the haven of working-class and transient people. Geneva was a port of call on the canal system, its protected harbor the place where canal boats moored overnight and holed up for entire win-

6. "Harbor of Geneva, New York, 1872." Canal barges are shown docked to various piers; the long L-shaped pier protected the canal harbor. The flat, composed largely of wooden structures, was the site of frequent fires well into the twentieth century; the area just below the photographer's position became one of few neighborhoods in which new African Americans could find housing in the twentieth century. *Courtesy Geneva Historical Society; gift of Mrs. George Klimes.*

ters. It had two churches that served as missions to the mobile canallers; one of them had an outside stairway from the canal towpath to a second-floor hall of worship. The hotels and tenement houses on Exchange Street and the smaller streets running east to the lake's edge boarded boatmen, railroad workers, clerks, maltsters, furnacemen, and others who worked in the fledgling industries near the canal, railroad, and lakeshore. Newspaper accounts of canal accidents and downtown fires document the presence of many strangers in the village—tramps, prostitutes, people down on their luck who lived in canal barns, and men like the boatman Patrick Conners, who had "no fixed home" and no known relatives.[23]

By all accounts, transience was high among the unskilled laborers who worked in transportation and personal service, loading and unloading boats and rail cars, picking up baggage and passengers at the steamboat dock and railroad depot, hauling lumber, produce, and meat from agricultural areas, driving cattle and sheep from these hinterlands, and cleaning, washing, and cooking in hotels, on steamboats, and in the homes of people who could afford help. Before the mass immigration of Irish and German people in the 1840s, white labor was scarce and expensive throughout the North. This scarcity created work in both unskilled and skilled trades. African-American men were able to work as blacksmiths, cabinetmakers, harnessmakers, and butchers in these years; but because of the unfortunate association of African Americans with unpaid labor, they probably often worked for lower wages than native whites would accept.

Moreover, New York State as a whole was a relatively hospitable place for African Americans.[24] As fugitive slave traffic increased and the gradual emancipation legislation of many northern states took effect, various northern legislatures sought to restrict the movement of free blacks into their states and to curtail their rights. Pennsylvania disenfranchised all black males in 1838, even those who, because they owned sufficient property, had been able to vote since 1815.[25] Such laws responded to numerous anxieties. White unskilled and skilled workers voiced their concern that competition from black labor would depress wages and heighten unemployment.[26] Legislators expressed fears, largely unfounded, that a labor glut would cause an increase in the government-borne costs of poor relief. Less openly, they also worried that the movement of free blacks into a place would, if not somehow encumbered, be so massive as to affect its political life, even so much as to shift the balance of power away from whites.[27]

The New York legislature appears never to have considered seriously any proposal to limit African-American immigration and in fact defeated an effort in 1813 to require certificates of freedom of blacks who wished to vote. New York State blacks apparently were not required to register themselves or post bonds, and from 1808 they were protected, at least in statute, from kidnapping. In upstate

New York, they were by all evidence not often subjected to attacks by whites, as African Americans had been in Philadelphia, Connecticut, New York City, and even rural New Hampshire during the 1830s. The state's developing cities promised more opportunity than did much of New England, the only other northern region that offered a comparably open political environment. As one of Harriet Tubman's nineteenth-century biographers put it, New York State must have seemed "the land of Canaan."[28]

Before 1850, Geneva's prosperity coupled with New York's political climate to attract African-American settlement. Indeed, until the 1950s, the black population never again grew as rapidly. Some blacks continued to come from the East and Mid-Atlantic states: the Arnolds and the Condols claimed New England origins, and Anthony Jupiter, Moses Ray, Samuel McIntire, William Bainbridge, and Anthony Baldwin listed Pennsylvania or New Jersey birthplaces in censuses. The names of other African Americans whose origins are not known suggest some movement from Albany and the Hudson Valley—Mary Van Rensselaer, Thomas Waggoner, John Van Horn, Richard Bogardus.[29] Gillams, Blands, Kenneys, Lees, Grahams, Duncansens, Gatens, McKenzies, Dorseys, Douglasses, Nobles, Prues, and Tompkinses, and some of Geneva's Browns and Taylors, came from Maryland or Virginia.

Part of the growth in numbers of African Americans was the result of another characteristic antebellum population movement— from farm to town. Slaves brought to upstate New York by southerners were often settled in rural areas—Seneca, Fayette, Ovid, Huron, Sodus, Phelps, Farmington—and were surely farm laborers. Slave women in rural areas probably did farm chores and worked as domestics in the homes of well-to-do farmers and village merchants, though rural white girls were as apt to hold such positions and probably predominated, owing in part to their far greater numbers.

But as commerce mushroomed in such places as Geneva, many white and black rural laborers moved into villages, into an economy increasingly oriented to cash and endemically short of labor. The movement of newly freed African Americans into prospering villages may have been more profound, in terms of both the proportion of the black population involved and its psychological meaning. Manumission and the statewide emancipation in 1827 brought with it a chance to start a new life, take a new name, abandon the associations of thralldom (such as agricultural work), and move about at will. This farm-to-town migration, which probably peaked between

1830 and 1840, is thought to have been responsible for creating African-American populations in towns such as Ithaca that had not been settled by slaveholders. Moreover, villages with existing black populations probably seemed particularly attractive, compared to the isolation and, possibly, the ostracism blacks might have confronted in the countryside.[30] Eighty-two African Americans—only fourteen still enslaved—lived in rural Fayette, just east and south of Geneva, in 1820. But by 1850, only fourteen remained there, while the African-American population of Geneva had grown from 131 to 317. Geneva must have been regarded as a place of real opportunity among blacks. Nearby Waterloo, also on the Cayuga and Seneca Canal and just then beginning to make use of its waterpower, had only sixty-five African Americans in 1850. By 1860, Ontario County had a black population of 639 people, the largest of any western New York county; almost half of this population was in Geneva village.

The official 1850 enumeration of 317 African Americans in the village may well have understated their actual numbers in Geneva, a possibility suggested by several sources. One list of students in the Geneva Presbyterian Church's Sunday School classes for African Americans in 1829, 1830, and 1831 contains forty surnames, fifteen of which never show up in pre-1850 censuses. Only two of those fifteen appeared in post-1850 listings. Another list of African-American names, commissioned in 1846 by white abolitionist Gerrit Smith, also suggests that a significant number of black residents escaped the notice of census takers. At Samuel Ward's request, Geneva's James Duffin, an African-American barber and political activist, surveyed several western New York counties to find and recommend to Smith sober and industrious black men who owned little or no real property. Smith's plan was to give these men enough land to enable them to vote in New York State, a move provoked by the defeat that year of a statewide referendum that would have extended the suffrage to disenfranchised black men. Duffin sent Smith the names of twenty-eight Genevans, twelve of whom were not listed in the 1850 census only three years later, and none of whom had settled on their Hamilton County lands by that time.[31] Property transactions, church registers, and newspapers establish the presence of at least twenty other African Americans who were not recorded in federal censuses through 1850.

African Americans suspected at the time that their numbers were not accurately recorded in official enumerations, a fact probably caused by both the inefficiency of census takers and the tendency of some blacks to, as Loguen put it, "keep as much out of sight as they may." For it seems likely that a significant portion of this pre-1850 population growth among African Americans was the movement of fugitive slaves. The romance surrounding the Underground Railroad has made it difficult to connect many people and places to this clandestine northward movement. Like the places where George Washington slept, homes with tunnels and hidden rooms throughout central and western New York have been alleged to be fugitive hiding places and "stations." But relatively few have a documented place in the history of the fugitive slave exodus, largely because such key station "masters" in the network as William Still in Philadelphia, J. W. Loguen in Syracuse, and Frederick Douglass in Rochester continually emphasized the necessity for secrecy.[32] Most reputable accounts of Underground Railroad activity do not mention Geneva, and none of the four principal routes through New York State passed through the village. The nearest approach was a spur from Syracuse to Skaneateles and Auburn, Harriet Tubman's home.[33]

Still, letters that fugitives wrote to Underground Railroad operators show them to have settled in many towns off the main-traveled routes. Because steamboats were popular means of escape in other places, it seems at least plausible that fugitives hid themselves on Seneca Lake steamers, particularly before the Erie Railroad spur from Watkins Glen to Canandaigua was built in the early 1850s. Elmira, the next major village to the south between Watkins and the Pennsylvania border, had become a major Underground depot in the 1840s after increased slave catching diverted fugitive traffic from New York City. Word-of-mouth accounts do assert a role for Geneva on this network. An article in the 3 May 1918 issue of the *Penn Yan Democrat* claimed that "the Rev. Mr. Logan," probably J. W. Loguen of Syracuse, had a cabin in Geneva to which fugitives were sent from Branchport by Dr. Wynans Bush, an "ardent Garrison Abolitionist." And regional popular historian Arch Merrill claimed in 1963 that Genevan Josephine Johnson had given him family records documenting that her family's Pulteney Street home had harbored fugitive slaves. Merrill also described the visit of a "Negro youth carrying a large and lumpy bag over his shoulder" to the Geneva home of George Giffing on North Exchange Street; inside is said to have been an escaped female slave who had become too weak to walk and thus was concealed and carried for miles in a bag.[34]

More solid evidence of the possibility that fugitives sometimes sought a safe haven in Geneva exists as well. Within months of the emancipation of African Americans in New York State, a fugitive was captured in Geneva and returned south.[35] In addition, Gerrit Smith had a long connection with Geneva. He owned land in the village, and both his son Greene and a nephew, named for him, lived in Geneva before the Civil War. After the war, so did his daughter, Elizabeth Smith Miller, a reformer and associate of Frederick Douglass and Mary Church Terrell. Smith was a frequent visitor to Geneva, both to carry on his huge business in land and to participate in the meetings of the reform movements, including abolition, that occupied so much of his energy. Preserved among his abundant correspondence is a letter from Genevan Edwin Barnard, a jeweler and a Presbyterian (turned Congregationalist by 1846) who was active in the Sunday School movement in Geneva, where many of the village's African Americans received the only education available to them before their own school was founded. Barnard wrote to Smith at his Peterboro home on 30 July 1852. Because the letter is torn around its edges, some words are missing, but Barnard's message seems clear:

> I learn from J. W. Duffin there has been a fresh importation of *Human* [torn] & that you have the care & direction of them. [torn] supposing that your aim is to locate them [torn] the best advantage for themselves. [torn] two friends living in Hamonds Port [torn] Co. Wm Hastings & LD Hastings, both wishing [torn] Domestics in their families. My object in [torn] ascertain if there are any & if they can [torn] from that quarter it would be natural [torn] that among the number (50 I learn man [torn]) there would be some that are accust[torn] and would like this employment. they are men [torn]lling to care for them & do well by them [torn]uld be glad to have an answer by return mail [torn] are here now & should it be favourable [torn] one of them will come and see you.
> Yours for Humanity Edwin Barnard[36]

In all probability, Smith had received at his Peterboro home fifty fugitives, both male and female, and Barnard's wish was to place them in upstate homes sympathetic to their plight and financial need. Although most fugitives were bound for Canada, especially after the 1850 passage of the Fugitive Slave Law, some stayed in New York villages when they could find work, or work could be found for them. Edward Lewis, who had changed his name to William Brady when he escaped, told Still in 1857 that he had chosen to stay in Skaneateles upon hearing from Loguen and others at Syracuse that "times are rather hard in Canada."[37]

At least three fugitives settled in Geneva. One was Aaron Lucas, who, according to his daughter's biographical sketch in an 1893 Ontario County history, escaped from Virginia "by the underground railway" and came to the village in 1825. Another was John Prue, born in Virginia in 1795 and sold to a new master in Kentucky, from whom he later escaped. He settled in Geneva by 1838. The third was Peyton Lucas (not a known relative of Aaron Lucas), who changed his name to Charles Bentley and appeared both in the 1850 Geneva village census and the 1847 list of disenfranchised black Genevans whom Duffin recommended to Gerrit Smith for grants of land. Born in Leesburg, Loudoun County, Virginia (the home of some emancipated slaves who settled in Geneva after the Civil War), and owned by a Baptist minister, Lucas was hired out as a blacksmith's apprentice at the age of fifteen. In 1841, Lucas's sister, a servant in his owner's house, overheard his master attempting to negotiate her brother's sale. Within a week, Lucas and two others escaped. Evading slave catchers and their dogs, they traveled only at night and eventually found a safe haven with two people who told them to tell anyone who inquired that they were on their way to a camp meeting on the Susquehanna River. In this way, Lucas and his friends reached the "track of the underground railroad" and, eventually, New York State. Stopping in an unnamed village and working in his trade, Lucas was warned by a friendly druggist that an advertisement seeking his capture had been posted at a nearby tavern. Sometime before 1855, at his final stop in Toronto, Lucas told antislavery sympathizer Benjamin Drew the conclusion of his story:

> My friends advised me to remove further. I worked in Geneva, N.Y., until the passage of the fugitive slave law, when my friends advised me to go to Canada, with which advice I complied, at a great sacrifice, on account of some property which I was trying to buy.
>
> I feel that I am out of the lion's paw, and I feel that THERE IS NO CURSE ON GOD'S EARTH, EQUAL TO SLAVERY.[38]

The most profound growth in Geneva's African-American population in the nineteenth century—a 61 percent increase from 193 to 311 persons between 1830 and 1840—must have resulted partly from the temporary presence of fugitives. In this decade, population in the village as a whole rose only 31 percent. If Geneva's black families were larger on average than Geneva's white families, natural increase might have accounted for the faster growth of the black population; however, if anything, the average black family in Geneva appears to have been smaller than the average white family at the time.[39] Fugitives came to the village as late as 1862. On 6 March, Adelaide Prouty of South Main Street recorded in her diary, "Tonight two fugitives came to us & begged assistance. They were to have been sold, & ran away to escape it.—Strange that a man must flee in this free & equal country, to be saved from cruelty & oppression."[40]

Before the Civil War, transience was slightly more common than persistence (fig. 7). More than half of all African Americans listed in a census between 1800 and 1875 appear in only that census and no other listing such as a city directory, a church register, or the vital statistics that newspapers published (New York State did not mandate that local governments keep vital statistics until 1882). But among the slightly fewer than half listed in a census and at least one other source, permanence is more remarkable than transience. Just 11 percent of these African Americans stayed in Geneva less than five years. Fifty-five percent stayed twenty years or more, often living all or nearly all of their lives in Geneva. And within this prewar group there was a statistically small but nonetheless interesting tendency to return to the village. James W. Duffin, who emigrated to Haiti in 1861 (perhaps with other Genevans), returned to the United States by 1863 and apparently to Geneva in the early 1870s. Nancy Lucas Curlin, born in Geneva in 1832, emigrated to the West Indies after 1853 but returned to the United States in 1878. She had returned to Geneva by 1892 and remained in the village at least until 1900. Josephine and Mary Henry, both born in the West Indies, had come to Geneva in 1854 with James Symons, an Englishman who quickly became prominent in Trinity Episcopal Church. Symons's wife and aunt, who were white, were natives of the West Indies, and it is possible that the Henry sisters, who were black, were domestics in that family before they emigrated. They stayed in Geneva at least until 1860 and then left—perhaps with Duffin or Curlin—for the West Indies. The Henrys returned to the United States between 1887 and 1890 and to Geneva by 1892, when Curlin also returned.

But after six decades of steady growth, the African-American population of the village and of other northern places—particularly those close to Canada—dropped between 1850 and 1855, no doubt

7. Unidentified woman in Marshall, Michigan, 1870. On the back of this photograph, preserved in Geneva's Kenney family, is the last name "Gillam." It may depict Mary Douglass Gillam, wife of Joseph C. Gillam, but the fact that it was taken by a photographer in Marshall suggests that it may be Douglass's sister Maria, wife of John Duer. In 1835, Duer, then a resident of Seneca County, purchased 160 acres of land in Fredonia, near Marshall, an Underground stop and home to a sizable black population; Duer moved there by 1840. His son Albert, also living in Fredonia, may have married a Gillam; in the 1850 Calhoun County census, both are listed as New York natives. *Courtesy John W. Kenney.*

because of the Fugitive Slave Law. More than 130 members of one Baptist church in Buffalo went immediately into Canada after the law's passage in 1850; in Rochester, 112 of 114 Baptists and their preacher abandoned a church and fled to Canada. An estimated fifteen to twenty thousand blacks migrated there in the 1850s alone.[41]

Because the law permitted no recourse to the free black "mistaken" for a fugitive, abolitionists regarded it with horror and disgust. Samuel Ward called it "the darkest page in my native country's history . . . her deepest degradation." It was doubly damaging because it not only drained African-American populations all over the North; it also crippled their leadership. "We have lost some of our strong men," Frederick Douglass wrote in his *Frederick Douglass' Paper* in 1851. "Ward has been driven into exile; Loguen has been hunted from our shores; Brown, Garnet and Crummell, men who were our pride and hope, we have heard signified their unwillingness to return again to their National field of labors in this country. Bibb has *chosen* Canada as his field of labor—and the eloquent Remond is comparatively silent."[42]

Seven years after the Fugitive Slave Law, the decision of the United States Supreme Court in the Dred Scott case—that African Americans "had no rights which the white man is bound to respect"—similarly scandalized free African Americans, and it came to have particular meaning in Geneva after the sensational kidnapping of two African-American men only eight months after the Court handed down its decision.[43] The perpetrator was a twenty-one-year-old white man, a dry goods clerk named Napoleon B. VanTuyl, who convinced two African-American men, John Hite and Daniel Prue, that he could secure them well-paying waiter's jobs at his uncle's hotel in Columbus, Ohio (figs. 8 and 9). At that time, Hite was eighteen years old and worked in the home of Genevan Robert Lay. He had been freed nine years earlier in the District of Columbia and had come to Geneva with his mother, Mary Ann. Prue, the eldest son of the fugitive John Prue and his wife, Sarah, was twenty years old and lived in his parents' home on North Main Street. He may not have been employed at the time, as Irish and German immigrant labor had begun to shrink the pool of jobs open to African Americans. On 16 November 1857, Prue and Hite left with VanTuyl on a westbound train. Within a week, John Prue received a letter from his son. Hastily written in pencil, the letter explained that he had "met with bad luck," that VanTuyl had tried to sell him, that he had lost all his clothes, and that Hite "has gon on to Kentuckey."

8, 9. Daniel Prue and John Hite, about 1857. These daguerreotypes were collected and preserved by Samuel Hopkins VerPlank, local chronicler of the kidnapping. The prints are not marked, and it is not known which is Hite and which is Prue. *Courtesy Mr. and Mrs. H. Merrill Roenke, Jr.*

Samuel Hopkins VerPlank, a cashier at the Bank of Geneva when the kidnapping took place and self-appointed historian of the event, collected Prue's letter to his father and all of the subsequent correspondence relating to his and Hite's retrieval. He also documented the role that Edwin Barnard, whom VerPlank described as "a man of 'advanced' views, an abolitionist in fact," had in arranging the state's participation in rescuing the men and bringing Van-Tuyl to justice. Barnard persuaded Governor John King to make Genevan Calvin Walker the state's agent in an effort to find and return the men; on 18 November, Walker set out for Ohio with Hite's employer, who also knew Prue. Within days, Walker and Lay found Prue working in a livery stable in Columbus and learned his story. VerPlank relayed the tale as Prue had told it to Walker:

While on the [railroad] cars in Ohio, Prue heard a man sitting behind VanTuyl ask him where he was going. VanTuyl said "To Cincinnati." This answer aroused Prue's suspicions and when the cars next stopped, which was at a station called Carlisle, he got off. A man whom he did not know got off the car and tried to induce him and finally to force him to get on again. In the struggle Prue's coat was torn. When the cars started the man jumped on, leaving Prue there. . . . In about an hour the man returned with another man who was covered with a large shawl reaching to his feet and with a long beard—Prue thinks this man was VanTuyl disguised. Anyway the first mentioned man came up to him at once saying "Now I have got you." The bystanders made some inquiry and said to the man: "He says that he is a free nigger." The man said: "No. He is not. I have got the papers here to prove he is not.", producing some papers.

As the papers were not proof of Prue's enslavement, he was released, whereupon he left on foot for Columbus. Meanwhile, Genevans had requested that a certified copy of Hite's manumission papers be sent to Walker in Columbus. Walker and Lay learned that VanTuyl had sold Hite on 19 November for about eight hundred dollars to Benton W. Jenkins, a slaveholder in Henry County, Kentucky, and had then fled to New Orleans. Jenkins had then resold Hite to a Judge Graves. After they persuaded Jenkins to refund Graves's money, Walker and Lay returned to Louisville, where they found Hite in a slave pen. They paid the pen keeper eight dollars, and Hite was deposited on "free Ohio soil" on 8 December. His rescue was celebrated at a Sunday School meeting in Cincinnati soon afterward.

By the time Hite was found, Jenkins had charged VanTuyl as a fugitive from justice and notified New Orleans authorities that VanTuyl also stood charged in New York State with "kidnapping a free black person and selling him into slavery in the State of Kentucky." By 12 February 1858, Barnard had news from New Orleans and immediately wired Walker in Cincinnati: "Vantuyl is arrested out on bail—Bring Prue home." Prue left for Geneva with Lay, and Walker turned to the task of finding VanTuyl. Several Genevans with Louisiana kin, including VerPlank, wrote to introduce Walker and to solicit their aid in Walker's search for VanTuyl. "Any assistance you give him will be a favor not only to him but to me & this whole village," VerPlank wrote his uncle in Baton Rouge, "for we all feel a deep interest in having the kidnapper brought to trial." On 8 March, Walker wrote Lay from the Ohio River steamer *Superior* to report that VanTuyl "is on board with us, *in irons*—but he is in custody of the authorities of Kentucky if they will give him up I shall bring him home." VanTuyl was held in Kentucky—allegedly in the same pen in which Walker and Lay had found John Hite—until his trial later that month. Walker wrote Lay of this, to which Lay responded on 19 March, "John is very much pleased that VanTuyl is in the same box that he was in while in Carrollton. Mrs. Walker says that John gets along very well and does all that she wants him to do."

By 31 March, VanTuyl had been found not guilty in Kentucky and was released to the custody of Walker, who delivered him to jail in Canandaigua. Charged not with kidnapping but with inveigling, VanTuyl was convicted on 11 April 1859, served two years at Auburn Prison, and died the next year in Penn Yan, only twenty-five years old. What happened to John Hite is not known, but his mother lived in Geneva until her death in November 1893. Daniel Prue also spent the rest of his life in the village, except for his service in a colored regiment during the Civil War. Wounded and evidently unable to work, Prue returned to Geneva and lived on his military pension. "It was his custom to lay in a stock of provisions for the family enough to last a month, pay off every dollar that he owed, and then 'blow' on the rest," his *Geneva Advertiser* obituary stated. "He would talk to a house, a tree or wagon and reason with it the same as with a man. But he never wrought injury to anyone." Policemen's books show him to have been arrested for disorderliness several times in the 1890s. Prue lived in his family home on Main Street with his sister Delia, a domestic, and died at his aunt's home in Canandaigua in July 1895.[44]

On the eve of the Civil War, Geneva's African-American population had edged upward to near its 1850 height, which seems extraordinary in view of its sharp decline between 1850 and 1855 and the events that seemed to put the lives of free African Americans at considerable risk. The population stood at 302 persons in the 1860 census and was 6.2 percent of the total population of the village. The number of black Genevans would not exceed 302 again until 1960; not until 1980 would African Americans again hold a 6 percent or greater share of the local population. Geneva's African Americans may have viewed their lots in favorable, if surely ambiguous, terms before the war, but the circumstances in which they lived became more clear-cut, and less inviting, afterwards.

1860–1915: Emancipated People

As Union troops occupied slaveholding areas, a small number of African Americans began to move north into the industrializing and urbanizing post–Civil War economy. After the war, the Freedmen's Bureau and labor agents hired by northern construction businesses and hotels found work in larger northern cities for newly freed people.[45] Geneva's John Smith Duffin, one of James W. Duffin's sons, wrote to Gerrit Smith in 1873 asking him for a loan of four hundred dollars with which he hoped to set up a business placing freed people in northern jobs. "I see a open field before me with Success staring me in the face," Duffin wrote from the New York City and County Hall of Records, where he might have clerked, "and I only desire a little capital the business is to open an Intelligence office for to supply the great demand for southern help." Duffin told Smith that he would take out a life insurance policy in any amount as collateral.[46]

Southern blacks were drawn principally to industrial cities in New Jersey, Pennsylvania, and New York; and the character of this movement explains why Geneva's population of African Americans shrunk after the war even as New York State's increased.[47] By 1870, only 196 African Americans lived in Geneva, 35 percent fewer than had lived there in 1860. In Ontario County generally, the African-American population dropped by a little less than 1 percent over the next five years, although it grew modestly in rural Wayne County, just north of Geneva, and in Saratoga County, where heightened work opportunities in prosperous Saratoga Springs resorts drew migrants. Between 1870 and 1875, African Americans moved in greatest numbers to such cities as Rochester and Elmira, which were industrially vigorous and home to comparatively large black populations.

Like other northern cities, Geneva was on the brink of an industrial boom after the Civil War, but it was not as well poised for this growth as it had been for commercial development. Like Buffalo, Geneva had no natural source of water power, and large-scale industrial growth depended upon the coming of electricity to the village in 1883. Its link to suitable materials and broader markets was made firm only six years earlier by a new railroad that ran along the west side of Seneca Lake to Pennsylvania coal fields and tidewater cities. Its most significant industrial growth was thus a feature of the 1880s. At the beginning of that decade, Geneva had only eleven factories, whose collective product was assessed at $58,940. In 1890, thirty-seven industries—malt houses, stove and boiler manufacturers, cereal companies, lens makers, and boat builders—produced goods worth more than $2.5 million. Between 1880 and 1900, the village's population rose from 5,878 to 10,433, and by the end of the century Geneva legally became a city.[48]

But the village's African Americans had found their primary occupational niches in transportation and domestic services, and here opportunities narrowed drastically for them after the war. The carriage of coal and such raw and heavy materials as sand kept barges competitive with rail transport well into the twentieth century, but weather could affect the water carriers more seriously than it did the railroad: in 1872, a lengthy drought lowered the water level in the canal so greatly that 250,000 tons of freight, mostly coal, could not be shipped by barge. The profitability of the Cayuga and Seneca Canal plummeted as far fewer boats and goods were moved on water. In 1870, only eight years after a state-financed project deepened the channel for heavy coal barges, Cayuga and Seneca tolls were $23,000, lower than they had been in 1847. By 1882, tolls fell to just $1,300.[49] The decline in barge traffic must certainly have shrunk opportunities for cartmen and draymen, and the increase in rail traffic probably meant more and steadier work only for those whom the railroad already employed.

Moreover, by the end of the Civil War, Geneva's far larger Irish population—which had in fact grown more than 9 percent between 1870 and 1875, faster than the total growth in population in both Geneva and Ontario County—was sufficiently well established to compete effectively with blacks for jobs on every front, particularly in the village's new factories. Before 1893, no African Americans are known to have worked in Geneva's largest industries—the Nester malt houses (opened in 1871), the New York Central Iron Works (founded in 1851 and immensely profitable after the war as demand increased for steam-heating boilers), Herendeen Manufacturing Company (1878), Phillips and Clark Stove Company (1885), and Patent Cereals Company (1888).[50]

The general emancipation had provoked another wave of fear in the North about the potential competition of cheaper black labor, feelings exacerbated by the use of African Americans as strikebreakers in iron and steel foundries and coal fields during the 1870s and 1880s. Animosity toward freed blacks was also fueled, ironically, by the postwar constitutional amendments guaranteeing equal rights for African Americans. Overtly in the South and more subtly in the North, an intricate system of social constraints upon their actions, justified by the growing popularity of Darwinian-influenced ideas about white superiority, replaced prewar legal constraints.[51] Uncertainty about what places in Geneva society freed blacks, their numbers newly supplemented, would occupy expressed itself in the bitter dispute over school integration and in disparaging editorial snipes at black suffrage and the federal government's efforts to help new freedmen through the Freedmen's Bureau. Yet, a stable core of African Americans remained in Geneva from its prewar years, their persistence strongly associated with their ownership of property.

Most of the large increases in New York's African-American population between 1870 and 1875 occurred along two corridors— one from Pennsylvania through Binghamton and Cortland and thence to Syracuse (now the approximate path of Interstate 81), and the other from Pennsylvania along the Chemung and Cohocton rivers, through Corning, through the rural Genesee Valley and Livingston County, and on to Rochester (Route 17 and Interstate 390). At least one African-American family in Geneva may have come to the state along the more westerly of these paths. By 1870, Minor Linzy, born in 1851 in Virginia's Loudoun County, was a single farm laborer in East Bloomfield, a farming village on the northeastern edge of the Genesee Valley. George Payne, a thirty-eight-year-old day laborer from Orange County, Virginia, lived in West Bloomfield with his two daughters, Dolly and Jennie. In July 1875, Linzy and Dolly Payne married in Auburn (not close to the Bloomfields, which suggests that kin already lived in the region) and rented a house in West Bloomfield. By about 1903, Linzy and his family rented a two-acre farm on the western outskirts of Geneva, property he bought in 1919. His son Daniel had married Lula E. Ray, daughter of African-American teamster William Ray, and was boarding at the Ray's Pulteney Street home in that year. Ray's wife, Amanda Gates, had been born during the Civil War in Oaklona, Mississippi, and probably came to Geneva with her brother Charles sometime before 1875. And by 1905, Minor Linzy's half-brother, also named Daniel, lived in Geneva with his Virginia-born wife and four children. Family legend has it that though Minor and Daniel Linzy shared the same African-American mother, Daniel's father was African American while Minor's was white—in fact, his mother's owner. Descendants of both Linzy branches remain in Geneva, and Minor Linzy's granddaughter Dorothy Cooke is usually entrusted to relate the story of the kinward migration and the lore about the mulatto children of white plantation owners.

My grandfather, and grandmother, apparently came from Virginia, and the name that sticks in my mind, that I've heard over and over again, is Loudoun County, and then somebody said something about Culpepper, Virginia, so I have to check that all out. My grandmother and her sister and brothers apparently left a plantation with their whole family and came north, and they came through Washington, and they said that my grandmother's mother, well, she got pneumonia coming across the Potomac River, and she died. And they continued coming. My grandmother's sister went to Canada. . . . Now, my grandfather, as you can tell, was mulatto. What the interesting part was, when they lived on the plantation, they said that he looked exactly like his master's son, exactly, they looked alike; it got to the point, I guess, where people were taking him for his master's son, doing things for *him*, you know, so it got too much for his father, so he apparently asked him to leave. So that's why he left the plantation and came north. And then they also said that after he got up here and got settled, he went back to look for that brother. He could not find the brother, because the brother—I don't know exactly what happened, but he changed his name, anyway, and he couldn't find him.[52]

Like Minor Linzy and Charles and Amanda Gates, most of the small number of African Americans who came to Geneva after 1875 were single. Six single or widowed women, born in Tennessee, Alabama, Maryland, Virginia, and Pennsylvania, had moved to the village by 1870, two living and working as domestics in the homes of white people, four boarding with African Americans. Only one couple and one family group had come from the South to Geneva by 1870, and nine persons had moved there from other places in New York State. But the greatest part of this postwar migration was single men, eight of whom married women who were native New Yorkers. Henry Scott, born in Maryland in 1825, had come to the village before 1870 and had married the widow Permelia Hardy, who had three teenage daughters. By 1870, Wesley Robinson, born in South Carolina in 1836, had married Harriet Gillam, a native Genevan who must have returned home from Utica after her husband, Thomas, died there in 1867. African-American women had long outnumbered African-American men in Geneva, a disproportion that had grown more pronounced. In 1840, 54 percent of the local black population was female; in 1870, 60 percent was. The migration of single men helped move the balance closer to parity: by 1900, women were just less than 53 percent of Geneva's African-American population. Of the thirty couples whose birthplaces were listed in the 1900 census, ten included men born in the South whose wives were born in New York; two couples were male New Yorkers and southern-born women, and sixteen marriages were between native New Yorkers.[53]

Small as it was, the rate of this migration slowed between 1870 and 1900. Thirty African Americans, almost all of them from other places in New York, had come to the village between 1860 and 1865; only sixteen came over the next five years. By 1900, the migration from the South to Geneva fell to a trickle, even as twenty-one thousand blacks moved into New York State between 1890 and 1900.[54] Just less than a quarter of African-American adults living in Geneva had been born in a southern state, and all of the children listed in the 1900 census had been born in New York.

By 1900, inmigration had become barely noticeable against the tide of outmigration. By 1905, the population reached a low of about one hundred; not since the decade between 1810 and 1820, when the village was still small and young, had there been so few African Americans in Geneva. Then, their share of the population had been between four and 8 percent; by 1905, African Americans were not even 2 percent of Geneva's total population. By 1915, even though the black population had grown in real terms by sixty people (about 27 percent), the growth in the white population was so much faster that African Americans composed barely 1 percent of the population. Newcomers were 29 percent of the total population; they had been only 8 percent in 1870. It would appear, then, that even though a small group of longtime residents remained in Geneva, many of their children did not. Confronted as they were with far fewer chances for employment and home ownership than their parents and grandparents had been, they experienced a curious kind of downward mobility in an era when the American gospel of the self-made man reached its apogee.

1915–1940: Industrial Laborers in the "Great Migration"

None of the nineteenth-century migrations of African-American people had changed the basic historical geography of their settlement pattern in the United States: by 1910, seven million blacks still lived in the South and fewer than one million in the North. But the "great migration" between the world wars brought nearly one million African Americans into large northern cities and factories. The urban and industrial nature of this movement was far more pronounced than it had been after the Civil War. Impelled by the boll weevil infestation, Jim Crow, and intense competition of white rural laborers for the South's new industrial jobs, southern African Americans accepted the mass invitation proffered by northern capitalists and railroad companies to take low-level factory jobs traditionally filled by European immigrants, whose entry into the United States had been curtailed during World War I.[55]

Factory jobs also opened up to women, which created a shortage in the domestic labor market. In December 1917, an African-American newspaper, the *Chicago Defender,* reported that the New York State Employment Bureau hoped "to effect a partial amelioration of the domestic problem by cooperating with Rev. L. B. Brown, pastor of Olive Baptist Church, to bring about 75 here from the south to take places in households, which it has been found next to impossible to fill. Seventy-five women are wanted here from 18 to 30 years old. Part of their fare will be paid. Women workers are in great demand. Such places are open: shirt makers, bindery workers, laundry workers, weavers, pastry cooks, children's nurses and laundresses."[56]

The great migration was more oriented to kin than earlier ones had been. Throughout the North, the post–Civil War movement had established networks of relatives and former townsmen that sometimes drew entire families and virtually entire towns to the area in the new century.[57] But in these years, Geneva offered neither substantial industrial opportunity nor the lure of a sizable African-American community. The small group of African Americans who persisted in the village, supplemented though it was by a smaller group of new southerners after the war, formed a weak host. Those few drawn to Geneva between the wars tended instead to come from other northern places. About 21 percent of the 161 African Americans listed as Genevans in the 1925 state census had settled in the city since 1915. Only 2 of these 34 new residents were single people. Fully half of them were northerners who were related to each other, but who lived in three separate households; rather than moving toward relatives already settled there, in effect they transferred an entire kin network to Geneva.

Lena Brown Dunham and Manuel Brown were siblings. Born in Corning, New York, in 1881, Brown worked as a mason at United States Radiator (formerly Herendeen Manufacturing Company) and lived in Geneva with his wife, his nephew James Tyson (also employed at U.S. Radiator), and Tyson's wife, who worked as a domestic. Lena Brown Dunham lived next door with her four children and William Cuffe, a cupola tender at the same foundry, whom she apparently had taken as a second husband. Lena Dunham's eldest son George lived and worked at a nearby "auto laundry" with his wife, two children, and two stepchildren. At some point before 1936, Lena and Manuel's mother, Clista Louckes Brown, born in 1854 in Sharon Springs, New York, had come to Geneva to live as well. Like the Dunhams, the family of Richard Jackson had also come to Geneva since 1915 from New York's southern tier. The remaining eleven newcomers were childless couples or small families, and only one is known to have come from Virginia.

By 1930, Geneva's black population had again fallen to just fewer than 120 people, living in only 30 families. These African Americans accounted for less than 1 percent of the total population of the city, and, compared to black populations in large cities, they were a minuscule group. Even compared to other New York cities of similar size, Geneva's African-American population was abnormally small. Of all cities in the state with fewer than one hundred thousand inhabitants, only Oswego had a smaller number of black households. Saratoga, a smaller city than Geneva in 1930, had more than five times the number of black households; Ithaca, with only 40 percent more households than Geneva, had more than four hundred times the number of black households. In Auburn, only 63 of 9,053 total households in the city were those of African Americans; in fact, black Auburnians may have been a smaller part of their city's population than black Genevans were. Still, Auburn seems to have been the city to which Genevans were most apt to go in these years for social life, and the difference between 30 households and 63 must have made Auburn seem a different world, both qualitatively and quantitatively.[58]

By the time the great migration began, Geneva's industrial base had already begun its long, slow slide. Some of the city's older industries, such as U.S. Radiator, Andes Range and Furnace Corporation (formerly Phillips and Clark), Patent Cereals Company, and Geneva Optical Company (later Shuron Optical Company), still prospered; new ones, such as American Can Company, had chosen to locate in Geneva. But many others had closed or relocated. A strike among workers at Alfred Catchpole's foundry, by then owned by Syracuse plumbing and pipe manufacturer Pierce, Butler, and Pierce, provoked the company's return to Syracuse after 1903. Samuel K. Nester's malt houses, claimed to be the nation's third largest in 1892, closed in 1910, two years after Nester's death. The New York Central Iron Works moved to Hagerstown, Maryland, in 1912, and boat and engine building at the reconstituted Fay and Bowen Engine Company, opened in 1904, had closed by 1937. By this time, too, the downtown section of the Cayuga and Seneca Canal, immediately obsolete when the New York State Barge Canal chose to locate its terminal at the Seneca River outlet at the northeastern edge of Seneca Lake, had begun to be filled in with all manner of dirt and debris, choking off a century of active water transport and commerce.

Skilled and supervisory positions in industry remained largely unavailable to Geneva's African Americans, and for those uninterested in or unable to afford college but disinclined to take foundry or domestic work, opportunities in Geneva were virtually nonexistent. The small size of the African-American population compounded the problem. In Geneva, blacks were isolated in two senses of the word—they were easily singled out, and they were set apart because of it. Dorothy Cooke, one of three African Americans in the Geneva High School graduating class in 1934, described the situation she faced at the time.

> I was supposed to go to college. Uncle Stanley was all set to send me. I wanted to go to Howard University. It just sounded like a fascinating place to go, I guess; we knew quite a bit about it. My courses were preparatory to going to college . . . my mind was set for it; I was all set to go. And he died in 1932, and I graduated in '34; well, that was all lost. So the courses that I took did not prepare for the working field, 'cause I should have taken typing and courses like that. I didn't. I took the romance, the liberal arts, and English. I loved English, and I was an A student for four years in English.
>
>   . . . I didn't even try [to get a job in Geneva after high school]. I just didn't want to stay here because I didn't want to be around the people I went to school with, 'cause I couldn't have done anything but domestic work, and I certainly wasn't going to work for the people I went to school with. Just pride. I couldn't do it. I'm still that type of a person. I went to Rochester, because there was nothing. . . . My mother decided to go, so just my mother and I went. My father was living in Elmira at the time. I think we rented a room at first, and she got a job in a private family, and I think I did, too.

Charles Kenney, who graduated from Geneva High School a year later, was a basketball and track star, played and sang leading roles in high school operettas, and wanted a career in sports or music.

> There was a lot of industry here; principal was the American Can Company, but they didn't want any blacks. They had one; he was a janitor.
>
> . . . The cynical thing about all of this—the Hovey family here in Geneva owned the Market Basket chain, which was a grocery chain. This was their headquarters here, and they had a big complex years ago where they ground their own coffee—big, big, huge place, big place for business. His kids used to play here, and I used to go up there and play up on Castle Street. He had a basketball court up in the attic, and, you know, we were like this. You would never know there was a color line. And actually, between us kids, there wasn't.
>
> When it come time for me to get a job, un-unh. They didn't want any part of any black. And it was like that generally all over. When I got out of school, if I wanted to work, I had to go over and work in the foundry, where my brother John went. I didn't want any part of that. If that's what you're adapted to do, fine. I wanted to continue sports activities, or vocal; you see the caption under my thing [his high school yearbook picture], they expected great things from me. But it didn't last very long, because in those days Cab Calloway used to come here, couldn't stay in the hotels, Duke Ellington, Jimmy Lunsford, they couldn't stay in the hotels. . . . They were shoved around terrible.
>
> . . . I did a stint in Temple, not for long, 1935, '36. They had a good basketball team and a good basketball coach, Pop Warner. In those days it cost, what, five hundred bucks. My father had just finished putting my older sister through Geneseo Normal, and helped her with her master's; and then the crash. I couldn't take it down there, expense-wise. So I came home, and that's when I went to Rochester, and I worked for a women's apparel store called Wilbur Rogers that used to be on Main Street, and I worked for them as a janitor, porter, you name it.[59]

For John Kenney, staying in Geneva was not so much a matter of will as of necessity. Two years older than his brother Charles, he was one of the first blacks to be hired at Geneva Foundry, where he worked most of his life. By 1933, the year he graduated from high school, his older sister and brother had left Geneva, he had four younger siblings, and his father had just been laid off from his longtime job as checker at the New York Central Railroad freight depot.

Despite excellent high school grades and college entrance examination scores, his parents told him, "You help home."[60]

1940–1965: Construction Workers, Servicemen, and Farm Workers

Outmigration continued to chip away at the African-American population base in Geneva until World War II. In 1940, African Americans numbered only 109 persons, down from 153 in 1930, and constituted less than 1 percent of the city's population. Their vital statistics hint that further decline was likely. Fully 85 percent of Geneva's African Americans were fourteen years old or older, suggesting that fewer women were producing children. But with the emergency mobilization for war, military and commercial agricultural interests presented the region's first true overture to southern black labor. In the early 1940s, the northeastern shore of Seneca Lake was selected as the site for a huge armaments storage facility and a base to train navy recruits. Throughout the war and more intently afterwards, the state worked with farmers to bring agricultural workers north to do the still largely unmechanized tasks of harvesting and processing fruits and vegetables.

Conceived in 1940, Seneca Ordnance Depot ultimately covered a section of Seneca County eight miles long and four miles wide just southeast of Geneva. At the peak of its construction, the project involved more than 8,800 persons. The site was to contain five hundred igloos (most of them underground) in which military supplies would be stored, barracks for five hundred troops, and other buildings. About half of the four thousand people hired to build the depot by September 1941 were Genevans. Another 30 percent had come from towns within a fifty-mile radius of the site. Yet as employment mushroomed, some 2,800 workers came from outside New York State, including about 350 African Americans.

Construction at Sampson Naval Training Station began in 1942 within months of the completion of the ordnance depot. The navy estimated that building the station—more than four hundred buildings on 2,535 acres, including barracks, mess and drill halls, fire stations, a 1,500-bed hospital, and numerous recreational and support structures—would require twelve to fifteen thousand people. Commander J. C. Gebhard, the engineer in charge of Sampson's construction, acknowledged that the scarcity of workers in the region would compel the navy to bring in labor "from outside." The *Geneva Daily Times* reported in mid-1942, "Many of the workers coming in

10. Workers registering and taking quarters at Sampson Naval Training Station, 1942. *Courtesy Geneva Historical Society.*

from outside will seize the opportunity to bring their families with them into the vacation land of the Finger Lakes," and Gebhard estimated this time that as many as twenty thousand people might come to the region for the temporary work the project offered. Over the summer and fall of 1942, the shortage of white male construction laborers grew so severe that contractors began to recruit African-American men, principally from New York City; in the end, an estimated seven thousand of the twenty-five thousand construction workers on both bases were African American (fig. 10). Four thousand of these workers inexplicably left over the Labor Day weekend, near the peak of construction activity, as 15,500 workers prepared to open the base for its first training group on 15 September.[61]

In 1943, after the construction of both bases had been completed, many laborers stayed on as civilian workers, cleaning and cooking for the thirty-five thousand troops housed at Sampson (in

all, the base trained more than 411,000 sailors) and assembling armaments at the depot. After the war, the depot was expanded and
continued to be used for munitions storage. By the end of 1946,
slightly fewer than six hundred civilians continued to work there,
but the depot remained one of the region's largest employers.[62]

Perry Carter, Sr., born in Sanford, Florida, in 1922, was one of
many drawn to Geneva by the military construction projects. In
1939, he had moved with his family to Bristol, Pennsylvania, outside
Philadelphia, to work on a large commercial farm. He married in
Philadelphia in 1942, and in July, when contractors were hiring hundreds of laborers a day to build Sampson, he and his wife Margaret
moved to Geneva.

> The man that we were working with, he wanted somebody to work
> for a while, and they was paying twice as much as we was getting,
> so I came up there [to Bristol] in '39 to work, and then I went back
> to Sanford and I came back in '41 and stayed, spreading fertilizer,
> hauling beets and carrots and stuff. You load 'em on the wagon
> and you take 'em to the packhouse. My father got upset with farm
> work, so he came up to Geneva, and they were starting to build
> Sampson, so he started to work out there. And he wrote back, and
> so then me and my mother, we come over from Bristol. So I got a
> job out there . . . and then I sent back to Pennsylvania and got my
> wife. So I guess about a year or maybe two, anyway, my oldest
> brother James, he come to Geneva, and he brought John Henry
> Williams. Like Walter Stuart, he came to Geneva because I sent and
> got my wife.[63]

The migration that began about 1940 was a movement of both
single people and family groups. With her grandmother, Dorothy
Hill Eldridge, born in Osceola, Arkansas, in 1940, followed her
grandfather to Geneva. Later, her mother and father joined them.
Harry Gramling was two when his grandparents brought him and
his sister from Sanford to Wolcott, New York, and then to Geneva in
1940. Like the Carters and the Gramlings, Cora Moore Burke, born
in 1914 on a farm, came from Sanford.

> I came here in 1942, I think. My husband was stationed here, and
> after he retired, after that, he worked pressing clothes and sent for
> me and I came here. . . . I'm the only one [in my family] that living
> north, and I been here forty-some years.[64]

Alvin Robinson, born in Viadet, Georgia, in 1916 and raised in West Palm Beach, Florida, and New Brunswick, New Jersey, was sent to the area with thirteen other African-American soldiers for ordnance training at Seneca depot.

> I finished college at West Virginia State University. Then I kicked around for a couple of years, and Uncle Sam grabbed me. I went in the military in '41 and stayed until 31st of December 1945, came out, came back to Geneva, and decided to settle here.
>
> . . . I was married, and after I'd been here for a while my wife came up to set up residence. She went to work at the ordnance depot, and I left here to go to a port of embarkation. She remained here while I was overseas. I was overseas for two years and ten months, and she stayed here employed at the ordnance depot. And when I came back, it was a sort of decision-making time, as to whether we were going to stay here or go somewhere else. And one thing led to another, and—well, I can't truthfully say. I guess maybe we kept putting it off, and then I went to work for a place they called the Market Basket, which was a wholesale grocery concern. I went to work for them for about a year as a janitor, and I eventually worked up to the position of baker's helper, which is about one and a half steps above a janitor; you do basically the same things, except you learn how to make bread.
>
> . . . This was during a highly sensitive era in the history of the country, socially. Segregation was rampant, you know, and jobs were few, and of course there was quite a bit of competition for jobs. And the economic situation is always in my opinion seemingly being the pre-emptive thing that caused racial dissension and whatnot. Because it's a competition thing. If I think you're taking my job, hey, all of the sudden you become a you know what, you know. It was difficult to find jobs, mainly, I think, because those of us who had been promised the jobs we might have been in previous to going into the military suddenly found women in these jobs, who, having made money, were not willing to give them up. And rightly so; they had earned the right to have them. But it created a highly competitive market.[65]

War work gave new life to the region's stores and many local industries whose work forces had already been affected by enlistments and the draft. The draft coupled with the sheer volume of war-related manufacturing to exacerbate the labor shortage, and new federal legislation gave African Americans access to defense industry jobs. And the war emergency stimulated a far more extensive and organized drive to recruit African-American farm laborers to harvest New York crops when efforts to solicit help locally—shortening the school day so that students could work in the afternoons; mobilizing teachers, women, college girls, and prisoners of war; and importing workers from Jamaica and the Bahamas—failed to supply the amount of labor needed for the annual task.

New York had sought migrant farm labor to pick beans and peas since before World War I, but with the war the effort intensified. A network of crew leaders assembled and hired farm laborers in southeastern states and brought them north during slack periods in the southern agricultural cycle. By 1943, the state recruited "negro farm laborers" in large numbers.[66] The movement north is thought to have peaked in 1949, when fifty-eight thousand persons, most of them African Americans, moved up the Atlantic coast to camps throughout central and western New York State and on Long Island (fig. 11). In 1954, snap beans, sweet corn, tomatoes, cabbage, peas, and onions occupied the largest amounts of vegetable acreage. In central New York, much acreage was also given over to beets. The largest fruit belt was just south of Lake Ontario, where 70 percent of the total work in fruit was required to harvest cherries, peaches, pears, plums, and grapes. All highly perishable, these fruits and vegetables needed to be harvested rapidly and canned, frozen, or sold fresh; the canning factories near these crop-growing areas, concentrated especially around Rochester and Buffalo, also had high labor requirements. Like harvesting itself, much of the processing work in these plants was not mechanized until the late 1950s.[67]

In 1957, the New York State Department of Labor estimated that between thirty-three and thirty-eight thousand out-of-state, migratory seasonal workers were in New York State. Nearly 80 percent of them were "southern Negroes," the rest coming from Puerto Rico, Jamaica, and the Bahamas. Fewer than one thousand were white. Nearly 80 percent of migrant workers surveyed in a sample of registered farm labor camps, whose numbers had grown from 656 in 1953 to more than 1,000 in 1957, spent the winters in Florida; the rest wintered in Georgia, Alabama, North and South Carolina, Mississippi, and other states.[68] Charles Kenney, who had worked in Rochester and Auburn and returned to Geneva to live in his family's Castle Street home in 1951, described the migration from a resident's point of view.

There were migrant workers, generally from Florida, from Sanford, Florida; there was a big influx of them. This was before Sampson.

11. Migrant farm laborers at Wayne County Cooperative Growers and Processors Camp, 1955–1960. *Courtesy Agri-Business Child Development, Schenectady, New York.*

[The migrant camps] were all around here—King Ferry, which is just outside of Auburn, Savannah, and right around here, there were migrant camps. Initially, these people would go from camp to camp to camp to camp, until the season was over, and then they'd leave. Maybe one or two would stay, somehow. And then the next year, here they come again, and when the season was over, maybe three or four would stay, so that gradually they found things getting better, so that more and more stayed. They were able to get the foundry, domestic work in and around here; then Sampson came in.

Rosa Blue, who with her husband moved from Madison, Florida, in 1949 to join kin in Geneva, described the pushes and pulls of migrating north:

I think one of the reasons people left the South was as automation [came], small farms kind of went out of business, sharecropping kind of went out of business. Coming with the war, also, it opened up opportunities, better job opportunities, and people tend to seek them. And of course even before then, you've always known—you had a few relatives who had moved North and who showed when they came around that there was a better way of life. So it kind of encouraged you to think about doing something different. Many of the people who came here did not just come; I think the seasonal employment might have brought my sister-in-law's family here. People usually in the South might move from Alabama, Mississippi, Georgia, and go to South Florida, to do seasonal work, to harvest the fruit, the vegetables. And then that work as I understand it ended early spring, and there would be no more work until the fall. So people started migrating to the North to harvest the crops up this way. Those people usually went back South. But with the increasing of employment opportunities along with the war, and the need for help, people took advantage of those opportunities, and stayed. And as they told about the accomplishments, it encouraged other people to come to stay also. And then finally, the population grew.

In the agricultural migration, crew leaders were the liaison between southern agricultural workers and northern farmers. Virginia Peek, born in Perrine, Florida, in 1928 of Bahamian parents, finished the third grade before she began farm work at the age of eleven. She described how she happened to come to upstate New York.

We catch the truck around six in the morning, six-thirty in the morning; we get back home around five, five-thirty. Sometime if we get through with the field earlier we get home early, get home around three-thirty, four o'clock, you know. But most of the time it's around five, five-thirty. In Florida it ain't like up here. In Florida you works like most of the year round, dropping tomato plants, hoeing tomatoes, picking tomatoes, picking string beans. And when it's not time for the beans and the tomatoes you working in the peppers, sweet peppers, okra, different stuff. There's always something to do there. You picking berries or something because the weather there is kinda good, you know, the year round, compared to here. Here you got a little season, you gotta do what you gonna do in three months, and it's over, you know.

I left home and went to Fort Pierce, Florida, where I worked in beans, tomatoes, and stuff, you know, tomatoes by the bucket. I was around about fifteen. And we worked at Fort Pierce and then as you work there when the season go down there, there be trucks coming up on the season, right? So I thought I come up on the season and I met my husband. He come up along too but at the time I didn't know him. We all went to Lyons, New York, in '48. When I got over to Lyons, New York, that's where I met him at. . . . There was trucks, trucks load of people. I say about at least ten trucks was following one another, belongs to Blake. Henry Blake was the man that owned the trucks, bringing peoples up, you know, to work. He bring 'em up to Lyons and Phelps, New York, different places he had already set up for the people to live. Then you picked cherries, and you pick, oh, apples; whoever like to pick apples they'd pick apples, cherries, whatever.[69]

Not all migratory workers came specifically for farm work; in fact, few workers surveyed in 1957 preferred it. They aspired instead to "non-farm, steady jobs." Essie Tucker, born in 1912 on her father's farm in Bristol, Florida, came north because she wanted her children to have a better education.

People used to talk and talk about, you know, if you got your education in Florida and you came North, you have to take it all over again. After their father died, the kids, they got to worrying me. They wanted to come North. People talked about the North; they was making like it was so cold up there and I wondered was it colder up there than it was down here.

. . . Me and my kids [came]. See, I knowed some people over there in Lyons, and so I moved over there. K. P. Clark. They was from Tallahassee, Florida. One of the brothers, he used to work down there in pulpwood. I came in '57 to Art DeMay's camp. I run the camp. There were 'round about thirty people, some from Florida, some from Georgia, some from Alabama.[70]

According to Rosa Blue, the migration from Madison, Florida, was similar to the one taking place at the time from Sanford.

I grew up in Madison, Florida, and got married kind of young. My husband, Clifford Blue, and I moved here after we'd had our first child. He at the time had a sister, Edna Blue Tompkins, who lived here, with her husband, David. And I guess the reason that they moved here was because her husband's sister had lived here since the early '40s, Juanita Andrew; her husband was Gaston Andrew. So that's probably how I came to come here.

. . . We came to Geneva in 1949. Quite a few families who are not related to us, who did not come here because of us, were [from Madison]. Most people come this way seeking employment opportunities, and better race relations. And the employment thing is more essential than anything else. People just seemed to join each other, another member of the family comes. . . . After I came, my brother that's next to me came in 1956, I believe. When we came, there weren't many people here, period. And many of the people who came later, not only from Florida but Alabama, Mississippi— there were people from North Carolina—[came up] up the eastern coastline.

The use of better fertilizers, pesticides and insecticides, and more robust plant varieties increased yields so that demand for agricultural labor remained high into the early 1960s. But shortly afterward, the introduction of new mechanical harvesting equipment for corn, potatoes, beans, onions, and spinach began to lessen the need for imported labor. Still, Sampson, Seneca Ordnance Depot, and commercial farming created a population increase in Geneva, most notably among African Americans. The African-American population grew 62 percent between 1940 and 1950, an appreciably greater increase than the 10 percent growth in the city's total population in that decade. Continued recruiting of African Americans for New York State harvests brought far greater population growth by 1960. In Geneva, the African-American population grew 550 percent between 1940 and 1960: where only 109 lived in the city in 1940, 710 did in 1960. Elmira, Auburn, and Ithaca, all larger cities, experienced nothing like this rate of growth in their African-American populations, and Oswego actually lost eight of its tiny group of thirty-two.

Even as the post-1940 migration fortified Geneva's African-American population base, it changed its composition in ways that made it less accurate to think of it as a community than as an aggregation of persons of the same race. Half a century had passed since more than a handful of African Americans had settled in Geneva. By the 1950s, even those with southern roots were northern people. In large part, the postwar agricultural migration was composed of rural and small-town African Americans from the South who had had little or no contact with urban life and northern culture. For Genevans of both races, their initial transience was clearly unsettling, a traffic whose effect was amplified by the extreme mobility and explosive, though short-lived, population growth of the war years. Some African Americans who had lived a long time in Geneva welcomed the influx of new people, for it greatly expanded the possibilities of social and family life. Others perceived the interface between established African-American residents and newcomers more as a collision. Among themselves and to whites, Geneva's African Americans began to speak of the "old families" and the "new families," groups distinguished from each other in both articulate and inarticulate ways (fig. 12). The old families lived in neighborhoods on the bluff. They thought of themselves as more apt to own homes than to rent apartments. Their religious life was more sedate and canonical. They were emphatically not rural, even if they were not exactly urban. The new families, as seen through the eyes of old families, were ignorant of, and resistant to, the rhythms and codes of urban living. They rented tenements and worn-down, carved-up houses in the flat along Geneva's shoreline, an area far more industrial in character than residential. To some old families, their religious practices were jarringly enthusiastic.

Most significantly, the political ideas and practices of old and new families diverged inimically. Since 1855, the old African-American families had experienced the withering effect of every person who moved to another place. They could not sustain institutions they had earlier created. There was not enough sheer numerical strength to build new ones, as blacks in such other small cities as Ithaca and Auburn did after the Civil War. Even after 1900, when a noticeable number of new people came to town, their arrival was more than balanced by the departures of greater numbers of others. When these others were longtime residents or their children, the loss carried greater meaning and left in its wake a nagging effect.

In the 1840s, Geneva's blacks attended conventions. In the 1920s, they played cards in their homes. They were generations removed from the kind of political action that members of new families took not long after they had settled in Geneva. African Americans came from the South in years when a new, and newly combative, wave of civil rights activity had begun to grip their old region. For years, many of them had heard the myths of the North—the better schools, the absence of segregation, the freedom of movement. But the persistent discrimination and de facto segregation they instead confronted disabused them. Their immediate disappointment moved them to create the city's first known chapter of the National Association for the Advancement of Colored People and to use it to protest the limitations and conditions of the work, schooling, and housing available to them. They also organized marches in sympathy with southern civil rights struggles, a form of

12. Norman Kenney, Charles Moore, Paula Moore, and Harold Gates (Jim) Foster at 15 Grove Street, Geneva, 1932. All members of "old families," these friends stood on the lawn of 15 Grove Street, the property Norman Kenney's great-grandfather, William T. Kenney, purchased in 1869. Foster was the great-great-grandson of Anthony Jupiter, a Genevan since the 1820s. The Moores' father, Ernest, an engineer, had come to Geneva by 1915, married Geneva native Helena Ray, and bought a home in the High Street neighborhood. *Courtesy Geneva Historical Society.*

protest members of old families thought ill-advised because it demonstrated how little new families actually knew about Geneva. It was they, they reasoned, who really knew Geneva, who really knew how to get things done there, who really knew how to live there. To them, open protest blasted the potential effectiveness of well-taught and hard-learned ways of managing local white society. The conflict between old and new families became not so much the disjuncture of urban and rural ways, or northern and southern upbringing, though it certainly involved those things; it embodied more fundamentally a disagreement about how African-American people could live securely in northern places.

Old Families and New Families

Two days after the Fourth of July in 1853, African Americans from the eastern coastal states to Illinois arrived in Rochester to serve as delegates to the colored national convention that year. On the evening of the first day, they listened as the committee on social relations and polity gave a critical report on the population's general status, how the patent failure of "two distinct, yet inseparable branches of education . . . that of the *School-Room* and that of the *Fire-Side*" had set, and kept, the population adrift.

> It is lamentable to state, that not more than one in fifty of us possess our own hearth-stones; and this is not so much from the want of means, as from ill management.
>
> A larger number still live crowded, pent up, shoved back, and even piled up and this, too, at rates of expense startling to contemplate; especially is this true in larger cities.
>
> When we add to this the feebleness and instability, the utter helplessness of a floating people, not possessing the very roofs that shelter them, having no anchorage, hold, or even footing in the soil from whence they derive their subsistence—we would earnestly call attention to this matter, hoping that in some tangible form it may be brought to bear upon our people.[1]

The committee was particularly critical of the want of "fire-side culture," which, it asserted, affected the "present and prospective advancement" of the race in every respect. For home was where one imparted and imbibed "the great lessons of self-confidence, self-dependence, perseverance, energy, and continuity," those things that made a people seek "proper callings" and disdain "all such as tend to humiliate, depress, and degrade." But the absence of stable home life had made African-American youth "unsettled in purpose, and unstable in habits, not yet inured to proper labor," and "enfeebled" in mind, body, and character.

> They have emerged from homes surrounded by so few attractions, that they know little of the bliss of home, and shrink from the responsibility, or even the thought of providing them for themselves. . . . Of one thing we are certain; comfortable homes and hearths, and correct culture and habits, tend to the increase of a people; the reverse to their diminution.[2]

The importance the committee placed on owning homes was, in part, eminently Victorian; the idea of home as the source of moral instruction and respectability was endlessly repeated in popular American magazines and advice manuals. But among African Americans, wanting a home and a stable family life embraced something more than the indiscriminate acceptance of the values of white society. In a world where work was unstable, limited, and poorly paid and schools were "indifferent or objectionable" to African-American students, property ownership was the most accessible form of achievement. For blacks, as for certain other American ethnics to whom real occupational mobility has also been foreclosed, owning a home became a more profound signal of "success" than ascent of the ladder from blue- to white-collar work.[3] But a home was also a refuge, a positive center. The idea of home as a haven had currency among whites as well, but confronting so little reward in society at large, blacks found special meaning in it. And African-American family life offered special compensations, principally a more intricate and extensive system of kin, near-kin, and fictive kin than existed among whites.[4]

Property offered a security that no other form of investment could. For African-Americans, it also constituted a symbolic inversion of chattel status: where they had once *been* property, they might now *own* it. In fact, both Gerrit Smith and Henry Highland Garnet believed that until former slaves owned land, true equality would never be possible. "The chains of the last slave on earth may be broken in twain," Garnet argued, "and still, while the unholy system of landlordism prevails, nations and people will mourn."[5]

Property, Family, and Dislocation

But even as African-American leaders identified property ownership as a means to certain progress, as perhaps the only means by
which they might gain access to larger rewards, it was progress
made possible only at inhibiting expense. It sometimes depended on
what historian Tamara Harevan has called "ruthless underconsump-
tion" within the household.[6] For some, keeping a home meant sacrificing children's education to the greater necessity that they earn
wages, and it could have a disintegrating rather than integrating effect on family life. The economic realities of home ownership perpetuated some of the dislocation that had existed under slavery. As
owners could sell children and spouses, so the expense involved in
keeping a home could compel women to remain single, couples to
forego children, mothers and children to work and live in the homes
of whites, husbands to take jobs out of town.

Historians, and some African Americans in Geneva, claim this
dislocation to have arisen from the Atlantic slave trade. In September 1965, Geneva native Mildred Mathis wrote to the editor of the
Geneva Times, "There is no place for us to go, for we do not know
from whence we came."[7] Rosa Blue said, "My great-grandfather was
a slave, but you don't even know what tribe you fitted into. You
pull together what they teach you in school, which is nothing, and
what you really learn is probably what you learned from your great-
great-grandparents and what's been handed down." The American
plantation system perpetuated this disregard for social organization.
As Frederick Douglass observed in 1855, slavery had "no use for
either fathers or families." Douglass himself had lived apart from his
mother as a boy in the 1820s, and he did not know his brothers
and sisters. "*Slavery* had made us strangers," he wrote. "My poor
mother, like many other slave-women, had *many children*, but NO
FAMILY!" Countless sources attest the persistence of an endemically
weak sense of ancestry. In 1863, one Louisville woman was unable
to tell an interviewer her age. "This is what has grieved me a good
deal," she said. "I can't tell you my age to save my life. You know
when children are separated from their parents early, they don't
know how old they are."[8]

Fugitive slave traffic further affected family organization. Although some evidence suggests that the desire to keep families intact might actually have depressed the volume of fugitive slave
traffic, those who did escape tended to escape alone. Geneva's

Peyton Lucas ran away after one of his brothers, his sister, and her two children had been sold into Georgia and another brother had escaped to the North. And, once escaped, fugitives often suppressed information about their backgrounds to protect themselves. "In the state of New York . . . where we lived for many years," wrote fugitive Samuel Ward, "my parents were always in danger of being arrested and re-enslaved. To avoid this, they took every possible caution: among their measures of caution was the keeping of the children quite ignorant of their birthplace, and of their condition, whether free or slave, when born; because children might, by the dropping of a single word, lead to the betrayal of their parents."[9] Ward was never certain that he had been born a slave until he was twenty-four years old. Other African Americans, whether fugitive or freed people, looked back on servitude as a past best forgotten. Essie Tucker, a Florida native who came to Geneva in 1961, said, "My grandfather was a slave. They talk about it some, but in them times they didn't talk too much before children."

A range of family configurations in the North resulted from such disruptions. The Nicholas/Lawson slave register and manumission records show that single men, single women, couples, couples with children, and men and women with children whose spouses (if any) must have lived elsewhere had been brought to Geneva in 1803. Most of the African Americans in Geneva before 1850 were probably unattached people, living singly in white households. Indeed, fully 71 percent of all known black Genevans lived in the homes of whites, either as slaves or as free people, in 1810. In white households where blacks resided, only two—those of John Nicholas and James Rees—contained African Americans in sufficient number to have constituted families. Of the six black households in the 1810 census, only two could have contained families. The other four black householders lived alone.

By 1820, just fewer than half of the blacks listed in the village census still lived in white households, twenty-two of them in William Faulkner's hotel. Some of these twenty-two persons might have been family groups: four were children younger than sixteen whose fathers or mothers may also have lived and worked there. Dry goods merchant Elijah Gordon's household might have included a black woman and her two children: three African-American females, two of them younger than fourteen years old, were listed there in the same census. The number of African-American households had climbed to twenty, twelve of them probably two-parent households with children. In nine of these homes, no child was older than four-teen, suggesting that these families were relatively new ones, per-haps created by former Rose Hill or White Springs Farm slaves.[10] Compared to the ages represented in the village's black population as a whole, fewer persons younger than fourteen and older than forty-five tended to live in the homes of white Genevans. Whites thus tended to house only those blacks who were in their most pro-ductive years, and the preponderance of people between fourteen and forty-five living in white homes might have limited the ability of the village's blacks to form families. In the village as a whole, a rela-tively larger group of blacks than whites were in their child-bearing years, but a smaller proportion of the black population was younger than fourteen. Geneva's African Americans either lived in newer families or were not in families at all.

By 1855, the living situations of African Americans had changed dramatically. Only 29 percent lived in black households in 1810; by 1855, more than 80 percent did. Even so, nearly one in five African Americans still lived in a white household. Albert Arnold's fifteen-year-old daughter Joanne lived with Eleanor Wheeler, a fifty-one-year-old white widow with four children. Mary Bland, who was seventeen in 1855, was a live-in servant in the home of widow Sarah Hemiup and her three children. The sisters Margaret and Emily Douglass lived in separate white households, and Margaret may have continued to do so even after she bought a $250 lot on High Street in 1852. The 1855 state census listed Arabella Brown, the el-dest of hackman William T. Brown's six children, both at her father's home and at the home of dry goods merchant David S. Spier, whose wife was a Southerner. Born a slave in Maryland in 1805, Brown was evidently prosperous enough to build a brick home valued at fifteen hundred dollars and to purchase the freedom of his enslaved par-ents. But the fact that Arabella worked and perhaps boarded outside her home suggests that the size of her parents' household was large enough to compel her to earn her keep.

In the twentieth century, many domestics listed as living in white homes kept residences of their own as well, even if they had little time to spend in them. Dorothy Cooke's father, Joseph Scott, was a chauffeur and butler; her mother, Mabel Linzy Scott, was a live-in cook and, later, a cateress. But because her parents lived in or worked out of town, Cooke was chiefly raised by her grandmother and her aunt, Laura Linzy Scott, at her aunt's 24 Dorchester Avenue home. Her parents boarded at 24 Dorchester when she was small, but Joseph Scott had left town by the time Dorothy was eight. Three years later, both of her parents were in Geneva, but they lived in at the home of retailer Richard R. Roenke. By this time, Mabel Scott had apparently begun to rent the first floor of a house on Geneva Street, close to the city's commercial center. Still, Dorothy continued to live with her aunt. By the early 1930s, when she was in high school, her parents had permanently separated, and she and her mother boarded with her uncle James Linzy. In the 1970s, Dorothy Scott returned to Geneva to care for her mother in her aunt's home, where she lives today.

> This was my aunt's house, and I think my aunt invited my grand-mother to come and live with her. They weren't getting along, my grandmother and grandfather, as I understand it, so then she lived right here also. [My mother] lived in New York, [so I didn't see her] that much, not until they came back to Geneva. I'm not too sure when they came back; I think it was after grade school. I don't know what they did in New York City.
>
> [In Geneva] they worked for private families. They worked for a couple of the oldest families in Geneva; one was the Roenkes, and the other was the DeZengs. But most of the time they worked for the Roenkes. He [my father] was a chauffeur, and a butler; my mother was a cook and a housekeeper. They lived right where they worked.
>
> . . . For a while they had an apartment. Well, actually it was a half of a house; we had the downstairs. She was up there [at the Roenkes'] too, but they liked to say that they had a home some-place else; so they had it didn't mean that they were there that much. It's just that that was a convenient address, you know, to say that was their home and where they lived. But they didn't actu-ally live there, because if they worked seven days a week they had one day off, Thursdays off; and then on Thursdays, of course, they would go home, but they had to be back there next day. When they were working, I was here; I couldn't be there all by myself. I was here, still here with my grandmother, and my aunt, and my cousin. Here most of the time.

Married women were sometimes able to manage raising children and working as live-in domestics if an older child could take care of younger ones, or if her spouse's schedule could be fitted around hers so that he could be with the children whenever she could not. But many women who confronted less flexible circumstances might have found it hard to form or build families. Dorothy Cooke's parents had only one child; her aunt, who also had one child, never remarried. Katherine and Lawrence Kenney, who lived for years as servants in the home of Hobart College president Murray Bartlett, had no children. Margaret Kenney Hardy had only one child, perhaps because she had been responsible for raising her younger siblings after both of her parents died in middle age. Katherine Kenney's sister, Nancy Yancey Hogan, also lived in for a time at the Bartlett home and had one daughter. Gerry Munn McBroom came to Geneva in 1953 with her daughter and did not remarry until 1967.

I was born in Daytona Beach, Florida, March 4th, 1928. Unfortunately I was adopted. I did live in an orphanage up to about age nine, and then I was adopted. I lived with them—let's see, they both died when I was about age sixteen, and then I went to live with other relatives at that time. But then I was able to meet my real family members, and I got to know who they are; they contacted me through the high school. And they were very educated people; they were all teachers and professors in Florida.

I went for a year to college. I took a secretarial course in typing and shorthand. I did not pursue that because I wasn't that interested in a secretarial course. But then I started working at one of the resort areas in Daytona Beach, as a salad girl, waitress, whatever, and that's how I met the Roenkes. They would go down every winter to this resort right on the beach. They wanted to know if I would like to come up and work for them. I thought about it and thought it would be something nice, a nice change; maybe I could go up to New York and, well—they say go to California and get your gold? Well, anyway, I thought it might be a nice change. At that time I wasn't married, and I had one child. My husband and I were divorced. So I did agree with the Roenkes that I would like to come up and give it a try. They gave me my ticket to come up, for my daughter and I to come up, and we did get up here and moved into their home on South Main Street, down by the colleges.[11]

In the 1800s, female-headed households were apparently no more common among African Americans than they were among whites,[12] but being raised by one parent may have become more common by the twentieth century. Marie Whitaker, one of six children of Cary and Bernice Johnson Whitaker, was born in Geneva in 1907 (fig. 13). Her father was killed in a freak railroad accident while working at U.S. Radiator, across the street from his 12 Washington

13. Hermine and Marie Whitaker, about 1914. Two of the three daughters of Cary and Bernice Johnson Whitaker, Hermine and Marie posed for a photographer against a rural backdrop. Originally, a cardboard mount probably concealed its edge—as well as the girls' well-worn shoes. Unlike their dresses and bows, shoes could not be made at home. The Whitaker family rented throughout its life in Geneva. *Courtesy Frances Craven.*

Street home, in 1919. Marie married before graduating from Geneva High School. Soon afterward, the marriage annulled, she moved to Rochester to live with her sister Maude and her husband. Marie remarried, had four daughters, divorced, and then moved to the village of Leicester (in rural Livingston County) at the beginning of the depression. An elderly woman, remembered only as Miss Phebe, moved with the family from Rochester to take care of the girls while Marie worked.

Others were brought up by kin who were not their parents. Clarence Day, born in 1914, was raised by his aunt.

> I was born down in Virginia. My mother died, my really mother died, when I was about three years old. My aunt adopted me then. She was living in Pittsburgh. So she adopt me and she took me to Pittsburgh, Pennsylvania. So I lived in Pittsburgh with my aunt, but I called her mother. Because she raised me ever since I was three years old. . . . I hardly remember my mother, I hardly knew her, you understand my point.

Alvin Robinson, born in 1916 in Georgia, was also raised by an aunt, though his mother lived in the same house for a time.

> I was raised by my aunt who lived in West Palm Beach, Florida, and I sort of moved between various aunts and uncles. But the stable element of my life was the aunt who lived in West Palm Beach, Florida. She was a domestic. This was quite some years ago. I sort of fluctuated between West Palm Beach and New Brunswick, New Jersey.
>
> I had [in New Brunswick] at the time my mother, my real-life mother, an aunt, and several cousins. And the aunt who lived in New Brunswick, New Jersey, was sort of like the matriarch of the family. At one time or another, most of us, I mean the younger kids, the nephews and nieces and things of that sort, lived with her. It's sort of a traditional thing with southern blacks.
>
> . . . My parents were separated-slash-divorced when I was quite young. My father lived in St. Petersburg, Florida, and my mother worked in New Jersey. My mother was a rather frail person at my birth and had some difficulties, so that began the cycle of being cared for by other people, because my mother was in no position to care for me. So an aunt would take me here this time, another one would take me; and I guess at some point in my life my Aunt Catherine decided, well, she was going to "adopt" me, so in effect she became my mother. And she replaced whatever was lacking as far as a mother image was concerned. And until her death I always regarded her as my mother, even though I was aware that she was not. My mother and I grew up as sort of good friends, brother-and-sister attitude, as opposed to any relationship

between a mother and a son. My mother was fifteen and a half when I was born and my father was seventeen. So they were not a hell of a lot older than I am, which seems ridiculous, but that's the way things went.

Harry Gramling was raised in Geneva by his grandparents; his mother later joined them.

I never knew my father. My sister and I was raised by my grandparents. My mother, she being young at the time, she lived in New York City, and we were raised here by our grandparents because of the lifestyle in New York City. Neither my grandparents nor my mother wanted us raised in the city. She had a job there, and she left us with our grandparents.

The precariousness of nuclear families was partly ameliorated by such extended families, which were more characteristic of African-American family life in Geneva than female-headed families were. In 1855, 18 percent of all African-American households in the village were extended families; 65 percent were nuclear families.[13] By 1925, extended family households were fully 30 percent of all households, more plentiful than they had ever been; 47 percent were nuclear.[14] Moreover, marriages tied families to other families in intricate ways, as the relationships between the Hardys and the Kenneys illustrate. Present-day Hardys in Geneva are among the ten children of Thelma Williams and George W. Hardy (born in 1903) or her second husband, Herbert Kenney. Present-day Kenneys are among the nine children of Josephine Lepeon and Herman F. Kenney (fig. 14). George W. Hardy's father, George L. Hardy, married Margaret Kenney, sister of Herman F. Kenney. George L. Hardy's sister Gertrude married Charles Wallace Kenney, a member of the other local branch of the Kenney family. Herbert Kenney was one of Charles Wallace Kenney's sons. These families may have been connected several times before. George and Gertrude Hardy may have descended, though not lineally, from Salaby Hardy, who married Nancy Kenney, a child when Robert Rose manumitted her with her parents and siblings in 1816. Nancy Kenney's brother, George N. Kenney, may have been the father of Charles Wallace Kenney.

Extended households offered a safety net for members whose fortunes were unstable. The Foster family's origin in Geneva is traced to Anthony Jupiter, born in 1793 in Pennsylvania. Jupiter

14. The family of Herman F. Kenney, Sr., 261 Castle Street, Geneva, about 1930. *Standing, from left:* Norman, Mrs. Gordon (Elsie Glover), Mrs. Herman, Jr. (Beulah Marshall), Gordon, Herman, Jr. (Pat), Charles, and John. *Seated, from left:* Ann, Elouise (Mrs. Angus Carter), Angus Carter, Floyd, Herman, Sr., Mrs. Herman, Sr. (Josephine Lepeon), and Fred, son of Herman, Jr. *Courtesy John W. Kenney.*

made his way from Philadelphia to Geneva by 1830 with his wife Susannah, born in New Jersey. Like fellow Philadelphians James Cicero, William Scipio, and Joseph Caesar, Jupiter might have taken a new Christian name and used his slave name as his surname.[15] A teamster, farmer, and laborer, Jupiter bought land on the southeast corner of St. Clair and Pulteney Streets, at the edge of the Hobart College campus, in 1843. The property remained in the family for more than a century. Jupiter's granddaughter Susannah Ray (probably named for her grandmother) lived there in 1860. His son

Harvey, a hostler, lived in the house until he died in 1864, only twenty-six years old. Jupiter's elder son, Benjamin, also lived at home until he joined a colored Civil War regiment at the age of thirty.

Jupiter's youngest daughter inherited the house. A domestic, Harriet Bethena Jupiter married the Syracuse laborer William Henry Foster in about 1860 and had one son, George Harvey Dwight Foster. The boy's middle names, apparently given him as a child before 1870, honored his uncle Harvey and his aunt Mary Jane Jupiter Ray's son Dwight, both of whom had died by then, before they reached the age of thirty. George Foster married Ida Hardy, George L. Hardy's cousin, in 1886. The couple had eleven children, many of whom lived all their lives at the Pulteney Street house. The youngest, Emily, born in 1909, recalled living there with her parents, some of her siblings, and the family of her brother George C. Foster, who had seven children.

> I lived at 429 Pulteney until I got married. My brother George and his wife Helen and some of his children—Juanita, Gabby, and Tony, or Antoinette—[lived there], and some of the other ones went off to war—you know, his son George, and Harold, too, he was killed over in France; they called him Jim—My mother just worked at home and took in laundry for the college students and like that.
>
> . . . I had to drop out when I was in high school because my mother became ill, and since I was the youngest, you know, I had to stay home and take care of her. . . . She didn't seem to really care about living after my father died. My brothers, some of them [lived there then]—George and Paul and Fred—they weren't much help. I don't know where Joseph disappeared; he went away one time and never came back.[16]

Working out of her home as a laundress, Ida Foster was able to raise a large family. But among domestics, the search for someone to take care of one's children may have been partly responsible for the rise in nonkin and extended households in the twentieth century.[17] Child-care options were limited in large and small cities alike: there were no day nurseries to serve the twenty-one thousand blacks in the District of Columbia in the early 1920s, and more than 30 percent of black married women (as opposed to 3 percent of white women) in New York City left their children in someone else's care while they worked.[18] When Virginia Peek began day's work in Geneva homes in the late 1940s, she said, "I used to tote my kids around the corner to a lady named Miss Liza Williams. She was the babysitter. She was black. She was living in the place I moved out of. She was living at 16 Exchange Place and I was living at 16 Tillman. . . . When I'd get off from work, I'd go by and pick them up."

The households of the children of Cary and Bernice Johnson Whitaker helped support each other in various parts of the region. As a single man in his twenties, Cary Whitaker had come to Geneva from North Carolina by 1900 and had married Bernice Johnson, one of at least five children of James Johnson, born in Virginia in 1836 and a long-time resident of Rose, a village north of Geneva in Wayne County (fig. 15). Bernice Johnson's sister and three of her brothers married Genevans, and all of them lived in the city during some part of their adult lives. The families formed a supportive structure for Bernice Whitaker's daughter Maude, whose husband, Genevan Lester Reed, left Geneva to work in Victor, some twenty miles west, shortly after their daughter Ernestine was born in October 1923. Maude and Ernestine first boarded with Zeffa Linzy and her family at 11 East Washington Street, around the corner from the couple's first apartment on South Exchange Street. The next year, Maude and Ernestine, together with Maude's widowed mother, her brother James, and her sisters Marie and Hermine, all moved to the 40 Evans Street home of Mae Williamson, a white woman who waited tables at the Kirkwood Hotel and who had three children of her own. Maude Reed's kin supplied her with many necessities after Ernestine was born. The two often visited relatives in Geneva and spent their Christmases with relatives in Pittsford, a Rochester suburb, and Philadelphia.

In 1926, Lester Reed was reunited with his wife and daughter, and the family moved to Rochester. The Reeds then took their turn as host to Maude's sisters Marie and Hermine Whitaker. After 1930, when Marie and her daughters moved to Leicester, her brothers James and Cary, Jr., lived with her periodically. Marie worked steadily as a domestic and farm laborer; her brothers got odd jobs and probably helped raise her four daughters. Another brother, Charles, became the stable nucleus of the extended Whitaker family (fig. 16). A laborer since his teens, Charles Whitaker became a chauffeur in his early twenties for Thomas Kane, a municipal judge who was physically disabled. For twenty-two years, Whitaker drove Kane around Geneva and the country and carried him to and from his wheelchair. Whitaker's wife, Capitola (or Cappy) Davis, a native Genevan, was a caterer. Both steadily employed, the Whitakers

15. James Johnson, Rose, New York, about 1920. Johnson, born about 1847 in Virginia, migrated to Wayne County by 1870 and married the African American Isadore Treadwell, born in Elbridge, Seneca County, New York. Their children Charles, William, Frank, Bernice, and Jessie all married Genevans, and by the early 1920s James Johnson moved into the city as well to live with his daughter Jessie Johnson Hackett. *Courtesy Frances Craven.*

owned a house next door to Laura Linzy Scott on Dorchester Avenue. Marie Whitaker and her daughters often visited her brother. Her daughter Frances Craven described his role in the family.

> They always helped us, because my mother was the one with all those "kids." So they'd always send us a box at Christmas and things like that. They were nice. He was like the patriarch of the family, you know; he didn't care how old the sisters got, he'd tell them what to do and when to do it.

For James Henderson, who came to the Seneca Army Depot as a serviceman in the early 1960s and married Beth Kenney, his South Philadelphia neighborhood served the function that Charles Whitaker served for his extended family.

16. Charles F. Whitaker, about 1915. The only one of Cary and Bernice Whitaker's children to stay in Geneva, Whitaker began to work in his teens and became a chauffeur in 1926. His wife was the great-granddaughter of Baptist minister Rufus Derby, a Genevan since the early 1840s. *Courtesy Frances Craven.*

I was the oldest of four. My parents were separated, and my mom basically raised us, along with a very mothering grandmother that lived a few blocks away.

. . . In South Philadelphia, my perception of the neighborhood was the street I lived on. There were on the street blacks who were married, who worked; also, there seemed to be a lot more sense of selflessness. There might have been a neighbor whose gas or electric might be turned off, that neighbors would either organize a block party to help that person, or if they had a little extra money, to help that person pay their gas and electric. And there was never a sense of "you owe me." There seemed to be a lot more integrity, there seemed to be a lot more consistency, of doing the right thing, of knowing right from wrong, because it seemed that everyone in the neighborhood was your mother and father. And they all had permission to beat your butt if you stepped out of line, and then to tell your ma, and she'd beat it again.[19]

Such networks of fictional kin have functioned as families since slavery. The tendency to affix the terms "aunt," "uncle," or "mother" to unrelated persons who perform the roles of kin attests this way of thinking about other people. Frederick Douglass recalled how such terms signified the respect accorded older slaves who held important positions in the plantation community; in 1863, white southerner Lucy Chase had noticed that the male servant in her household called the family's older female servant "aunt" even though they were not related.[20] This practice survives among African Americans in Geneva, although some who are called "mother" or "mom" have acquired the title from their roles in Pentecostal churches. Trudy Spencer, born in Geneva in 1936, recalled visiting the Worthington Avenue home of her grandparents, Charles Wallace and Gertrude Francis Kenney, as a child.

I had lots of aunts and uncles who were around, and they were probably maybe fifteen, seventeen years older than I was. I remember my Aunt Vilette; we used to call her "Fiji". . . . There was an uncle we called—people were like uncles and aunts even when they weren't relatives; it was very confusing, because people didn't want you to call them Mr. So-and-so, or Mrs. So-and-so; they became Aunt Betty and Uncle Lou—there was an uncle, I remember, I think they called him Horny; I remember he was probably in his twenties, and then he had gone to Rochester. There was Uncle Mose . . . there's my Uncle Harry, there was my Aunt Loretta, there was Aunt Connie, there was Aunt Mildred.

The use of kinship terms and nicknames may have helped both to identify and to solidify an extended network of support among African-American Genevans. Vilette Kenney's family called her "Fiji," the Kenneys of Castle Street called their brother Floyd "Klondike," Beth Kenney's brothers call her "Pudge"; Ernest Moore was known as "Skabooch" by his friends, the McDonalds, who called their father "Coachie," their eldest sister Margaret "Paula," and their youngest sister HenryEtta "Hankie." Hermine Whitaker was called "Babe," her brother Cary was called "Bus," Horace Cook was known as "Yit" or "Horny," and his grandfather Charles W. Kenney was called "Gunnar." White Genevans often knew one of these names, either a given name or a nickname, but usually did not know both. Few whites knew Mose Kenney's true first and middle name, nor Bose Foster's, nor Bing Foster's. Few knew that Jim Foster's real name was Harold Gates Foster. Today, few know Alvin Dion Robinson as anything other than "Robby." Nicknames probably served and continue to serve as a language that only few whites are permitted to learn and that thereby strengthens the positive sense of alliance that some of Geneva's African Americans feel with others.

The use of nicknames shows an association between unrelated people that, if short of a blood tie, was far more than neighborly.[21] When the widowed barber Theodore Duffin died in 1913, Douglass Claggett, "Mr. Bland," "Miss Duffin," and Samuel Grant Lincoln handled the funeral arrangements. In 1917, Mr. and Mrs. Joseph C. Gillam ordered and arranged the High Street Chapel funeral for Walter E. Johnson, a native Genevan, retired porter, and Civil War veteran who had boarded with the Gillams in his old age. Antoinette Foster, one of the six children of George and Helen Gates Foster, was the godchild of Joseph and Nettie Dugan (whom some called "Mom Dugan") and lived with them during high school instead of living at her parents' and grandparents' Pulteney Street home.

Property and Persistence

In 1942, when Antoinette Foster was a high school senior, her grandparents died within months of each other, and the taxes on the family property had not been paid in years. Antoinette's oldest sister, Clara, a beautician in Rochester, paid the back taxes and then sold the worn-out house to Hobart and William Smith colleges, which promptly tore it down. The expense of owning property must have weighed heavily on the Fosters, but the house and land are probably what kept them Genevans for a century. For in Geneva, as elsewhere, property tended to tie people to a community.[22] Nearly all of the African Americans who owned real estate in Geneva in 1865 remained in the community until they died, at which point many properties passed to relatives. Benjamin Cleggett's home was occupied by his youngest daughter until she died in 1960. William T.

Kenney's Grove Street house, which he bought in 1869, passed after his death to his daughter Margaret, who lived there until she died, also in 1960. Part of the Gillam family lived on High Street from about 1822 at least through 1934.

From the 1820s forward, the clear trend of African-American investment in Geneva was real property. In a culture still skeptical about the real value of currency, owning land had solid appeal to both whites and blacks. For black New Yorkers during most of the nineteenth century, land was a literal entitlement: no African American was a legal citizen without it until 1871. And unlike savings or investments in stocks and bonds, property ownership is tangible wealth. Because it visibly demonstrates economic competence to oneself and one's peers, it has a certain symbolic utility.[23] And for blacks in particular, property was the most pragmatic of investments, far more sensible than investing in a business. A home was one's own; once acquired, keeping it did not depend directly upon the patronage of whites. But a business needed customers. In a village whose African-American population was as small as Geneva's always was, no business pioneered by an African American could hope to survive on the commerce of blacks alone.[24]

From what living conditions Geneva's African Americans came into property ownership can only be imagined. John Nicholas's slaves are said to have built and lived in a frame dwelling that still stands about two miles from the main buildings of White Springs Farm. Two accounts state that Robert Rose's slaves lived in cabins near the shore of Seneca Lake. In his quasi-fictional *Allerton Parish: A Tale of the Early Days of Western New York* (1863), John Nicholas Norton recalled walking "along the lake shore, and through the green meadows, in the shady corners of which a negro cabin would be hid" at Mortimer, Norton's pseudonym for Rose Hill. Local historian George S. Conover stated similarly in an 1883 letter he wrote Arthur Patrick Rose as the latter prepared to give a talk on "Slavery in the Early Day" at the Geneva Historical Society:

> It was a fortunate circumstance that Mr. Rose brought slaves here, for the swamps and marshes at the foot of the lake made not only that locality but Geneva and also Rose Hill Farm very unhealthy— the air was full of malaria—its effect was truly bad on the white people—the blacks however were not affected and there were many cabins along the foot of the lake near the outlet where they lived with impurity and thus time was covered until clearing up the

brush, woods, &c, and letting in sunlight, together with improvements finally overcame the source of malaria. At that time Rose Hill
Farm could not have been worked by white people as well as by
the blacks—Dr. Coventry had tried and failed—This I think an important item and should be noticed in your paper.[25]

Some African-American people lived in the homes and hotels
where they worked; others lived in boarding houses, at least one of
which was specifically operated for African Americans. Still others,
possibly many others, lived "pent up, shoved back, and even piled
up" in places local census takers missed. In 1849, African-American
preacher J. W. Loguen described the conditions he had come upon
in a place forty miles from Syracuse, where he then lived. Here he
found twenty African Americans, "principally women with children," in a "miserable shanty" abutting the Erie Canal towpath. He
wrote in a report to the *Impartial Citizen*,

> Would you see them you must not keep upon the highways of our
> country towns, among the wealthy farmers, or comfortable livers;
> but you must go into the by-ways, the most unfrequented roads,
> that lead to the tracts where the soil is sterile, or not easily culti-
> vated. In our villages and cities you must seek these forlorn beings
> stowed away in cellars or garrets, or abandoned out-houses, in nar-
> row lanes or back yards.[26]

Theoretically, anyone who did not own a home was subject to
the idiosyncrasies of landlords, most of whom were white, and to
the variable conditions of those rental properties they could afford.
The 1853 colored people's convention had estimated that only 2 percent of all New York's African Americans were homeowners. Geneva's African Americans appear to have been better off, if only
slightly. They owned land from as early as 1813, and from 8 to 10
percent of the village's black population owned property in 1855.
Eighty percent of the recorded African-American population in the
village lived in these thirty homes, and all but three of them were
valued, with their land, at more than $250.

Some bought land with remarkable alacrity. On 15 January 1817,
just fifteen days after he was manumitted, the African American
Moses Lee bought a little more than an acre of land in Seneca
Township for $100.[27] John Graham, probably the "John" whom
Nicholas freed in 1818, bought an acre of village land for $80 the

same year. Land prices varied so greatly before 1830 that one cannot know whether they paid going rates: Willis Lee, a former Nicholas family slave who bought more than six acres of rural land three miles west of Geneva between 1813 and 1820, paid $100 for five acres in 1816.[28] Alexander Graham, the first African American to buy village land, paid $394 for the five acres he bought from John and Eliza Woods in 1818, seven years after Nicholas freed him.

From 1818 through 1824, John and Eliza Woods sold eight lots to the Grahams and three other African-American men in the unsettled "western outlots" that bordered the core of homes, shops, and streets of the village proper (fig. 17). Woods was not the only white to sell to blacks, but he somehow passed into local legend for having *given* land to African Americans soon after their 1827 emancipation in the state. Despite the fact that at least one historian presented evidence to the contrary, this notion has persisted to the present, perhaps through the sheer will to believe in a tradition of white benevolence.[29] Woods, an Episcopalian like most other slaveowners in early Geneva, had himself owned slaves through at least 1810.

These western outlots became the High Street neighborhood, a four-block area that actually began on West Street where it intersected with High. Most African-American people who bought land in Geneva before 1834 bought here. Alexander Graham's six acres extended westward along High Street and southward along West Street, both streets probably little more than cart paths in 1818. John Graham's acre was just south of this lot. Before 1822, the African Americans John Bland and Philip Gillam, Jr., bought the next two lots along West Street, and in 1822, 1823, and 1824, John Graham bought a second West Street lot and added another acre to his earlier purchase. Charles Kenney, whom Robert Rose manumitted in 1816, bought an acre of land on West Street for forty-five dollars in 1822 and another four acres in 1830, and John Bland bought another acre for sixty-five dollars in 1824. Before 1829, Geneva merchant William Tippets sold John Duffin (probably James W. Duffin's father) a lot on the north side of High (then Oak) Street, just east of the West Street intersection, and in 1829 he sold the fugitive slave Aaron Lucas three-quarters of an acre just west of Duffin's lot. Also before 1830, Tippets sold a large lot to Salaby Hardy (Charles Kenney's son-in-law) that may have extended from West Street to the line of what became Nursery Avenue.

The spate of land sales taking place after 1822 may demonstrate the response of the village's African Americans to the revised New

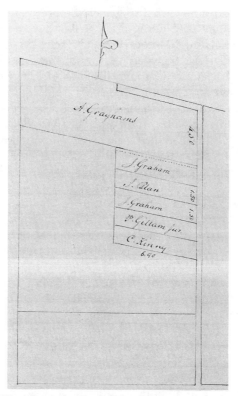

17. Map of West Street house lots, 17 May 1823. The map appeared alongside a deed from John and Elizabeth Woods to John Graham, "man of colour." *Reproduction courtesy Ontario County Records, Archives, and Information Management Services, Canandaigua, New York.*

York State constitution as much as it reflects their growing financial competence. Before 1821, men of either race could vote for state assembly candidates if they owned a freehold valued at $50, rented a tenement for more than $5, or had been a freeman in Albany or New York in 1777 and 1775; any male who owned property valued at $250 or more could vote for senator and governor. Although earlier state legislators had resisted attempts to restrict free African Americans, the prospect of impending emancipation apparently moved the 1821 state constitutional convention to lift suffrage restrictions for white males and stiffen them for black males, who thenceforth could vote only if they had been New York State citizens for three years and owned $250 worth of real property.

In 1825, only 298 African Americans in the entire state—hardly 1 percent of the total black population—owned enough property to be voters, and not until 1871 did disenfranchised black New Yorkers become legal citizens.[30] In Geneva, possibly only Willis Lee and John and Alexander Graham owned property of sufficient value. By 1849, three years after the defeat of a statewide referendum to rescind or lower the property qualification, the village assessor's rolls showed that twelve African Americans owned more than $250 in real property. No one who owned less property was listed (a person who owned $250 worth was taxed only 43 cents), and so the list did not include all African-American property owners in the village at that time; deed records exist for some whose names do not appear on the assessor's rolls. The properties taxed at the assessor's minimum were probably only one-fifth of the total black households in the village at the time.

In this early period, like no other, it is possible to view Geneva's African Americans as having been segregated, though it cannot be known if this pattern of settlement was voluntary or compelled.[31] Deeds and village meeting records had called the West-High area the "African" or "black" settlement since the early 1820s, and there is some evidence that deliberate white exclusion had planted it there. In 1822, only a year after white colonizationists had purchased Liberia with the intent of resettling the country's free blacks there, the village plotted "Liberia" (later West) Street from Washington Street to what would become High Street. The village's blacks evidently felt that white Genevans viewed the area as a kind of local exile. In 1845, a group of neighborhood residents petitioned the village to change the name of the street from Liberia to Bland. John Bland, then the largest property owner in the area, was a positive symbol of the progress of their race, not a negative symbol of their infamy. But village trustees declined to rename the street. They chose instead to lay the petition "upon the table" and never officially took it up again, though the road was renamed West Street by 1856.

Still, by the 1830s, Geneva's African Americans carried on a thriving business among themselves buying and selling land, particularly in the "African settlement" at West and High Streets. This commerce suggests that their residence there was neither passive nor grudging, as do their repeated efforts to improve the area. In 1832, unidentified petitioners asked the village to lay out a road "running from Pulteney Street west to the black settlement," which became High Street sometime after 1834. In 1849, both black and white residents of this neighborhood approached the village trustees with another proposal, this time to run a new road from West to Grove Street through the rear of the lots that faced High and William streets. Village trustees, however, rejected this petition, just as they had tabled the petition to change the name of Liberia Street four years earlier.

By 1855, the neighborhood was almost entirely African American, and it was the site of a segregated district school and two churches (fig. 18). African Americans had moved into the neighborhood from the rural hinterlands, from the east, and from Rochester, where Frederick Douglass had settled in 1847. Some were agents and missionaries. Jason Jeffrey, a porter at Rochester's Eagle Tavern and a subscription agent for Douglass's North Star in 1848, had moved to Geneva by 1845. Jeffrey was also prominent in the Western New York Anti-Slavery Society and might have served its interests in Geneva. Benjamin F. Cleggett, who had moved either from Canada or from Boston to Rochester in the same year Douglass moved there, had married the sister of William C. Nell, Douglass's assistant editor, in 1849, and moved to Geneva by 1858. And by early 1850, Henry Highland Garnet was sent by the American Missionary Association as the home missionary for the Geneva African-American church on High Street.[32]

Yet by the 1850s, whites had begun to realize the commercial potential of the western outlots, no longer peripheral to the growing village. By 1850, English nurseryman Thomas Smith had purchased Alexander Graham's large lot; and by the turn of the century, Hammon and Willard nurseries occupied land that had formerly belonged to the Bland family. By 1900, too, much of the rest of the neighborhood had been populated by whites, who had always owned homes on High Street south of its intersection with Grove Street. African Americans continued to live in the West-High neighborhood, but by the 1920s only a few still had homes there. By World War II, none of the homes on West Street that had originally been built and owned by African Americans remained in African-American families.

The likelihood that blacks willingly settled in this neighborhood, increasingly identified with the "old families," is strengthened by the fact that at least some other areas were not closed to them. From the 1820s onward, they bought land in other sections of the village,

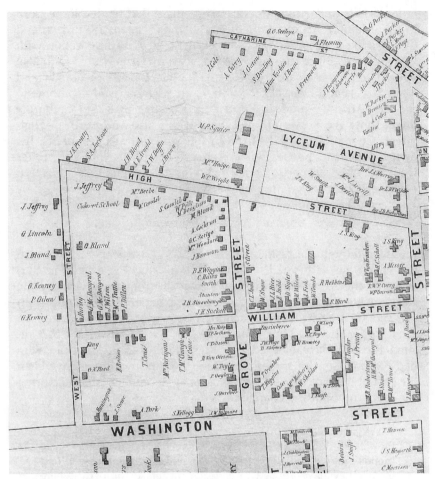

18. Detail of High and West neighborhood from "Town of Seneca and Village of Geneva," 1856. At the time, Mrs. Beebe and J. S. Prouty were the only white residents on High Street above Grove; only whites lived on William Street, but West between William and High was entirely African American. On Catharine Street at far right, J. Gaton, A. Freeman, and W. Johnson were black householders. *Courtesy Geneva Free Library.*

little pockets of African-American settlement that tended to be close to the original "African settlement." Blands, Gatens, Kenneys, and Condols lived on Washington Street just east of its intersection with West Street. Since the mid–1830s, African Americans had also bought lots in and around the quadrangle formed by Castle and Main Streets and Dorchester Avenue, an area that was also home to the first African-American Baptist church after 1838. On Catherine Street (now West Avenue) just west of this area and north of High Street, George Gaten, Edward Johnson, and Edward Tompkins, Jr., owned land and houses, Gaten as early as 1829. Anthony Jupiter was the only property owner who lived outside these western neighborhoods.

Steering Toward Segregation

Even though the residential distribution of African Americans in the village never formed a "black section" such as existed in Syracuse by the 1870s, their dispersion was far from even. And by the 1890s, evidence that African Americans experienced difficulty renting and owning in certain sections of town began to emerge.[33] In 1895, under the headline "This is Queer," the *Geneva Advertiser* related the quandary of Frederick Riggs, an African American who had come to Geneva sometime before 1892 and who may have been the first of his race to work as a molder at Herendeen Manufacturing Company on South Exchange Street:

> There isn't a steadier man in Geneva than he is. But he has hunted the village thoroughly for rooms where he and two other male friends can live and board themselves, and they are unable to find them. They have applied to a dozen owners of property where signs are exhibited "Rooms to Let," but have been turned coldly away. In this particular he finds no difference between republicans and democrats; they are all alike, and have all the same answer— no rooms, yet the signs remain in the windows. Don't talk to us about outrages upon negroes in the South, when a decent and orderly colored man receives such treatment in an orderly Northern city. There is a prejudice against the color, and this prejudice will not down. Fred. Riggs feels it keenly, not on account of his color, for he does not try to push himself forward into white society, nor try to get board along with white boarders. He is retiring in his nature, and wants to rent rooms or a cheap house where three of them can live by themselves. Isn't that fair?[34]

In its description of Riggs's quandary, the *Advertiser* suggested that residential segregation was clearly the rule in Geneva by the end of the century: the editors could support the man's case because he did not attempt to live among whites or to "push himself forward into white society." Riggs eventually managed to find housing with African Americans who were also relatively new to Geneva. At the turn of the century, he lived in two of the three neighborhoods on the bluff west of Main Street in which African-American renters and homeowners tended to be found. In 1899, he lodged on Cortland Street in the home of Daniel Coleman, a Kentuckian who had come to Geneva about 1889 by way of Auburn and had married Ida Lewis Binks of Canandaigua, whose mother was the Genevan Rebecca Gillam. In 1900, he boarded in the West Street home of Stephen Ambush, a teamster who had been born a slave in Maryland, had also married a Genevan, and had apparently settled there at about the same time Riggs did.

If they were sufficiently prosperous, African Americans new to Geneva after the Civil War tended to buy in one of these two neighborhoods or in the Main-Dorchester-Castle Street area. Charles Gates, who had come from Mississippi by 1875 and had married Geneva native Josephine Hardy, bought the High Street house and lot of the widowed Catherine Polk, who had lived there since at least 1840. Reuben Hawkins had come to the village from Virginia in 1886 and married Margaret Condol, daughter of Joseph Condol, who had lived on High Street since his father William brought the family to Geneva about 1843, when he was thirteen. Hawkins bought the High Street lot next to the one his father-in-law had purchased from James W. Duffin in 1864. Even without the marriage ties to High Street, Gates and Hawkins probably would have bought property there. Both men were hardware clerks—they were in fact Geneva's only African-American clerks—and it made sense that they would buy property in the city's most established African-American area.[35]

By the turn of the century, these three areas west of Geneva's Main Street, the physical and psychic dividing line between the bluff above and the flat below, had become increasingly associated with the old African-American families. New families who had not married into old families were more and more apt to be relegated to new peripheries; even members of old families who either could not afford the bluff or could not buy property at all ended up in the neighborhoods that developed in commercial and industrial areas in the

19. Johnson, Whitaker, and Hackett cousins on the Johnson porch, 36 Bradford Street, 1907–1908. Bradford Street terminated at the canal harbor and was lined with boiler shops, the buildings of Patent Cereal Company, tenements, and at least one brothel. *Courtesy Frances Craven.*

flat. One neighborhood developed near the rail yard and foundries that had anchored the northern end of Exchange Street since the 1840s; by World War II, it had become a particular residential and social enclave for new and transient African Americans (fig. 19). Another was the area directly across South Exchange Street from the U.S. Radiator foundry, one of the few industries in which African Americans could get jobs at the time; blacks had been living in the frame tenements across from U.S. Radiator since at least 1894. From about 1920 until they were razed during urban renewal in 1967, these dwellings—especially 686 and 658 South Exchange Street and 11 East Washington Street—became virtually exclusive African-American addresses. In 1921, Robert Linzy and his family moved to 11 East Washington Street; seven years later, after Linzy and his wife separated, George W. and Thelma Hardy and their large family moved into the house. One of their children, Leona Hardy James, described growing up there.

> We lived where the Rec Center is now—there used to be houses there—at 11 East Washington, and next door we had Ida Foster's daughter, who married Devoe Linzy [Robert Linzy's son]. . . . I do remember that now [that Robert Linzy lived there earlier], because there were stories that said they used to sit there with their guns and shoot the rats in the house.
>   We rented it from George I. Tieder. He used to be a lawyer. Spencer Morgan got it after we moved out. He bought it. It was a two-story house, but with all us kids, there wasn't much room. It was in bad shape, and Mr. Tieder didn't fix it up; well, we painted, he gave us money for paint and everything, but at that time, when my father died and then my mother had to go on welfare, we didn't have much money to do much fixing. But we did paint. I remember—I think there *were* rats.[36]

By the time Clifford and Rosa Blue came to Geneva from Florida in 1949, they confronted a tight and dismaying housing situation in which 11 East Washington and 686 South Exchange were among the few rental units available (fig. 20):

> I lived in a house called 686 South Exchange Street. The address is now the skating rink. And that was a big house owned by Spencer Morgan, who was another black man who had moved here from South Carolina. And I don't know how long ago Spencer had been here, but he was a progressive black person who obviously had had some terrible times, housing problems, trying to find a place. And once he had got himself established in the U.S. Radiator—that was my husband's first really long-term employment here—well, he then invested some of his money into housing. And housing was one of the worst problems in the Geneva area when we moved here.
>   . . . To find a place to live was really a luxury, and it was purely discrimination. Even if you had a job and the money, you just didn't usually get the apartments. We lived in one bedroom

20. 686 South Exchange Street before demolition, 21 March 1965, photograph by R. E. Doran. *Courtesy Geneva Historical Society.*

and shared a kitchen and bath. I had one baby, three months old; when we lived down at 686 Exchange Street, that house was perhaps originally a two-family house, and it had been divided up into a four-family house. It had stairways, two apartments upstairs, two downstairs. I remember well the outlay was a living room-dining area, kitchen, and two bedrooms, and one bath; that's the way each apartment was divided. Each apartment had separate entrances, and back doors. Had a back yard, kind of, that went up the hill there, because it's right off the back of South Main Street, so we had space that we could plant gardens, hang clothes. So we shared that apartment with my husband's sister and her husband until they left; they returned to Florida. There was another house on Washington Street between Main and Exchange Street, and that house had also one bathroom and one kitchen, and it must have had about eight families. Might have been 11 East Washington.

After they left 686 South Exchange, the Blue family moved to the 300 block of Exchange Street. Rosa Blue described the housing conditions there:

We moved to 310 Exchange Street, which was another apartment building; I think it had about three rooms. It's a parking lot now; it's down near Lake Street, right around the corner from Tillman Street. And I remember when I got that apartment I had three children, and I was so delighted to find an apartment. You had to have a good reputation to even get the apartment. The rent was not exorbitant, but the landlord—you had heat, and water and the necessities—he would do repairs, but he would not do anything to improve the property. He wouldn't paint it. He praised you if *you* did. The kids, the only place they had to play was on the sidewalk. The back was also a parking area.

Now around the corner where Sam's Bar and Grill is on Tillman Street, between Sam's and the restaurant there on the corner—I think it's Rintino's or something like that, used to be Madia's—there used to be other apartments, and I'm talking about some that were really like chicken coops, almost, that responsible people, white people owned and rented to black folks. And usually the only time that black folks were able to live in a place was when the landlord decided that he wasn't going to do anything for it, you know, it wasn't good for anybody else, and sometimes these apartments were infested with rats and roaches and what have you, even bedbugs sometimes. Across the street from us at 310 was 308 Exchange Street, and that was another unit that was filled with black folks. You know, you knew about where black folks lived, because as one came, they probably got housing through another, and they were limited. There were ads in the newspapers, but if you called—and quite often people couldn't tell who you were, from your voice—people would say, "Well, yes, we have apartments for rent." But when it was time to look at them, they'd take one look at you and say, "Oh, no, I just rented it," or, "No, I don't have anything," or some would even tell you, "Well, we don't rent to colored folks." So housing was one of the most serious problems encountered in Geneva.

Racial discrimination in housing was a statewide problem, as the state-appointed Commission on the Condition of the Urban Negro Population had officially acknowledged in 1939. But, commission members averred, the housing problem was one whose solution would have to wait until "the basic handicap of inadequate income was removed." Accordingly, the commission recommended that ra-

cial discrimination and segregation be banned only "in public housing projects or those enjoying tax-exemption."[37]

By 1940, the 300 block of Exchange Street contained what little
commercial and social life existed among African-American people
in Geneva, and city officials at the time indicated clearly that additional housing for African Americans was not available. The city's
housing stock, already almost completely occupied in 1940, was se-
verely strained by the influx of construction workers to build Seneca
Ordnance Depot and Sampson Naval Training Station. State housing officials intervened, urging Geneva and other nearby cities to
register all available rooms and encourage homeowners to convert
garages and rooms in their homes into rental units. In August 1942,
one state official noted the effect of the housing shortage on the
labor problem at Sampson:

> Mr. Handley has asked that New York City send no more negroes
> because the local housing facilities for negroes apparently are full.
> Insofar as he knows the nearest housing now available for negroes
> is in Rochester, where the wage rate is so much higher than on the
> Naval Base, that he is sure that if negroes were housed there, they
> would soon secure better paying work there. He apparently regret-
> ted not being able to employ more negroes, as he stated that they
> have always found that they are pretty good workers.[38]

A report later that month to the state war plans coordinator stated,
"Colored labor has been housed to some extent in Ithaca, but with
the later increase in hiring this type of labor many have been housed
in the barracks of the Naval Training Station."[39]

Still, Exchange, Canal, Bradford, and Tillman Streets housed
many African-American newcomers and transients. Here was the
short-lived Harlem Lunch Room and the Carpenters Hotel, run by
Marie Gray, who had operated a commercial laundry in Canastota,
New York, before coming to Geneva in 1933. She and Spencer Morgan were the only known real estate entrepreneurs among Geneva's
African Americans in the twentieth century.. African Americans had
bought and sold real estate among themselves before, but in the
1900s it began to seem to be one of the only ways in which they
could gain access to homes of any kind. Marie Gray's daughter,
Edna Dunham Hansen, described their family businesses.

> When they started building Sampson, my mother was the first
> black to room the blacks who came in to work out at Sampson. She

had that building right on the corner of Canal and Exchange; I think she had 24 rooms. So she housed them. And the beds never got cold. They worked around the clock, you know. Then about three or four weeks later, my husband and I started a hotel down in the next block; it became the Central Hotel. We had it first. We had a full-fledged hotel. When I say full-fledged, I mean we had the rooms, we had a dining room, and we had a bar. It was probably in the beginning of the forties.

. . . There was twelve rooms there. My mother gave us the money to get started there, because my husband was making fifteen, sixteen dollars a week at that time working at Firestone. . . . During this same period of time, my mother bought two houses on Clark Street, 2 and 4 Clark and number 9 Clark, because she had a contract with the United States Radiator that they brought in these men from Barbados, and we housed and fed them down there. . . . This was during the war, and they got at that time you had to have food coupons to buy meat and sugar and stuff like that, and United States Radiator furnished us with the books to get meat.

. . . My mother owned those houses [on Clark Street] seven, eight years or more. My mother was always trying to help people. She bought several houses and resold them. She bought these for the newcomers, to give them a start. She'd buy a house for maybe two, three hundred dollars down. It was all black people that she gave a start to. Maybe they'd give her a hundred dollars down. Then if their rent was thirty dollars a month or fifty dollars a month they'd give her ten or twenty or something extra to apply towards their downpayment. She had what I guess you'd call a second mortgage. She bought a house on Middle Street, . . . then she sold a house to Spencer Morgan way up on the upper part of Exchange Street, the last house on the street [686]. And then she sold the houses on Clark Street to the Carters; she sold number nine to the father, and she sold the two and four to the son. And then we had a house on Evans Street. . . . Those were the houses that I can remember.

The substandard condition of the housing available to African Americans by 1940 was revealed in the number of fires they suffered. Early in January 1945, an oil stove in a second-floor room at the 14 Tillman Street tenement is thought to have started a fire that left several African Americans and a "Negro religious group" (probably Mount Calvary Church of God in Christ) homeless. Six days later, a fire in an Exchange Street tire store spread to the Carpenter Hotel, "driving approximately 30 to 40 persons, all Negroes, from their homes," the *Geneva Daily Times* reported. The Salvation Army housed the lodgers until "fellow Negro workers" got off their shifts and came to take them in. In May 1946, a property "until recently operated as a rooming house by Mrs. Marie Gray and her daughter Mrs. Edna Dunham" at 4 Clark Street—sold three weeks earlier to Perry Carter—left twenty African Americans without a place to live and left one man with serious burns. In 1948, 14–16 Tillman Street burned again; again, an oil stove explosion was thought to have been the cause.[40]

The New Periphery: The Rise of the Sixth Ward

Gray's Clark Street homes were in the city's new sixth ward, an area that became known as the "butt end" of town. The section probably first acquired this reputation because of the concentration of industrial, rail, and canal facilities that sprawled along the flat, marshy northern lakeshore. The neighborhood was divided by the vast plant of the Andes Range and Furnace Corporation, and by 1915 African Americans had begun to live in neighborhoods on both sides.

South of the sprawling Andes complex were the railroad tracks, the canal, Lake Road, and then Seneca Lake. By the 1920s, Lake Road, the main entry to Geneva from all points east, was crowded with gas stations, car and tire dealers, fuel storage tanks, bars, and a vacant lot between the road and the canal where large trucks parked. Past the gas stations were small frame dwellings—newspaper editor Edgar Parker called them "shanties" in 1910—packed in a row along the road's northern edge. Their back doors opened almost literally onto the canal, and their front doors were exposed at all times to the wind and waves of furious storms coming off the lake.[41] Turnover was high in these houses, probably because they were among very few that families new to town, black and white, could find to rent. By 1915, the families who formed the bulk of the small "great migration" to Geneva had settled in these dwellings. But these structures were clearly marginal, and by 1929 the city thought them an unbecoming introduction to Seneca Lake Park, which it had begun to develop just east of Geneva. The homes were razed in 1930.

African Americans had begun to live in the neighborhood north of the Andes plant in about 1925. This area shaded into Seneca County at a sparsely settled section known as Border City; the city's old fair grounds, where both whites and blacks had gathered for various nineteenth-century celebrations, stood on this still-rural border. But by the early 1940s, the fair grounds became the site of the city's first public housing project, and the area's already inglorious image was tarnished further by the popular associations of public housing and the peculiar origins of this particular project.

Popularly known as the Dixon Tract, later as Dixon Homes, the project was built in 1943 originally to house defense industry workers and military personnel stationed at the Seneca Ordnance Depot and Sampson Naval Training Station. In 1941 and 1942, housing in the region was in such short supply that many construction workers lived in tents, sheds, cars, barns, and in a hastily constructed trailer park in neighboring Waterloo. Because virtually all of these thousands of laborers were expected to leave the area after construction was complete, their housing needs were viewed as temporary; accordingly, the 250-unit Dixon Tract was built to last only ten years.

By March 1944, the first fifty apartments in the one-story, concrete-block units composing "Dixon Victory Homes" became home to defense industry workers and to officers and civilian employees at both bases. But just two months later, nine of the project's buildings were given over to house 240 German prisoners of war brought in by Geneva Growers and Processors Inc. to do agricultural work in nearby fields and factories—work that African Americans were also invited to do. These buildings were encircled by a barbed wire fence, flood lighting, and wooden guard towers that stood on stilts.[42] By 1955, the Dixon Tract was vacant and vandalized, but the need for housing in Geneva remained so acute that the Mayor's Council for a Better Geneva recommended that three of its units be rehabilitated "to help relieve the housing shortage."

The fact that housing was not only limited but substandard had attracted much publicity in Geneva during and after the war. Servicemen and construction workers with families, most of whom had to live off the bases, complained bitterly about the conditions of Geneva's rental property. One 1962 study of the effect the military bases had on Geneva noted that 30.6 percent of its dwelling units lacked private baths and toilets and were dilapidated, a higher percentage than prevailed in both Waterloo and Seneca Falls, where rents were also appreciably lower.[43] That African Americans were among the primary occupants of this housing stock by the mid–1950s was intimated by the Reverend John C. Laske in a guest editorial in the *Daily Times* two days after the announcement about the Dixon Tract.

Christian people in larger numbers in Geneva should be working away at this blight of poor housing. Actually poor housing is too mild a term. Most of us would not live one hour in some of the "apartments" that are located in our city. A human being is a human being whatever his income, the color of his skin or his religious preference.[44]

Another tacit acknowledgment of how centrally the housing problem affected African Americans was the appointment of Charles Kenney to the Geneva Housing Authority in the 1950s.

I was on the housing authority at the time; there's a plaque down there at Chartres Homes with my name on it. Bing Rogers was the mayor, who was a friend of our family. And heretofore I guess there had never been any blacks appointed to any of the commissions here in the city. Since apparently I was in the spotlight around here because I had formed a couple social clubs that had to do with kids and the black population, and I was a member of the Elks and a big church man and all that stuff, I guess he thought at the time that I might be a good subject to be on the housing authority, so I was. It was the early fifties.

We orchestrated the redevelopment of that whole [Dixon] tract. Of course I tell anybody today if I had to do it all over again I would never have put a project down there, but at the time, at that particular time, that was it. Lots of room. But I wasn't well enough addressed in the subject of "Gee, here you got a congregation of all poor, blacks and white living together, no transportation"—you know, it's way out there. I wouldn't do it again, but at the time it was the thing to do.

My first knowledge of it, you know, it was a former prisoner of war situation down there, and it was just concrete floors, bare walls, the bare minimum of utilities; they had a latrine, and a sink, and a bed, and that was it. Nothing exciting, for the prisoners. And then at the close of the war, I guess, they did away with that and here was an empty tract with some buildings. And so that was the beginning of the project. You couldn't ask any legitimate citizen of the community to live in the place, but it was all right for the prisoners. Yeah.

Gloria Peek, born in 1951 in Geneva, moved with her family to the Dixon Tract from 16 Tillman Street when she was about four years old.

We lived downtown. I remember the house and what it looks like, but it's a parking lot right now. There's an Italian restaurant on the corner. There was a big house in back of that, and that's where we lived. My family's never owned property. I guess my clearest recollection was when we moved to the projects, Chartres Homes, and I guess they called it the old Dixon line or something like that. And I remember us living there the majority of my childhood. We were in the projects until the new projects were built, and we moved from the old projects into the new projects. They were right next to each other. So you're talking about a couple of steps. And I was there until I moved away from home.

They weren't all that new. I remember the projects as being—they always reminded me of the Indian huts that I used to study when I was in school, the long ones, you know, the long huts, because that's what they looked like; they looked like the long Indian huts. And they were little apartments. They were concrete, and the way they were made were like the long Indian huts, okay, but apartment sections. One story, one side, like a motel. And there might be five apartments on one row of houses, and then right in front of it was another row like that with five, with a little road that came with it, a deadend. And out from each apartment was like a coal bin. I called it a coal bin; it was like a woodshed; you could store wood or coal or put storage stuff; I really called it a cave, because as a kid it reminded me of a cave, and that's where I used to hide and play. They were attached to the house. . . . If you went in there was only one way out, and that was a little door.

There had to be a couple hundred or more families there. And it seemed like all the blacks in Geneva were congregated in that project. I remember as I was little families staying there for long periods of time. To move out meant to move up, okay, and I just didn't see a lot of that. When we moved from the one projects to the other ones, the families I knew moved too. We all kind of moved together. It was like a migration, but it was a migration of maybe a hundred feet. It was weird.

Gloria Peek's recollection that the Dixon Tract was called the "Dixon Line" probably conflates her childhood perception that all of the city's blacks lived there with what she must have learned in school about the Mason-Dixon Line. Her memory may also attest the alienation and lack of contact between new and old African-American families. For in its early years, the project was racially balanced, and, compared to available South Exchange Street rental property, Dixon Homes seemed a distinct improvement (fig. 21). So did its successor, the John J. Chartres Homes. Cora Williams Wells, born in 1936 in Sanford, Florida, lived in both the 300 and 600 blocks

21. Ruth Sellers and her sons Herbert, Albert, and Larry at Dixon Homes, June 1957. *Courtesy Rosa Akins Blue.*

of Exchange Street as a child and moved to Dixon Homes after she married.

> We moved to the old Dixon Tract. There were a lot of black families living out there when we went there. The rent was cheaper, you know. It was just like any other project—your neighbors were right there *with* you, close. But as I remember, we were young and it was nice. We had some nice neighbors. It wasn't bad at all. But the place needed a lot of work on it, so they built the Chartres Home.
> . . . Along in then, a lot of low-income people really liked the

apartments because they were roomy. And it was probably the first nice apartment, looking back on it—well, it was; I thought it was great. I thought it was a great apartment, you know; I could fix it up and do what I wanted to. It was a nice place to live; they had their own rooms, their own apartment. You had to meet the criteria—you had to be low income, you had to show birth certificates of your children, all that stuff. I think that they wanted people in there that were going to pay their rent.

Like Wells, Virginia Peek lived in both projects.

Me and my husband moved off of Tillman Street, and we moved out in the old Dixon Home. See, they knocked that down, and they built Chartres Homes, and the people what was living in the old Dixon Home moved over in Chartres Home. It [the Dixon Home] was just like the project at Chartres Homes; only thing different you could drive up to your door. To me it was much better, because when you got your groceries, you can drive your car up to your door and unload your groceries and everything. It ain't like Chartres Homes—you got to unload your grocery in the parking lot and try to lug it home, and all that, you know. It [the Dixon Homes] was much better. When I went to having children I needed a bigger place to live. You could have got up to four bedrooms, but I got three—three bedrooms, living room, and a kitchen. I liked it better than I did Chartres Homes. They was kinda long, you know, but they was connected together. Like I live right here and maybe you live right there.

Complaints about the conditions of living at the Dixon Tract were aired in the newspaper through 1955, though the housing shortage might have suppressed criticism: one city councilman expressed his suspicion that more tenants would have reported problems if they were not "afraid to complain because they thought they might be evicted." Electric current to run refrigerators and other utilities was insufficient, and aldermen acknowledged the source of this particular problem to be the fact that the supposedly temporary housing used "cheap materials, especially the house wiring," when it had been built by the federal government. Tenants themselves had to operate street lights by flicking a switch that hung from an electrical cord only six feet from the ground. Cockroach infestation had also been reported.[45]

By 1960, the housing shortage, conditions at the Dixon Tract, and public health problems elsewhere in the city, including several cases of meningitis in South Exchange Street tenements, compelled the city to seek public housing funds from the state. By August 1961, the 124 units at the state-financed John J. Chartres Homes opened on a site adjacent to the Dixon project. Dixon Home residents—"provided they can qualify," the newspaper stated—were given first priority for the new Chartres apartments; by December 1960, 107 of the 120 Dixon Tract residents had applied for them.

For those like Virginia Peek who had moved from area migrant camps into Geneva, the Dixon Homes seemed almost luxurious.[46] Peek described the camp in Lyons.

> It was houses, you know, like you see these houses that the people—they not no project. They wasn't no project. They was long houses and they had rooms, you know. They wasn't no back door or nothing. There was one little window and one way in and one way out.
>
> It was made out of wood, mostly—what is it they call it?—beaverboard? Yeah, beaverboard; it was made out of that. . . . Some of them have like twelve rooms on this side and then over on the other side there's twelve, you know. And it was divided. And it holds a cot, a cot or your single bed, table, and you have your two-burner stove in there, you know, maybe setting up on the meter box or something, and you have another little table sitting in the corner at which you write on or whatever, you know. The bathrooms was outside. There not no bathrooms inside, no. You ain't have no kitchen facility. You had a live-in kitchen, dining room and everything else—bedroom, dining room, kitchen and all was combined in that one room. That's right.
>
> You called them your house, you know. I didn't never know the name that they called for it. To me it was just, you camping out, you know.

The state acknowledged that the 287 farm labor camps within its jurisdiction were problematic as early as 1943. One state health department report noted that camps in Wayne, Oneida, Madison, and Erie counties especially anticipated "large numbers of southern Negroes and whites" in the coming harvest season and that "sanitation has always been below the desired level" in the camps to which they were brought to live. Three Wayne County camps operated by canning companies had been operating without permits and in violation of state sanitary codes. In the fall of 1942, the district office of the state health department found nearly 42 percent of 851 Wayne

County African-American migrant workers to have been infected with syphilis, whose spread is hastened by overcrowding and poor sanitation. Syphilis plagued New York's upstate military bases and the cities near them as well. Complaints about the camps compelled a revision in the state sanitary code in 1944 to effect "a higher quality of housing" in the camps, but poor conditions persisted. Edward R. Murrow's "Harvest of Shame" documentary, aired on Thanksgiving Day in 1960, brought them to national attention; seven years later, Robert Kennedy's visit to a "deplorable" Wayne County camp brought the continuing scandal uncomfortably close to home.[47]

Moving off the Flat

By the mid-1950s, the migration of African Americans from the South coupled with the very existence of Dixon Homes to make the distinction between old and new families seem more real to white and black Genevans alike. It accordingly became increasingly difficult for African Americans to buy even in those areas in which they had lived for generations.[48] When Mildred Linzy married Clyde Mathis in 1945, the couple moved farther up North Wadsworth Street from where Mildred had lived with her mother. The Mathises rented there until 1957, when they were able to buy a house on the north side of High Street, across from the High Street School. The house, originally in the Bland family, is probably the only one still standing from the nineteenth-century African-American neighborhood at High and West streets. Mathis recalled having to work intently with her realtor to get a house there in the 1950s, by which time the suspicion that Geneva realtors were steering African Americans to the sixth ward had become common among the city's blacks.

> I was this type of person—like I told the real estate girl that took me out, if she started showing me areas where I wouldn't live, "Now, I'm gonna tell you right now; I'm not living down below the tracks, and I'm not living in no house sitting on the street, you know what I mean, these narrow streets, that you wouldn't get a good price for if you wanted to sell it." So we just bought right from the owner, but at that time when we bought Sampson was still here and housing was hard to find. Everything was taken.

The reluctance to sell to African Americans persisted into the 1970s. Clarence Day, a veteran civil servant transferred to Seneca

Ordnance Depot in 1957, rented in Geneva with his wife until 1971, when he tried to buy a house near the home in which the Herman F. Kenney family had lived since 1916.

> I had trouble . . . the woman told me if she knew that I was black she would never have sold it to me. And I done made the down-payment on it, too. I bought it through realtors. And I told her if she back out I'm going to sue her pants off. She's still living, too. She questioned all around about me, she questioned *everybody* about me. [imitates her voice] "If I'd a knowed I'd a never want no black people in my house, oh, no, no, *no*." I had to have a ceiling put in this place, siding, panelling before I could move in it. That paper in the hall; she wanted to take that paper off. I told her if she take it off I'd *sue* her. That's old-time paper. She said she was of-fered a thousand dollars for that paper there.

After Jim Henderson and Beth Kenney married in the early 1960s, they were among the families living on lower Elm Street who were forced to relocate when the city chose the area for its first senior citizen housing complex. Kenney's father, John, who rented an Elm Street house across from the couple, bought the home at 116 High Street that belonged to his uncle, Art Kenney. But the couple found it difficult even to rent. Finally, a fellow Jaycee told them about an apartment for which Beth had earlier been told there was a waiting list.

> Two days later, my wife gets on the phone and says, "My name is so-and-so and my husband just got a job, we just moved to Ge-neva, and my husband has a job working at American Can, and we're looking for an apartment. Do you have anything available?" And the lady says, "Oh, yes." My wife says, "Are you sure, now? There isn't a waiting list or anything?" And she says, "Oh, no, please. When would you like to see it?" Now this was two days after telling us that there was this list. What I discovered later . . . was that [the Jaycee] had the audacity to canvass the *neighborhood* prior to telling us about the apartment he and his wife were mov-ing out of, canvass the neighborhood, to see if they had any objec-tions to a black moving in, and my mother and father-in-law lived one block away.
>
> . . . We told Mr. Mathis that in the situation we were in we could buy a home according to federal guidelines within that target area. . . . So he said, "Jim, I'm gonna take you and show you what you're up against." He took me down to the real estate place on Castle Street, he walks in, introduced me, you know, he knew the

lady and stuff, and he said, "This young man and his wife are looking for a place." She said, "Well, what price range?" And I said, "Well, I'm not sure, we're not even sure what we want, but we'll know it when we see it." So that left a wide spectrum right there. Suddenly we noticed that pictures of homes and things and listings were all in the fifth and sixth wards. And Clyde picked up on it, too. So Clyde started to smile, and I said, "Excuse me, ma'am," I said. "These seem to be only homes in this one area here. Do you have other homes?" "Oh, no." I said, "You know, I find that hard to believe, that in Geneva, that the only properties you have in terms of homes that are for sale are in the fifth and sixth ward. So in the first, second, third, and fourth you have nothing?" "Oh, no." And then Clyde started laughing.

. . . Then we went back to trying to find a place to rent again. This was documented—the number of places we looked at, the people we took to the Human Rights Commission—and then, I mean, I'd been working up at American Can and stuff, and when Beth and I got married, we had a 1958 Oldsmobile. And what we did, we went looking for a new car. So we got a brand new 1967 Grand Prix. It was beautiful. Guess what the talk in the neighborhood was? The people there were still in the process of selling their homes to the federal government. "My God, look at that—they can go out and buy a brand new car, but they can't find someplace to live." And you know, I told Beth, I said, "This town is ignorant," I said. We knew all the attempts that we made. And they had no concept of discrimination. But it was something like—it was a mindset, I don't know where they got it, of the stereotype of somebody owning a Cadillac and they have no place to live; they eat and sleep right there in the Cadillac.

Clearly, the construction of Chartres Homes had not ended the housing shortage in Geneva, at least for African Americans. If anything, the total stock of rental units probably declined afterward. In 1930, the Lake Street houses had been razed and not replaced; in 1967, when 11 East Washington and 656, 658, 672, 683, and 686 South Exchange were torn down, urban renewal plans made no provision for building new rental housing despite official acknowledgment that it was in critically short supply. "At present there are 15 units occupied by Negroes that are being relocated under Urban Renewal," Geneva urban renewal director David B. Aldrich stated in 1964, "and there are not 15 vacancies to accommodate these people."

The housing shortage and its unfortunate racial associations were among the motive forces behind the creation of the city's first Commission on Human Rights in 1964; it was the complaint of an African American to this commission that eventually gave the Hendersons access to an apartment on South Main Street. But the commission's existence had little apparent effect on the overall conditions in existing rental units or on fulfilling the need for additional income-based public housing after Chartres Homes opened. In the late 1970s, Geneva Mayor Helen Maney called the city's reluctance to enforce its building codes on Exchange Street apartments "humanitarian" because no alternative housing then existed, and she presented a justification for why no new housing was being contemplated. "There's only so much one community can do," Maney was reported to state in the *Finger Lakes Times* in 1978. "We cannot supply housing for other areas that haven't done anything in low-income housing. Many are not Genevans, but they find it nearly impossible to get into these other communities so they settle here."[49]

Since the 1850s, African-American leaders had deplored segregation not only because of its inevitable association with poor housing conditions, but also because of the broader social damage it could cause. Samuel Ward believed that blacks who had deliberately settled themselves together in 1850s Canada hurt whites as well as themselves because "some of their white neighbours need to be taught even the first ideas of civilization, by being near to enlightened progressive coloured people."[50] But in Geneva, residential segregation persisted, and it forced a reenactment of the 1870s battles over school segregation. In the 1960s, Geneva's "modified Princeton Plan" shattered the historic relation between primary school districts and neighborhoods because residential segregation had created serious racial imbalances throughout the school system.

The Costs of Owning

Over time, it may have become somewhat easier for African Americans in Geneva to buy houses wherever they chose to live, but the intervention of whites was necessary for others into the 1970s.[51] And home ownership was never easy at any point, in either century. In 1847, when James W. Duffin submitted the names of twenty-eight Geneva blacks eligible to receive land grants from Gerrit Smith, twenty-two owned no property at all, and the other five or six, he wrote, "have each of them a house and lot but upon each there are mortgages varying from $200 to $500 dollars. I supposed that such could not be considered in easy circumstances."[52] In the 1800s, those few tradesmen whose enterprises required some capital investment tended not to own homes or lots in the beginning of their careers in Geneva; laborers, whose work required no investment, were more apt to be homeowners.[53]

However, real estate was rarely the type of investment that led to greater wealth among the village's African Americans. Some few, such as John Bland, had been able to accumulate acres of property. But most owned small amounts of land and devoted varying amounts of their lifelong income to keeping it. Some blacks left household inventories and savings: Anthony Jupiter left two stoves, three beds, a full range of other household furnishings, more than $350 in the bank, $55 in cash, and more than $400 in debts owed him and notes he held. Delia Prue, a single woman who had inherited her Main Street house from her parents, left an inventory valued at more than $900 when she died in 1893. Her home appears to have been furnished according to conventional Victorian taste: her inventory included an array of parlor, dining room, and sitting room furniture and gimcracks such as mantel ornaments, wall brackets, a mounted deer's head, and about twenty prints and pictures. Margaret A. Freeman, a laundress who probably inherited her uncle Samuel A. Jackson's High Street home, left an inventory of similar size and character, as well as nearly $500 in savings and $120 worth of stock.

However, most other property-owning people left much less. When Salaby Hardy died in 1869, he left his West Street property to his surviving wife and unmarried children and left his married daughters Harriet Gaten and Mary Allen five dollars each. At his death in 1857, Doctor Merriweather (not a physician; "Doctor" was his first name) left his trunk, all his clothing, his shoes, hats, and tools to his friend Edward Tompkins, Jr., a cook and laborer who by that time had bought a house and two lots on Catherine Street. When Tompkins died in 1869, he left to his "beloved sister" Eliza, then a cook in her late thirties, whatever remained of his estate—the real property alone valued at approximately one thousand dollars— after his debts were paid. After her death, the estate was to pass to his adopted son Henrico Freeman, then ten years old. However, Tompkins's executor found no personal property "except an old shawl and an old pair of shoes of no value" and was evidently compelled to sell his property, despite the provisions of the will. In late November 1870, the executor presented an equivocal justification for selling only the vacant lot to the Ontario County probate court:

> In regard to mortgaging the premises I cannot find any one to lend money on the property and there is no source from which to pay interest. I couldn't lease the property to much advantage. The house might bring $40 a year over & above the taxes if the rent was not lost. I couldn't get a very good class of tenants. I think the vacant lot is not getting any better. The fence is partly gone. I think it would be better for the boy & all to sell the lot rather than to rent the house. . . . The sister of deceased, Eliza Tompkins, has a life estate & occupies the house. She is sickly & has difficulty in getting along, and could scarcely make a living without the house. It would need some repairs in order to rent it. . . . The sister's health is so poor that I think if she is deprived of the house, & is taken worse she would be thrown upon the Town.[54]

By March 1871, some and possibly all of Tompkins's real estate had been sold and the proceeds distributed to his creditors. The $52.10 surplus from the sale was invested for Eliza and the interest paid to her "from time to time" until about 1 September 1880. By the time of her death in 1896, Eliza Tompkins rented a room or an apartment on Dorsey's Alley in downtown Geneva. According to her death record, she died of "senility and malnutrition."

A random survey of housing values listed in the 1875 census indicates that black homes were, on average, worth about $1,700; the average home owned by a white person was worth about $1,000 more. Clearly, simply buying and keeping a house could foreclose the possibility of improving it, and it might utterly exhaust one's capital. When John Bland's heir, George J. Bland, died in 1886, he owned three dwellings and more than six acres in the High Street neighborhood. But he was cash-poor: five years earlier, Geneva physician N. B. Covert wrote on the back of Bland's $28.50 bill that Bland "couldn't pay under a year / Had nothing to pay with." After his death, Bland's wife had to sell nearly all his property to pay his bills of $315.52, including one for more than two years' worth of stove coal, Covert's bill, and another medical bill amounting to $161.47.[55] In 1899, Margaret Douglass died poor despite the fact that she owned her High Street house and lot, two acres north of the village that her older brother Charles had deeded to her in 1868, and half of a thirty-acre Seneca Township lot that her father had originally purchased in 1843 (fig. 22). In her 1893 will, she directed that her real estate be sold to pay her debts, including "whatever may be from this time, advanced to or expended for me by the Trustees of the Presbyterian Church of Geneva from its poor fund."

In the twentieth century, the constricting effects of property ownership were still apparent. African Americans in Geneva continued to forestall property improvements, either from sheer lack of resources or because other expenses, such as college educations, took priority. When Alice L. Cleggett died in 1960, her house was not wired for electricity; she evidently still used kerosene lamps. The Castle Street home that Herman and Josephine Lepeon Kenney began to rent in 1915 and then bought from the estate of O. J. C. Rose in 1929 had neither central heating nor electricity until after Charles Kenney returned in 1951 to occupy his childhood home. In the 1960s, John Kenney bought his uncle Arthur's house on High Street, once well and amply furnished in Victorian style by his wife Mary, a chiropodist and hairdresser. But Art Kenney's income was not sufficient to pay for the house's upkeep.

> I used to stop off and see how Art was doing, because my aunt had died. And I knew that any money that was there was left by her; he inherited the house. The day that they told me Art's furnace blew up and the welfare was looking for someone who would take care of Art—I couldn't take care of him; I had a family to take care of. The welfare commissioner had already decided to put Art up where I worked, at the county home. The furnace blew up, and he used most of the money that she left him, and all that was left was the property. When the money she left him ran out, the property had to be disposed of to pay for his fee. So we bid on it, and we got it; it was quite a chunk for us. It proved to be quite profitable, because it was a home.

However African Americans have managed to secure houses in Geneva, the meanings they have attached to having them have clearly extended beyond the simple necessity to have a roof over one's head and beyond the common knowledge that it makes more economic sense to own than to rent. For blacks far more than for whites, owning a home provided a stable, rooted center amidst an uncertain and conflict-ridden political, economic, and social environment outside. And however difficult they were to keep, homes secured families. In them, families could create and sustain a social

22. Margaret Douglass, about 1875. Born in 1820 after her parents were freed, Margaret Douglass worked as a domestic and laundress in Geneva until her death in 1899. *Courtesy Geneva Historical Society.*

world that was positive and complete. Trudy Kenney Spencer described the effect of growing up in her large family:

> A lot of time people will say, "They were poor." There were ten of us. I was so surrounded by love that a lot of things didn't even touch me from the outside. I know that we were not rich, but I

think we had something that a lot of families don't have today and a lot of families didn't have back then, too. When you don't have transportation and you don't have a lot of money, you're sort of together a lot, and you figure out things to do that won't hopefully get you into trouble outside the family. When you've got four sisters and five brothers you're kind of insulated from a lot of different things. . . . *Now* I know that we were not financially well off, but I never remember being hungry, I never remember being cold, I never remember being without touching, without feeling, without feeling really good, a lot. So it's kind of hard for me when people say, "You're really underprivileged." I just go, "Really?" Maybe it's because we do accept what is and we don't expect what could be, but there were so many great times that we had growing up that I can't seem to find any underprivileged information in it.

Still, for some, their awareness of the world surrounding these domestic havens tinged the positive values they attached to homes with ambivalence. Dorothy Cooke grew up in her aunt's Dorchester Avenue home at a time when the dwindling number of African-American families found it impossible to sustain an institutionalized social life in the community at large, an isolation that her feelings about the house still reflect.

This house is a drawing card. It's just inbred, because when I come in I see my relatives, in a way of speaking, you know, my grandmother, my aunt, my uncles, they used to come over here and bring all their instruments and we'd sit, because the family was so large we never needed any outsiders, you see, just the family. We'd either be here or we'd be out to Wolcott. We always had music. This house—I often think if I were to move if I could just take this house with me I would go someplace else but Geneva.

Just What They Could Get to Do

You could never get a job in a five-and-ten or soda
fountain or anything like that. We always had to go
for the housework. There was one time I couldn't
even get a job working as a maid in a hotel, till later;
then when they began to need more help and everything they started hiring blacks in this area. Now
you take the South: blacks was the ones that got
those jobs.

Mildred Linzy came of working
age in the 1930s. She wanted to be a nurse; but because her family
needed her income, after she graduated from high school she took a
job as the downstairs maid in the home where her mother cooked.
Since she was small, Geneva's best hotel, the Seneca, had not hired
African Americans to do its service jobs, though when her mother
was her age nearly all of its help had been black. As World War II
drew white women into defense industries, the Seneca once again
began hiring African-American women.

African Americans have long been accustomed to the effect labor
shortages have had on their access to work. It was easier to get jobs
in the 1830s and 1840s, before the mass immigration of German and
Irish people; during the wars; and when commercial harvests after
World War II were too large for local farm laborers to handle. African Americans often found the same work that new immigrants did,
filling jobs at the margins of the economy, jobs they could easily lose
when work was scarce and other laborers competed for it. In many

respects, they saw few differences between the northern capitalist economy and the southern plantation: North and South, whites typically knew only as much about blacks as would make them useful, and whites used the labor of blacks to enhance the profits that accrued to ownership. North and South, African Americans epitomized alienated labor, realizing rewards far slimmer than their vast investment of effort led them intuitively to expect.[1]

The steady devaluation of manual labor, despite how essential it was to building wealth in the urban industrial economy, had multiple effects on black Americans. As brain work and leisure became associated with heightening status, African Americans stood on the other side of the mirror. They did the necessary work whites believed to be beneath them, and they were disparaged for doing it. And the devaluation of manual work of course had economic as well as social effects. Because it carried such low wages, African Americans began their working lives earlier and ended them later, took several jobs at once, and combined the wages of as many in a household as could work.

No aspect of their lives brought them closer to white people than work, yet it was here that the psychic distance between the races was most assiduously maintained. The jobs that were open to African Americans consistently emphasized how whites both commodified them and categorized them in a social hierarchy of which both were manifestly aware. As Frederick Douglass said at one 1855 meeting, "Here at the North, our white friends—not our friends but our fellow citizens—have a regard for us—like us very well in our places,—and they have selected our places for us, and they have marked out the boundary lines for us,—and while we remain in the narrow circumference they describe for us, we are 'good fellows,' and they pat us on the head and say we are good boys."[2] In similar terms, Frances Craven described going to work at the downtown Rochester department store Sibley, Lindsay, and Curr in the 1940s:

> I got hired at Sibley's, because it was the war years and things were tough. And they hadn't hired too many Negroes, only in the kitchens and things like that, you know, behind the scenes. And so when things got a little hectic, they began to hire them in other parts. I worked in the buffet.
> . . . First they started us out as bus girls—we didn't have sense enough to do anything but pick up the dishes off the tables—and so we did that. And then after they saw that we knew how to handle ourselves and we wouldn't be breaking all the dishes and

falling down on the floor or whatever, they divided the tables up
into sections, and we became waitresses. And then after they saw
that was going good, they put us on the counter, and so then we
went behind the counter and we took people's orders.

In work places, each race formed its principal ideologies about
the other. Whites saw blacks as fit to do little other than the work
whites allowed them to do. And despite the lengthy debate on labor
issues in the African-American community from the 1830s onward,
blacks confronted unerring constancy in the nature and content of
their labor and a deadening absence of true economic and occupational progress. Middle-class whites are taught to view work as ex-
pressive, as self-actualizing, and some blacks have certainly seen
their work in that light. But for many, labor may actually have functioned as a negative center, the necessary support that has permitted the construction of more positive contexts of meaning.

The necessity to work within a framework of white ideology
combined with skill and need to help determine what kind of work
one would do within the narrow universe of opportunity available
to African Americans. For many, especially women who entered the
work force before World War II, domestic work appeared to be the
only opportunity. Among men, to spend one's occupational life in
heavy, unskilled work on the farm or in the factory was equally
common. Newcomers could usually get this kind of work because it
was work that whites put behind them as soon as they were able. In
Geneva, newcomers were also more likely to take service jobs in
hotels. Those who had lived longer in the village structured their
working lives in particular areas of personal service based largely on
the extent and quality of their connections to local whites. But employment in skilled trades and professions varied more historically,
both tending to be more prevalent before 1850 than at any point in
the century afterward.[3]

Historically, talent in sports and music opened doors for some
African Americans in Geneva, but it rarely provided a sustaining
income. Even Henry McDonald, whom many sources claim to have
been the nation's first black professional football player, often
earned only ten dollars a day at his sport and spent the rest of his
working career as a janitor at the American Can Company. Many
African-American barbers and bootblacks were also musicians who
used barbering in part to promote and develop clients for musical
engagements and, in turn, used performance fees to supplement

their barbering income. J. C. Gillam, Edward Liberty, Samuel Lepeon, Lewis Scott, and Art Kenney were among them, but evidently only Gillam was able to support himself on his musical ability. A barber in the village in 1841, Gillam went west before 1850 and formed the touring African-American Ethiopian Serenaders, who returned to Geneva for two concerts at Ramsey's Hall in November of that year.[4] But for most, these aptitudes became a sideline to other work and even proved to be a way to develop other work. Will Gillam and John Bland were acclaimed Seneca Lake oarsmen, a fact that probably encouraged them to assume that their 1879 restaurant and catering business would have the white patronage it needed to succeed. And Arthur Kenney's notoriety as a member of the Geneva Colored Boys Quartet and as one of the originators of barbershop singing in Geneva helped him get the waiting and bartending jobs that enhanced his income from shining shoes, blocking hats, and cleaning local banks. McDonald raised a little extra money by training his sons Edward and Edgar to box against each other in rings all over the region, as Edward McDonald recalled:

> Since we were small we were boxers; my father taught us how to box. And we boxed right up until we went to college. We made a lot of money out of it, too. My brother and I being twins, my brother had a trainer, and my father was my trainer, and we were hired by different lodges and places—in fact, we went by Pullman all the way to Pennsylvania just to put on a show. And when we finished they would throw silver dollars or half dollars in the ring, and we made lots of money like that. And we enjoyed it until we went to college.

Geneva's first business directory, published in 1857, and the 1855 state and 1860 federal censuses permit the first clear view of the kinds of work African Americans did in the village, a profile that differs little from what pertained in other cities throughout the North.[5] Servants were between 36 and 43 percent of all those whose occupations were listed in these sources. Men working for a day's wage in unskilled labor were about 20 percent of all working people, and men in transportation jobs—driving teams, hauling goods and materials, driving public coaches or hired carriages—were another 6 to 8 percent. In 1860, farm laborers were 13 percent of all African-American workers; barbers were about 8 percent. Six percent worked in skilled trades or were teachers, clergy, or musicians. Only one African American, the furnaceman Henry Swan, did factory work, probably in one of the village's foundries. Some details of this profile changed over the next eighty years, but its basic features remained unaltered.

Farm Work and the Production Ideal

Certain issues about labor attracted debate among both white and black people in nineteenth-century America. Just as Jefferson and de Crevecoeur extolled the virtues of agrarianism, so too nearly every colored people's convention before 1860 exhorted African Americans to turn to a farming life. The 1847 convention at Troy pointed out that, for all its civic and moral benefits, farming had practical assets of special meaning to blacks.

> The farmer is an *independent man;* the man of no other pursuit is so much so. He may do without what men of trade and traffic have to dispose of, and upon the disposal of which, depends their very living; but they cannot do without what he produces. To him they must come for the very things upon which human existence, under God, is absolutely dependent. Without him, they have neither house, home, food, nor clothing. They must have the bread he produces, the cotton, the flax, and the wool he grows. They must have the timber from his forest, the clay from his bed for brick, the sugar from his grove, his beet, or his cane. . . . Yea, the very articles in which they trade and traffic, are the fruit of the farmer's toil. If he toil not, then they trade and traffic not.[6]

African-American leaders viewed farming as the occupation singularly adapted to the task of changing the position of blacks in white society, of ending the continuing dependency that struck many as a discomforting and persistent legacy of slavery. "The estimation in which we would be held by those in power, would be quite different, were we producers, and not merely, as now, consumers," the black activist Mary Ann Shadd wrote to Frederick Douglass's *North Star* in March 1849. The occupations of the city were "precarious" by contrast, the agriculture committee of the 1843 convention maintained; those who held them were "subject to all the changes of fortune and of circumstances to which those who employ them are subjected, as well as to all the vexatious changes in the business affairs of the country."[7]

Fugitive slaves were also preoccupied by the idea that the mass participation of African Americans in agriculture could change the racial dynamic. Austin Steward was an urban merchant, but he nonetheless recommended agricultural work because "the farmer can live less dependant on his oppressors" in the country. And Samuel Ward openly regretted not having pursued an agricultural life. "Had I clung to the use of the hoe, instead of aspiring to a love of books," he wrote in 1855, "I might by this time have been somebody, and the reader of this volume would not have been solicited by this means to consider the lot of the oppressed American Negro." To Ward, as to Booker T. Washington a half-century later, actions spoke louder than words; the black man who proved his value rather than simply asserted it, he held, would be the one to win equality and respect for the race.[8]

A minority of politically active blacks, including Frederick Douglass, refused to accept the notion that agrarianism would change the equation of dependency, chiefly because most African Americans chose, for whatever reason ("perhaps the adage that misery loves company will explain it," Douglass once wrote to Harriet Beecher Stowe), to congregate in towns and cities. He also disputed the assertion that most African Americans could afford to buy and improve farm land as easily as they could pay rent and buy food in cities.[9] Indeed, even those African Americans to whom Gerrit Smith had given rural freeholds in 1846 and 1847 rarely settled down upon them to farm.[10] And the urban tendencies Douglass perceived among African Americans of his day only grew stronger.

Still, a statistically small group of African Americans have worked steadily in agriculture, in Geneva and elsewhere in the North, most of them for white farmers or on small farms of their own. Willis Lee probably farmed fewer than twenty-five acres in Seneca Township, and men who owned large village lots apparently used them for small-scale farming through the 1860s.[11] Parts of the Kenney and Hardy families appear to have preferred farm labor to working in the village, but by the end of the Civil War most had entered the village economy. Newcomers, usually from the South, were most apt to fill available agricultural jobs around Geneva from the 1870s forward. Frank Brown, a Geneva minister who had come from Hampton, Virginia, to Liverpool, New York, after the Civil War, worked as a farm laborer until he saved enough to buy a fifty-two-acre farm in nearby Clay. There he raised vegetables, tobacco, poultry, and some livestock. But his three daughters moved into

Syracuse to "work for the rich people" as domestics.[12] Minor Linzy, Sr., and his sons James and Stanley were postwar migrants who did agricultural work. Dorothy Cooke's description of her grandfather's enterprise reveals the persistence of positive values attaching to agricultural work at a time when negative associations had begun to cluster around this form of labor.

> I think they came about 1919. He bought a farm, a big farm. And he was a businessman and his sons all worked for him. And his business was plowing gardens. Way back then everybody had a garden. And he had the only business apparently in Geneva, and he was almost on contract from year to year to the different families in Geneva to plow their gardens. He had all the equipment. And at the property that he owned, he had a slaughterhouse on the property, and all the men who owned meat markets used to go up to him, go up there, get their meat from him. He owned horses, he owned wagons, and later years I understand he used to take people sleigh-riding, companies of young people. That was the thing to do I guess back in those days, in the winter, and he would be hired out to do that in the winter. So he really had quite a business.
>
> Apparently they were rather prosperous, because they said people used to come like—I guess tramps used to be prevalent at that time—and they said that they would come to the back door and she [Dolly Linzy, Minor's wife] would always give them something to eat. They had the reputation of apparently having things, having food, having property or money. . . . And they had a big table in the dining room, and the hired help would come in and she'd have meals for them. . . . He raised regular crops. I know he had pigs, cows, and horses. He was respected as just a farmer businessman.

By the time Marie Whitaker Van Cleaf began doing farm work in the 1930s, its status had changed, probably because visible numbers of migrant workers were being hired to do it.[13] According to her daughter Frances Craven, Van Cleaf did domestic work in rural Leicester until harvest time because, despite the fact that it was unpleasant work, it offered "ready money." In fact, migrants considered the wages of farm work its most, if not its only, attractive feature, and it continued to be the leading occupation of African-American women until at least World War I. By World War II, agricultural work became a major point of entry for southern African Americans into the northern economy. In trucks and buses, crew leaders brought southern workers by the thousands to Long Island

and upstate farms. Most worked on at least three farms each season. One 1957 survey found that no more than 20 percent of those interviewed would have chosen agricultural labor if other work—particularly industrial, construction, or transportation jobs—had been available.[14] Virginia Peek, who had been doing farm work since her teens in Florida, described the work she did in the North:

> We caught the truck in the morning and we go to work, and if we wasn't too far from the house we come home for dinner. If we was too far we didn't come home till that afternoon. And we pick up potatoes, we pick cherries—you did so many thing like work, you know. A lot of people pick apples and whatever, and whatever, and whatever, you know. . . . Farm work is hard and nobody know unless that you have did it, you know.

Essie Tucker, a Floridian who had run her father's farm when she was eleven and became an overseer on an upstate farm-labor camp, left the job after four years despite the fact that it paid better than the domestic work she did in Geneva.

> In '57 I moved over in Phelps and I run the camp. That was Art DeMay's camp. He's dead now; that old camp is *gone*. Round about thirty people was up there, some from Florida, some from Georgia, some from Alabama. I was overseer—go out in the field and boss 'em and see if they was doing their work.
>   . . . Most of the time I went right along with my crew. See, I had to see to them getting to work; I would have to drive them to work. And see after I get there I'd stay out there. We left 'round about seven o'clock, eight o'clock, [and stay] sometime until sundown. . . . If I had work for them to do, they couldn't go to no other camp to work; they had to come to me.
>   . . . I was there until '61, and then I moved over here in Geneva. I just got tired of it. . . . [Domestic work] is less trouble. You don't have nobody to bother with you, nobody to go and tell, you don't have to watch peoples—like picking tomatoes. You got a big basket, you pick so many a basket. If you don't know, those tomatoes and ain't no people watching, they put ripe one all the way around it, and then the bottom is green. And see I have went down the road and just turn the baskets over and tell 'em, "Go back and fill your baskets."

Migrant farming was hard, outdoor work that isolated agricultural workers geographically and socially. And because it involved African Americans almost exclusively after the war, both whites and long-settled blacks conflated race with the already strongly negative association between migrant farming and poverty, southernness, and ruralness. The size of the migration surely accentuated these feelings. But even without its social liabilities, the fundamental unpleasantness of the work was so profound that for many, including Virginia Peek, even domestic work seemed preferable.

> It was better than farm work. You know, it was much better because it was inside, you know, and cleaning inside the house is much better than outside. Outside you working in the sun, you working in the rain, you working in the cold. It's just hard. . . . You put in as many hours [doing housework] but then it's so much better, because if you know how to clean house it's easier to clean because you is inside. If it's raining you is inside. If it's real hot you *still* inside.
>
> Although the housework was hard because you worked for different peoples. Some of them was nasty to you and all they want was the housework. They didn't care nothing about you, but you go ahead and try to do it because you *got* to do it. Some of them put so much on you in one day that it's ridiculous; still you got to try to do it. Sometime you get home from the houses where you work you be just as tired or tireder than if you did the farm work. The only thing, it was inside and it was much better.

Domestics and Day Laborers

Nineteenth-century African-American leaders glorified agricultural work at the expense of the work African Americans seemed far more inclined to do—the panoply of labor and service jobs in the urban economy. The 1843 colored peoples' convention objected to "our people's clustering about the large cities, and picking up just what they could get to do"; Austin Steward deplored the fact that so many blacks "flock to cities where they allow themselves to be made 'hewers of wood and drawers of water.' "[15] Still, general service work and unskilled labor often presented, especially to newcomers, the only opportunity for income; nationwide, only farm labor was statistically more common from 1850 through at least 1910.[16]

The most plentiful group in the early years were day laborers. They did the general unskilled work that needed to be done in cities, whenever it needed to be done; in Massachusetts in the 1870s,

23. Paving Genesee Street, Geneva, 1898. About half of this paving crew were African American, many of them probably transient. Police mug shots at the time include one of an African-American man named Fred Edwards, who, police wrote on the back, "came from Coulombus Ohio to work on street paving." *Courtesy Geneva Historical Society.*

the average day laborer worked no more than 240 days out of the year.[17] In Geneva, they dug ditches and cleaned gutters; they loaded and unloaded barges, steamboats, and drays. After the village became a city in 1897, they worked on the crews of private contractors hired by the city to pave the streets, lay sidewalks, railroad track, and sewer pipe, and fill the swampy shoreline to make new public lands along the waterfront (fig. 23).

Even though African-American laborers were more apt to be homeowners before the Civil War than tradespeople were, their fortunes declined afterward. Day laborers' wages were probably so low and unpredictable that their income could not support their households. In Geneva in 1870, two-thirds of all black day laborers had other wage earners in their households, sons who also did day labor, daughters and wives who worked as maids or laundresses. By 1900, eleven of the thirteen African-American laborers listed in the federal census rented their homes. By 1925, no African Americans were listed as laborers in Geneva censuses, which may be more a matter of changing nomenclature than changing work; men were probably still doing the same sort of general labor for specific private enterprises, such as nurseries, coal yards, churches, clubs, and industries.

The only significant competition for laborers' jobs in Geneva came from Irish immigrants, who appear to have held the great majority of them by the 1860s.[18] The changing concentration of African Americans in domestic work also demonstrates how whites perceived the place of black labor in the economy. In Geneva in 1855, when African Americans were between 5 and 6 percent of the village's total population, they were between 9 and 10 percent of the total servant population in the village. Irish-born men and women were also slightly overrepresented in the servant population. But after the Civil War, their concentration in domestic work grew notably heavier. In 1870, persons born in Ireland were about 14 percent of the population of Geneva, but they held almost half of the available domestic service jobs. African Americans, then only about 3 percent of the village population, held only 8 percent of service jobs. Through 1900, domestic service made up an increasingly smaller share of all jobs held by African Americans in Geneva, though 8 percent of the domestic work force continued to be black through 1925. In Geneva and elsewhere, domestic work continued to be the main source of employment for black women even as other opportunities became available to white working women, and a much larger proportion of the black female population worked. By 1940, 28 percent of Geneva's total female population aged fourteen years and older was in the labor force, compared to nearly 39 percent of the black female working-age population.[19]

In 1820, seven African-American children aged fourteen or younger lived alone—that is, without a parent or a sibling—in the homes of white Genevans, which suggests that they must have been working as domestics there. African-American women probably also were maids in boarding houses. But they were most apt to be found in the homes of Geneva's elite and of its prosperous middle class. Many less prosperous people had live-in help as well. Some surely needed the extra household help: in 1855, twenty-one-year-old African-American Rosetta Armwood probably worked in the household of John Ackley, a widowed clerk with four children and an elderly female relative living with him. But others who were in less obvious need probably had live-in domestics because of what household labor had come to mean to middle-class women. Not only did female labor outside the home mark low status; working inside the home came also to signify the inability to meet one basic criterion of middle-class existence—living comfortably on one male income. According to this ideology, only working-class women did their own housework. In 1855, Elizabeth Bola, a twenty-one-year-old African American, was a live-in domestic in the home of Vermont-born clerk Matthew Allen, who had only a wife and a son in his household. Robert Lay and his wife had two domestics (one of them John Hite, kidnapped two years later). By the 1880s, perhaps as many as half of all middle-class families—those earning between five hundred and two thousand dollars annually—had one servant.[20]

After 1900, as electric appliances proliferated and household income was redirected to acquiring them and such other durable goods as automobiles, the number of servants declined rapidly. And as white women took clerical and industrial jobs, the domestic work force became predominantly black and married (fig. 24). In many northern places, living in was largely replaced by day's work by the 1920s, even though the demand for domestics to "sleep in" continued to be strong. Living in was isolating work, and it was work without end. Few married women were able or inclined to be perpetually on call.[21]

But in Geneva's prosperous first ward alone, there were 125 live-in domestics in 1925, to say nothing of the help that came in for day's work or of the presence of domestics in other areas of the city. More than half of the first-ward live-in domestics were white and American-born, 19 percent had been born in Ireland, and nearly 9 percent (eleven persons) were black. Harriet Bias, a single woman who inherited her grandfather's property on High Street, worked for Mrs. Frances Wells Shepard, Hobart professor William P. Durfee, and Trinity rector Samuel Edsall, all of whom lived on South Main Street (fig. 25). Katherine and Lawrence Kenney lived in with Hobart president Murray Bartlett, his wife, and their daughter. At the South Main Street home of Henry L. DeZeng, whose family had had black servants since the 1820s, Dorothy Cooke's father Joseph Scott was butler, and the sixty-year-old Amanda Ray was cook, though Ray was also listed at her own Andes Avenue home in the 1925 census.

Gertrude Sims and Zeffa Sims Linzy, sisters from rural Marengo, New York, both worked as domestics for wealthy Genevans; but only Gertrude, who was single, lived in, first as a maid in the

24. "On the front porch," possibly the home of Corydon Wheat, 561 South Main Street, Geneva, about 1900. The domestic may be Elizabeth Jones Ray, whom the 1900 census listed at both the Wheat home and her own home at 91 High Street. *Courtesy Geneva Historical Society.*

upper Castle Street home of attorney Charles Rice and later for the J. R. Roenke family on Delancey Drive. Zeffa Linzy's daughter Pearl also worked for Roenke, coproprietor of the dry goods store Roenke and Rogers. Roenke's son Richard employed live-in domestics well into the 1960s, hiring most of them during winter vacations in Florida: Richmond Mathis, Clyde Mathis, Mitchell Whitehead, and Ger-

25. Harriet Bias at age sixteen, 1886, photograph by Pomeroy, Rochester, New York. *Courtesy John W. Kenney.*

aldine Munn McBroom moved to Geneva after accepting Roenke's offer. Richmond Mathis married Pearl Linzy, and his brother Clyde, who followed him to Geneva, married her sister Mildred, then doing day's work with her mother at Harold Hovey's Lochland Road home.

> There was the Roenke family that owned the Smith's dry goods store, and they went to Florida every winter. They always had a help problem. And they were in the area where Clyde lived in Daytona and they just found Clyde and asked him to come live with them. That was back in the thirties. He did cook, butler work. . . . The first group of help that the Roenkes brought up were the Georges, from Clyde's home town, and the Georges worked here until they didn't want to come up no more. And Richmond come up with the Georges, and Clyde came up because of his brother.

McBroom lived in at the Roenkes from 1953 to 1960, when she had saved enough money to attend Geneva School of Nursing.

> A live-in maid is what it was all about. We lived right in. . . . A day would be getting breakfast, lunch, supper, or they might go out. If they had a party then they would call in a cateress. [Their parties were] maybe on the average of every other month; they might have one this month, one this month; it varied. The house on Main Street was just a two-story house, but they rented to a couple upstairs. Downstairs was just where the Roenkes were. And then the house on the lake, East Lake Road, was a big old home, beautiful home, beautiful landscape, but it was not hard to do. Because it was just the Roenkes there and my daughter, so it didn't get really dirty, so it was not a lot to do. I would general clean once a week, and then dust, you know, daily. They ate in the dining room; my daughter and I ate in the kitchen. My daughter didn't work for them; I didn't involve her in that.
> . . . The only thing I did for the Roenkes was clean the house and do the cooking. I had two days off a week, Tuesday and Wednesday, days together. I'd go into town with my daughter and go to the movie with her, or if there was some play or something I would go with her there, go shopping, and we'd stop in and have a chocolate malt or something.
> . . . I did not have a hard time working with the Roenkes. I left because I wanted something better for myself and my daughter. I knew that I didn't want to be a maid all the rest of my life. It was not because they mistreated me or whatever; it was that *I* wanted

something better. I really felt good; I didn't feel bad about my plight because I knew that I had a goal, and I was just working toward getting to this goal.

Many other domestics had little taste for live-in work. After leaving the migrant camp in Lyons, Essie Tucker came into Geneva and did day's work from 1961 to 1977.

There was quite a heap of people doing day's work. I just would see them, you know, and they would tell me they was doing day's work. They says now they pay more for day's work.

. . . I worked for Mr. Flanigan, lawyer Brinn, Doctor Newman—oh, I can't recall them all, and I worked for John Barrow, I worked for Jim Barrow. . . . I can't name the people I used to work for. They paid ten dollars a day. I just cleaned. I enjoy cleaning. I liked it. I didn't bother them. I knowed what I had to do, and I did my work; I didn't bother them. 'Course like my birthday and Christmas and things they'd give me money.

Mildred Mathis described the work she and her mother did for the Hovey family, owners of the Market Basket grocery chain, who lived in a forty-room home overlooking Seneca Lake.

My mother always did housework. She worked for the Hovey family for a long time, and she cooked for the old Elks Club, and she cooked for the fraternity on Main Street. She went from home to work; she never lived off. She wore just housedresses. My mother worked all her life; she never stopped; she didn't stop till she died. It was a necessity.

. . . I took care of the downstairs; I was downstairs maid. So I had to keep the living rooms and things clean, and then when it was meal time I served them at the table; my mother cooked. And that was a typical day. Finish up at night and go home. . . . Hoveys had three girls, and then they had Don and Harry and Gordon. They were teenagers when my mother went to work for them. This lady named Emeline Bergman [did the upstairs]. See that's when they moved out on Lochland Road. They had—all I knew him by was Jim; I never knew his last name—[as groundskeeper], and they had a chauffeur.

Mrs. Hovey was a very lovely person, and Mr. Hovey, he was a very staid person. I never cared for Mr. Hovey, because of the fact that he was like he was. And I'll never forget, my mother had a chance to buy a house, it only cost two thousand dollars, and she asked Mrs. Hovey if she would lend her the money to get the house, and she said she had to wait and ask Mr. Hovey. And Mr. Hovey said no, he didn't want us to have nothing. They were the type that they'd give you all the clothes and things you want, but they'd never give you money, because they know money is power. At Christmas, she'd go downtown and buy all the old junk, you know, but they would never give you a ten-dollar check or something that you could use.

You just know you had to work, so you worked. You worked or starved or whatever. My mother left from there. Once she quit the Hoveys, she got a job cooking at the fraternity house.

I wanted to be a nurse, but I knew I couldn't go because I had to help my mother. We had a niece that lived with us, Jean Paulette Matthews, but I had to help her pay the rent, buy food, you know. In those days you felt like you couldn't leave, especially since my father wasn't with us; she needed help.

People newer to Geneva often had a more difficult time with domestic work, perhaps because they expected better of the North. Virginia Peek went from migrant farming to day's work after she moved into Geneva. Her husband worked at Geneva Foundry.

At that time I was doing housework, you know, for different people. I worked for Rosenblooms and I worked for different people, a lady named Mrs. Brown. I worked for her two days and other people three days, you know, cleaning and dusting and ironing and stuff like that. Even some of them I had to fix meals. You might work as many days as you can and, you know, you got children you can't work; every day, say, from Monday say, to Sunday. Sunday you can't do it 'cause you got your children to feed; you got your house to tend to, though I used to do a lot of my work at night, wash and iron my clothes at night. Used to sit up all night and iron and wash and everything. I'd braid my kids' hair at night, and I'd have their clothes laid out for the morning 'cause they got to go to school, you know.

The people I worked with was okay. The Rosenblooms was real nice. I could work for them—I must have worked for them about fifteen years. They was nice. I could go to work when I got ready. Then I got my husband a job there. He would mow the yard and cut the hedges and stuff, you know. I'd go in to work for them, like if something came up and I had to be home in the day with the kids, it was okay. I had a key to their apartment. I go in at evening and I can wash, go down in the basement and wash their clothes and iron them and dry them and whatever, you know. If I had to go in put in some meat or roast or something for them I was able to do it, you know, and it was okay. It was all right.

We was Jim Crowed a lot. People was prejudiced; a lot of prejudiced people in Geneva, you know. . . . You go and work for them all day long some of them. You know, you can't come in their front door. You couldn't even eat in the kitchen. Now mind—you fixing their lunch for them, you fixing the sandwiches and the soup and everything and their coffee. In the morning you go in, you fixing their bagels and everything but you can't sit in their kitchen. The Rosenblooms were the only white people—and they were Jews—the only white people I could sit down to the table. They had little booths in their kitchen. I could sit down at that table with them and drink coffee or eat a bagel or whatever I wanted, you know. The rest of them white folks you had to go out and come to the back door. You can't eat—you had to go up on the tree, a pine tree, away in the back and eat or eat in the garage. And some of that stuff they fed you—if you would have ate it, it probably would have killed you. Some of it, I would just have got out the door and put it in the garbage, 'cause they done had it there in the refrigerator so long and that's what they fixed for *you*.

I used to work for some people . . . that was rich, rich people, but they was so Jim Crow. And when I went to work for that woman, that woman had grease on her stove that thick. It took me days to clean that woman's stove. Days. That stove looked like a brand new stove when I got through cleaning it. And that woman was so nasty, and she had two boys. I go there every other day. I have to pick up junk and funny books and so much a mess and that woman, I'm telling you, you try to clean that house—and that woman had met me downtown on Exchange Street, before she speak, she turn her head. And mind, I'm cleaning for her.

The Service Trades and White Patronage

Being at once in the most intimate and the most objectified relation with one's white employers was intolerable for some, but most African Americans had to take service jobs in order to survive. Some, particularly members of older families, organized their effort differently. Service work marked by some degree of independence and specialization—laundresses, cooks, sextons, gardeners, stewards, whitewashers—became increasingly better represented as a share of all jobs from the Civil War to the onset of World War II. Such work became more profitable the better one's relations with local whites were. Members of the older families were more apt to know the white people in town, who had the most money, who didn't like to do housework, and whose attitudes would make soliciting someone's work more trouble than it was worth. These service workers could, to some degree, set their own schedules and choose their own clients. They could work either in or from their own homes, for wages and virtually under contract. Usually, they did not move within the commercial economy. They depended instead on an extended domestic economy and fulfilled the special service needs of households and institutions such as the colleges, the churches, and the country clubs. And some of them, particularly laundresses and cateresses, became highly skilled workers with reputations that in turn sustained and increased their business.

These service specialties developed as the American middle class emerged and its boundaries began to be defined. No African-American women were listed as laundresses or washerwomen before 1860, none as hairdressers before 1875. But as middle-class whites grew conscious that the absence of toil had come to signify their newfound status, the number of African Americans working in service grew. Twenty-two percent of the African-American work force had service jobs in 1870, 32 percent in 1900, and 35 percent in 1925.

African-American men tended to take specialized service jobs in the village's commercial economy—barbers, bootblacks, bellboys, porters, hostlers, draymen, cartmen, waiters, bank messengers, retail clerks, and janitors. In particular trade related to the transportation of people and goods, Geneva's hallmark for the entire nineteenth century, provided an important work opportunity for African Americans, although notably few worked as boatmen.[22] Early Geneva merchants such as Walter Grieves and Elijah Gordon probably used slaves and free blacks as porters in the early days of the village's settlement, as did hotel proprietors and those whites involved in "forwarding" or shipping businesses before the canal and the railroad came to Geneva. Hackmen such as William T. Brown transported people, usually in a public coach or carriage. Coachmen carried them in more fashionable, usually private, vehicles; in the twentieth century they became chauffeurs, as Charles Whitaker did. Draymen such as Noah Polk carried trunks and such other goods as produce in low, heavy wagons to and from the depot and boat landing; cartmen drove two-wheeled carts and hauled lighter, smaller goods or refuse, manure, or rags. Stephen J. Ambush, listed as a laborer and a teamster in various censuses, worked largely for households. "I guess you would call him a truckman," Ambush's second wife testified in a 1901 hearing about his contested will. "He was around and hauled out ashes and cleaned up yards." Hostlers such as William Douglass took care of horses in hotel liveries; they often dressed in style and stood in front of the hotels that employed them, waiting for guests to arrive in coaches and carriages (fig. 26). Other hostelers worked in private stables around the village or in the canal barns. Teamsters did heavy hauling with teams of draft horses well into the 1920s, when they switched to trucks.[23] Harry Dunham, Paul "Bing" Foster, Alvin F. Kenney, Harry J. Kenney, Herbert G. Kenney, Richard H. Moore, Fletcher Simpson, and Walter Davis all drove trucks for freight companies or retailers between 1925 and 1965.

African-American men were less likely to hold transportation jobs after the Civil War. In 1870, slightly less than 3 percent of all employed African Americans worked in transportation service, and at least a third of the thirty-six transportation workers listed in the Geneva city directory were Irish. But by 1900, as Irish and Italian workers moved into the factories, these jobs were left for African Americans to fill. Thirty-two percent of all African-American workers were in transportation services by 1900. The share declined to 11 percent in 1925 as industry slowly opened its doors to black workers.

Some transportation service jobs provided a point of economic entry for newcomers, but the most successful of these workers were, again, those who were best connected to the white community. Transportation work had been the historic occupation of males in the Castle Street Kenney family at least since the 1860s. In the 1860s, William T. Kenney and his mother worked on the farm of Gerrit Smith, nephew of the abolitionist, and Kenney was probably known among Geneva's prosperous people by the time he took up his village trade. By the 1880s, he was a sexton at Trinity Episcopal Church and a drayman who handled much of the work of Hobart College students. Kenney's sons Herman and Arthur helped in the business as boys; Art Kenney surely learned one of his most legendary skills—running down and stopping frightened runaway horses in downtown Geneva—by holding the lines of his father's skittish horses as "Kenney's Express" made its way, loaded with students' trunks and dorm room furnishings, from the depot to the college.

When Kenney died in 1893, Herman and Arthur took over the business; Kenney's son-in-law George Hardy, also a drayman and a baggageman, might have worked with them. They were well known

26. William Douglass, 1875, photograph by Charles B. Sprague.
Courtesy Geneva Historical Society.

not only as baggagemen but as unofficial guardians for wayward, probably intoxicated, Hobart students. The 1902 Hobart yearbook, dedicated to Herman Kenney, proclaimed, "Kenney's Express is the authorized vehicle in which unruly freshmen are treated to nocturnal rides about the country near Geneva. So, it happens that Herm is an institution at Hobart, helping homesick boys to get settled or unsettled, as the case may be and lustily cheering for the teams of his Alma Mater whenever a game is taking place on the campus." Hobart seniors called the Kenney freight wagon "the time honored contemporary of Trinity hall or of Geneva."[24]

Kenney's association with Hobart might have helped him procure the contract as baggageman for the Brevoort Hotel, where his father had earlier established a shoeshine stand. Arthur Kenney took up this shoeshining work and also perpetuated the family's connection with Hobart both as a cheerleader and as a hired attendant at various college social events. The baggage work led to Herman Kenney's later employment by the New York Central Railroad and to his son John's work as a driver for Trinity Episcopal Church and country club parties. John Kenney also worked as a church sexton, a caddy, a drugstore porter, and an upholsterer's apprentice before he began to work at Geneva Foundry in 1938. He described the work he and his father did.

> He used to deliver baggage for the Brevoort Hotel. He used to pack baggage from the New York Central to Hobart College. He had a horse and a buggy. He would go as far east as Kendaia, across the lake, and his father had a little baggage transfer, so that Kendaia was known as something on the main line coming around the lake, and they'd transfer this freight from his wagon into other parts, from there over to there, and he would also baggage smash people out that way, farmers that lived out that way.[25]
>
> My father's father's business was [also] shoeshining, shoeshine parlor in the Brevoort Hotel, which was on Exchange Street. And there wasn't that much business. . . . They all were in this business. Art, he was always a shoeshine expert. It was my Aunt Mary that had the money.
>
> . . . [My father] was a checker at the New York Central freight house, which was on Exchange Street. A checker is a man that can read and write—I emphasize this because all them other men that were there couldn't until this Grady came from Auburn; he was the only other man that could read and write. There was not too much education down there. They had Italians that were newly in to Ge-

neva, and they'd take a cart and bring freight from the boxcars, and they'd line 'em up. Well, where the restaurant used to be, there was a rail switch that come out like this, and these boxcars, they'd push 'em in there, and they were all loaded, and these men would run to get their carts, because they were paid so much for so much freight. He had a, not a salary, but he had a time payment. . . . He could add, subtract, and he was very good with figures. So that was his job. While doing this, if there was a company such as Maxwell Bowen who wanted nursery stock or something, he had to catalog all of that and put it over here.

. . . I got my license and I drove the church station wagon for five years. . . . At that time I was working for St. Peter's Church. . . . I worked there and cut grass. As a sexton you had to bank the fire—it's just a glorified name for a janitor—you banked the fire, you shoveled the walk, you mowed the grass, you took care of the rector's house, and whatever things he had to do. Plus, Miss Rogers there knew that I sang at Trinity Church's choir and she wanted to know if I couldn't accompany the boys in their choir. These were all Syrian boys, by the way, in St. Peter's Church, at that time. They were called the poor ones; we were called the rich ones—Trinity. Hobart, you know, was supplemental to a lot of that.

Lady lives up the street hired me out to fix meals out at the Lakeside [Country Club] and sweep up and clean, open the building and close it when they got done. Empire Gas and Electric used to have dances out there, and then the telephone company heard about it, they wanted to hire me out. I used to make good money, sometimes thirty, thirty-five dollars a night, taking drunks home. In their cars; then somebody'd come and get me in my car. Took them home and soothed the tempers that flared, 'cause some were married, and some weren't. I lived quite a life then.

Herman Kenney's income was supplemented by the money his wife Josephine made, primarily as a laundress. By 1920, 70 percent of all laundresses in the United States were African-American women who, like Josephine Kenney, worked at home. Doing laundry was such tedious, heavy, time-consuming work that it tended to be the first household chore for which women sought outside help.[26] Its rigors, as well as a growing cultural interest in cleanliness, made laundresses among the steadiest laborers of all African-American people, but their livelihoods depended critically upon their connections with whites.[27] Josephine Lepeon married into the Kenneys' connections with Trinity Episcopal Church, her major client, and her father, the Honeoye Falls barber Samuel Lepeon, was a fiddler well known among whites throughout the region.

Laundresses who worked at home could supplement their labor with their children's. Emily Foster Linzy, whose father did gardening and household jobs for South Main Street homeowners, used to help iron and deliver her mother's laundry work to William Smith College students and South Main Street homes. Trudy Kenney Spencer used to help wrap the laundry her mother did. John Kenney described his mother's laundry work and how it helped satisfy the needs of their household.

As far back as I can remember she worked doing laundry. She had a tub here and a wringer here and a tub here, and a copper boiler on the stove, huge. The boiler was always on. We had to put that on the night before. We burned coal [at night]. . . . They burned wood all day long, incessantly. My brother and I, Charlie, we had to get out five-thirty, six o'clock in the morning and buck wood up so that she could [work]; we had a big crosscut saw, and . . . we had to get up in the morning and cut that up and split it before we could go to school.

See, you bank that fire off at night so it would heat the boiler and not burn out. Then my mother'd be up around four, quarter after, she'd be poking clothes out of that boiler into what we call the tub where she had bluing, and she'd spread 'em around there. Come out whiter than that. She'd do that for about two hours. [imitates her voice] "John? Charles? Gordon?"—wanted us to help her put it through the wringer, and then this tub, that rinsed it, then it come back through to the bluing water; that brightened it up a little.

. . . She spent pretty much the whole day. It would be around two o'clock. Gordon would get home from school about two, and there used to be long poles that you'd have to push to get the lines up—clothespoles. And sheets—if they ever got on the ground, boy, she'd burn you. It was good education. We had a cart, and we went to Bub Rose's house, we went to the various people that she washed for, and—I forget what that lady's name was—she *hated* her. Then she finally went into some people by the name of Caulfield and Meehan; she went to work for them; she'd get all her hats through Caulfield and Meehan, and she did their laundry to pay for the hats. And that's where we got to have good shoes, at Coniff. At Coniff's, she used to do his laundry, see, and, for pay, she'd save up enough for shoes for us. They had good shoes. The best. We never ate poor, but bread and milk was a staple with us. Crackers and milk was a luxury.

. . . She had various clients. The church linen came every other week—that was for Edsall, who my father didn't like; before that it was Dr. Sills, he's the one that baptized me; I have his picture. She did all of their surplices and cassocks. When they were due to come here, Mrs. Edsall saw that Josie—that's what they called my mother—had plenty of work. These were very delicate garments which they would bring. Bishop Brent when he used to come here, it was a standing order that he would have his cassocks and robes—they weren't the heavy ones, they were the lighter ones, whites and pinks, which they wore then—that she would do them, because he could never get them done the same as that. And she stood there with that iron—she had six irons—and they were cast iron; they had a flat back and a point in the front, and they had the most ungodly handle I ever saw. But that handle—she'd take what we called her iron mitt—we use them now to handle hot pans and stuff like that—she had arthritis in her hand, and she'd stand and iron at that ironing board, and the ironing board was yea wide, about foot and a half, and she was always burning old sheets that she'd put on, no covers like you have now; just sheets, and she'd fold them over so she got a good foundation, and they just hung down there; they weren't tacked or anything; they just hung there; and that's what she would iron these—and they come out beautiful. No coathangers; she'd fold everything, and put it in baskets. We had three laundry baskets, as I remember. Gordon tells the tale how he went out to Mrs. Gallagher; she had paid my mother, and whenever you took the laundry to her she'd give you a tip. And what we did, if we earned money, we would give it to my mother and she'd put it in the jar. We never saw it. We never saw the jar *or* the money. She was using it to keep food in the house.

. . . We went to the Market Basket. The man's name was Munzer; he was the manager, and if we ever ran short . . . he would trust us for maybe four or five dollars' worth of groceries, which was two bags, some crackers, stuff like that. He became very good friends with my mother, and it ended up that she did shirts for him. That was part of how we got food.

Thelma Hardy Kenney took over the job of doing Trinity's laundry after Josephine Kenney died; according to her daughter Trudy, she also washed for several families.

She had her way of doing things and she pretty much did them by herself. I remember we had a washing machine that was like ancient; it was like with the rollers and everything. Now I can remember once, before we got one that was electric, I remember having one with a crank, and I can remember she would let us do that, or sometimes she would let us do our things. . . . And I can remember in a real cold winter her going out to hang up these clothes, and the sheets would be totally frozen, and then she'd bring them in the house and thaw them out, but of course they were still wet. And then she'd drape them; upstairs there would be a room that she would have just lines on, and she would just drape the things across the lines, and then she'd fold them up, and then she'd bring them down, and then she sprinkled them and ironed them dry. Most of it was muslin or cotton and it didn't look good unless you wet it and ironed it dry.

She preferred not to use a dryer. Everything she did she did by hand. Even when we got a dryer, she would say, "Keep it for your things; I'd just as soon line dry." Her concession to something that might be convenient was getting a washer with wringers that were automatic.

Catering also relied heavily on the quality of one's clientele. John Bland was perhaps the best-known caterer in Geneva in the nineteenth century. Descended from the largest African-American property owner in the village, Bland began working as a day laborer in his teens but had turned to whitewashing by his early twenties. Whitewashing, like barbering, seemed to be a virtually exclusive province of African-American men in the 1800s, and, like laundering, it was a chore that homeowners often left to hired people.[28] Whitewashers generally worked on exteriors, such as buildings and fences. But when it was combined with sizing and coloring, whitewash became calcimine (or kalsomine), and using it to paint interiors was sometimes considered a great skill. In 1874, Bland's work in neighboring Waterloo earned the attention of the *Waterloo Register,* which called him "a colored artist" because of his work calcimining R. G. Smith's drugstore there. "John is a fine artist, as his work shows," the newspaper reported, "but he has so much business to attend to in Geneva that he cannot find much time to ornament Waterloo."

By 1879, Bland's business was evidently profitable enough that he and fellow oarsman Will Gillam were able to start a restaurant in downtown Geneva and a catering business "for balls, parties and private assemblies." That the *Geneva Gazette* acknowledged both enterprises confirms that Bland and Gillam sought white patrons. But Bland also catered African-American events, such as the supper for Penn Yan debaters in 1871, the regular masquerade balls, and probably emancipation celebrations.[29] By the 1900s, African-American women such as Laura McDonald, Laura Scott, Mabel Scott, and Capitola Whitaker had begun to cater country club, Hobart, and

South Main Street parties, teas, and dances. Edward McDonald described his mother's work.

> She was a cateress and a housemother at the Kappa Alpha fraternity. What she did, she planned and cooked all their meals; she had twenty-eight boys. She prepared with a steward—they'd have a different one each week—and they planned the meals for the entire week. And she cooked and then shopped—she called by phone, and they delivered and all that sort of thing. But she prepared all their meals and kind of mothered them when they'd need advice and stuff like that. They were, you know, grown kids. It was like a great big happy family. She'd come home every night; in fact, I used to go and walk home with her at night.
>
> . . . She used to do weddings, and those fabulous teas, dinner parties; many times she had dinner parties, and she had complete control. Some of the people would have guests coming in from different places, famous people, and they would always hire my mother, because they knew they would have a fine meal and everything. My mother would prepare it for them, and they really had a ball, just like being at one of the gourmet hotels or something. She'd plan out what to have with this, what to have with that, even down to the desserts, and even the punches.

The children and relatives of these caterers took obvious pride in the skills catering involved, as well as in the array of exotic foods to which they thereby became exposed. They also seemed to find meaning in the prestige of various clients. Certain people identified strongly with these clients—HenryEtta McDonald recalled on occasions when she encountered Charles Whitaker driving Judge Thomas Kane, "They'd drive down the street and you'd say, 'Hi, Judge,' and both of them would wave." Some African Americans no doubt understood emulation of this sort to be one of the few symbols of respectability available to them within the broader society. But they probably quite consciously built these reputations as a way to get the best-paying work they could. What many perceived as imitative behavior may have been so much role play, parts taken on as pragmatic business decisions.

Barbers also traded on the status of their customers. With caterers such as John Bland, barbers were the only African-American workers who received specific and approving mention in Geneva's newspapers, presumably because white men relied almost exclusively on African-American men for shaves and haircuts until the early twentieth century.[30] Although some African Americans disdained the occupation, barbering was evidently one of the more lucrative trades and carried with it some prestige. Barbers frequently distinguished themselves from other barbers by calling themselves fashionable. J. C. Gillam advertised himself as a "barber and fashionable hairdresser" in 1841. And when William Wells Brown became a barber in Monroe, Michigan, in 1835, he lured the business of his chief competitor by placing a sign over his door reading, "Fashionable Hair-Dresser from New York, Emporer of the West." Brown added, "Of course I had to tell all who came in, that my neighbour on the opposite side did not keep clean towels, that his razors were dull, and, above all, he had never been to New York to see the fashions. Neither had I."[31]

Even the *Geneva Gazette* allowed that barbering required skill and discernment. When Benjamin F. Cleggett returned to Geneva after the war, he went into partnership with Benjamin Jupiter, who had been a hostler before he entered the Union Army. The *Gazette* not only announced Cleggett's return (no other black Civil War soldier or sailor was welcomed home by the newspaper) but also observed, "Mr. Cleggett has already a host of friends, his former customers, and Mr. Jupiter, by his excellent shaving and the taste he evinces in dressing hair, is fast gaining them. We advise all who wish a good shave or scientific hair-cut to give them a call."[32]

Cleggett and his father were both barbers in Rochester, and his career attests the prestige associated with the trade. His first wife was Frances Nell, the sister of William C. Nell, a well-known black abolitionist from Boston who moved to Rochester to help Douglass edit the *North Star* in the late 1840s. When he set up shop in Geneva in 1860, he apparently worked on lower Exchange Street near Jackson Street, where he could surely rely on the trade of men who worked at the nearby foundries, rail yard, hotels, and canal harbor. After the war, the *Gazette* reported that Cleggett was working "at the old stand," but by 1870 he moved up the street to a more fashionable address, just across Franklin Alley from the Franklin House, where James W. Duffin had worked as a barber before he emigrated to Haiti in 1860. By 1875, Cleggett had become partners with Duffin's son Theodore and soon moved to the shop at 17 Seneca Street, where he remained for more than forty years.

By this time, Cleggett was probably serving many of Geneva's prosperous businessmen. It seems certain that Charles J. Folger was among them, for when Folger left the village to join Chester Alan

Arthur's cabinet as Secretary of the Treasury, Cleggett went with him to Washington to take a laborer's job in the treasury department. Like Edwin Barnard, the village's African Americans probably regarded Folger as a friend; once a Democrat, he switched his party affiliation because of his opposition to slavery. When Folger died in 1884, Cleggett was among the six African-American men (two of them servants in his Geneva home) who carried his casket into the church for his funeral. It was a symbolic service in death as in life—African-American pallbearers, among them Geneva's William T. Kenney and George J. Bland, also carried the coffin of Gerrit Smith when he died in 1874—that continued in Geneva well into the twentieth century.[33]

By 1911, Cleggett's daughter Mary had taken Arthur Kenney as her second husband, and Kenney began shining shoes at Cleggett's Seneca Street shop (fig. 27). By that time, Cleggett had retired. Only one African-American, Joseph C. (or Chris) Gillam, worked as a barber in the village by 1915. In that year, Gillam also had a shop on Seneca Street, but by 1925 he had moved the business next to his High Street home. By World War II, nearly all of Geneva's barbers were Italian-American. In the 1930s and 1940s, African-American men in Geneva could not get their hair cut in the village at all: John Kenney first met his wife when he, his brother Charles, Eugene Linzy, and Jim Foster were on their way to get haircuts in Syracuse.

In 1917, the year Cleggett died, Art Kenney set up a ticket agency for the trolleys run by the Geneva, Seneca Falls, and Auburn Railroad Company, which expanded the shop's business and made it even more of a stopping place than it had earlier been. His wife also worked. Mary Georgetta Cleggett Kenney was a hairdresser and a chiropodist; her sister Fannie and half-sister Alice also worked in the business, located in several second-floor rooms on Seneca Street (figs. 28 and 29). John Kenney, who later lived in the High Street home she bought and furnished, described her various occupations.

> Well, she owned one of the first Buicks in New York State. She was a chiropractor, she was a foot doctor, and she was a beautician. She was one of the only beauticians around for quite a while. As far as a foot doctor, she did all the Catholic schools, the nuns, the ministers, people who had money or access to money. A lot of the nuns that were here then came from rich families, at St. Stephens, De Sales—anyhow, she did their feet. This couch that's out in the barn

27. Theodore Derby and Art Kenney on Seneca Street, 1900. Derby was a laborer, and, by 1900, a cook at the Nester Hotel; Kenney was a porter and bellboy there. The Nester was several doors away at the intersection of Seneca and Exchange streets. *Courtesy Geneva Historical Society.*

28. Mary Georgetta Cleggett Kenney, 1911–1913. After the death of her first husband, Garrett Kenney's son William F., Mary Cleggett married Arthur Kenney, sixteen years her junior; this may be her wedding photograph. Her High Street property remained in the Kenney family until 1991. *Courtesy John W. Kenney.*

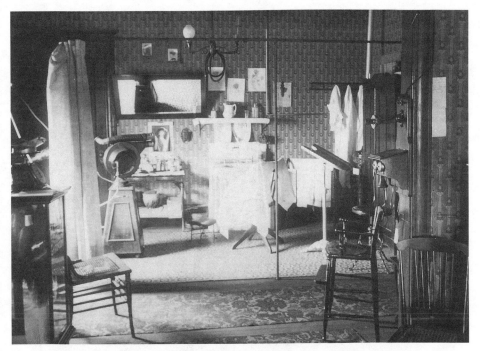

29. Mary Kenney's chiropodist and hairdressing parlor, Seneca Street, about 1920. *Courtesy Geneva Historical Society.*

is her receptionist's couch. She went to school; she graduated. You didn't get a job at those things unless you had a college education.

Those who tried to serve only the needs of the African-American community were few and their ventures short-lived. Martha M. Wright's 1849 boarding house "for colored persons" apparently operated less than a year; nearly a century later, Marie Gray's boarding house, the Carpenter Hotel, operated for less than a decade.[34] Only in those upstate communities with large African-American populations did black grocers and retailers thrive.

Despite constant encouragement from African-American newspapers and conventions, most of Geneva's blacks in both centuries surely recognized that competing with white businesses for local trade was a challenge too great to surmount.[35] They were accordingly much more likely to take service jobs in hotels, on steamboats,

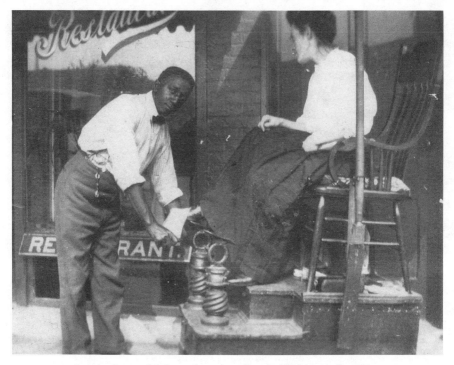

30. Lewis Scott shining shoes on South Exchange Street, 1909–
1913. *Courtesy Dorothy Scott Cooke.*

in banks, and in stores. African-American men were often bank
messengers, janitors, porters, and stewards in the twentieth century. Arthur Kenney was a janitor for Geneva National Bank and
Lincoln Rochester Trust. Kenney, Lewis Scott, and Charles Rice
were shoe shiners and bootblacks (fig. 30). Rice took over Scott's old
stand in the Linden Street barbershop, working at a chair in the back
corner until he died in 1953.

   In 1900, much of the staff of the Nester (later the Seneca) Hotel
was black, more than half of them new to the village. But by the
1920s, some recall, African Americans could not get work, much less
a drink, there. In the 1940s, the Seneca bar and restaurant were still
viewed as off limits to African-American patrons, but it had become
possible again for African-American women, including Margaret
Hardy, Mildred Mathis, Kate Haines, and Margaret Carter, to work
in the hotel as maids.

31. Charles Gates at Dorchester and Rose hardware store, Seneca Street, 1898–1900. *Courtesy Geneva Historical Society.*

At about the same time that blacks filled many of the service jobs at the Nester Hotel, two of the city's hardware stores employed African Americans as retail clerks. The backgrounds of these clerks may suggest how they came to be employed in such capacities. Charles W. Gates, who came to Geneva from Mississippi after the Civil War, worked as a porter until about 1890, when he was hired to clerk at Dorchester and Rose hardware store (fig. 31). Douglass Claggett, who had come to Geneva from the District of Columbia in 1898, also worked there in 1900. Perhaps as early as 1892, Reuben S. Hawkins, who had come from Virginia in the mid–1880s, and Frederick Riggs, a southerner who had settled in Geneva by the early 1890s, clerked at William Wilson hardware at 485 Exchange.

Longtime African-American residents of the village may have felt that such service jobs were demeaning, or they might have come to believe that clerking was one occupation they might never fill. Perhaps only relative newcomers felt unencumbered enough by local tradition to apply to be clerks. And it may be that southern blacks, acculturated to a more profound deference when dealing with whites than northern blacks were, were less troubled by the necessity to assume the deferential demeanor that may have been, in the eyes of store and hotel proprietors, a critical job requirement. Hawkins and Gates may have viewed it as a reasonable trade for what could have been a much improved life in the North. Both married into old African-American families; both owned homes in the best black neighborhood. But these positions remained open to African Americans only as long as the working careers of these men lasted. When they retired, their jobs were filled by white persons, and not until the 1960s would African Americans again work in retail positions.

The ironies of domestic and personal service cannot have been lost on Geneva's African-American people. The jobs available to blacks—cleaning whites' homes, shaving white men's faces, working on white women's feet, even carrying their bodies into church—exposed them to the most intimate details of white peoples' lives. But they also made manifest a social hierarchy that whites wished to preserve. The specific public posture of deference associated with shining shoes and blacking boots visibly demonstrated subordinance. And at least for a time, it must have reassured those whites who lived uncomfortably with the awareness that blacks indeed knew a great deal about them, that blacks recognized the meaning and effects of how whites controlled their economic lives, that blacks could not fail to think badly of them.[36] The inert demeanor blacks assumed in the presence of whites concealed both this knowledge and those judgments. Whites objectified blacks in order to avoid dealing with such social and ethical complexities; blacks in turn acted as though they were objects around whites. After the war, the arrival of new southern freedmen in the North—people whose new civil rights, at least in theory, were constitutionally guaranteed—multiplied the anxiety whites already felt about rising immigration from southern and eastern Europe. This uneasiness found expression in the growing body of pseudoscientific theories about genetic racial inferiority, ideas such turn-of-the-century spokesmen as Booker T. Washington tried to ameliorate.

Out of the Ranks of Service

Antebellum Geneva offered work to skilled African-American tradespeople, including the chairmaker Albert Arnold, the blacksmith Charles Peyton Lucas, and James Suzey, who worked as a cabinetmaker at Bennett and Bulkly's cabinet shop.[37] African-American professionals were also found in the village's occupational matrix: before 1860, there were two clergymen, a schoolteacher, a music teacher, and a violinist. But even then, when their occupational distribution was most balanced, their numbers were few among skilled and professional workers.

Some African-American leaders claimed blacks were so underrepresented in skilled trades and professions because they lacked opportunities to acquire occupational skills—"the door," as Frederick Douglass put it, ". . . by which we can escape our present menial callings." Whether training of this sort existed was debated in the African-American press and at antebellum conventions almost as often as the merits of agricultural work were. At the 1855 meeting of the National Council of Colored People in New York City, Geneva's James W. Duffin argued that in Ontario County, despite its being the "pro-slavery county of New York," such opportunities existed.

> It seems to me that there is not so much difficulty in getting our children into mechanics' shops as is supposed; in western New York, I do not know of any trade that the colored children cannot be instructed in. We can get all our children into the best workshops and into the public schools. So far as my experience has gone, I think that places might be attained to learn all the various branches of mechanics.

Two years before Duffin made this claim, the village had at last built a district school in the High Street neighborhood, which may account in part for his favorable assessment. But he had no apparent justification for his further claim that black youth could gain admittance to "any educational institution, from the blacksmithing to an entrance into Hobart free college"; only one African American, "a light-complexioned mulatto from New York," had been admitted to Hobart by that time.[38] Few at the council meeting accepted his assertions, Douglass in particular. Living only fifty miles away, Douglass claimed, "I know, for my own section of the country, that there are not those facilities,—that there are not the open doors, flung open wide to our children, and I must say that, so far as my own office is concerned, I have a difficulty to introduce a colored boy in my own office, where there are white men." John E. Brown allowed that though colored mechanics could always find work in Elmira, young

African-American men could not find places to learn skilled trades. John Bonner and Stephen Smith claimed that the same situation prevailed in Chicago and Philadelphia. Most African-American tradesmen in Philadelphia, Smith stated, had learned their skills as slaves in the South, just as Charles Peyton Lucas had before coming to Geneva. And some argued that education had no effect on the kind of work African Americans were able to get, even with the aid of the most sympathetic whites: Stephen Myers of Albany stated, "Go to the Abolitionists, and you cannot get your son, even with his collegiate education, placed above a porter."[39]

Nowhere did white workers more strongly and violently oppose the competition that African-American labor appeared to present than in skilled trades, and, indeed, African Americans in Geneva ceased to practice them after the Civil War. Arnold apparently could no longer sustain himself and his family as a chairmaker and began working as a porter at the sanitarium in nearby Clifton Springs. After the war, the proving ground for the debate about occupational skill switched from mechanics' shops to factories, and the coming conflict between black and white factory labor was an industrial version of the contention between black and white mechanics.[40] African Americans were systematically kept on the periphery in the North's rapidly developing industrial economy, either by unions or by practices that emulated formal exclusion.

As a rule, the "industrial opportunity" permitted African Americans was specific and circumscribed.[41] Not until the 1890s did any African American participate in Geneva's industrial boom: in 1892, Frederick Riggs worked at Herendeen Manufacturing Company as a coremaker, one of the most skilled positions in the foundry, and Charles Hardy was listed in the census as an iron molder. Most entered the factories either as janitors or in various foundry jobs. By 1905, Herendeen had begun to hire African-American men more regularly to work as laborers in its foundry. Cary Whitaker began there as a laborer and was stropping radiators by 1915; George Foster was a boilermaker there.[42] By 1925, Devoe Linzy and his brother Wesley, Cary Whitaker, Jr., Samuel O. Doctor, James Tyson, his uncle Manuel Brown, William Cuffe, George C. Foster, and possibly Earl D. Cook all worked at U.S. Radiator, as laborers, cranemen, cupola tenders, or mason tenders. The molder Edward Dorsey may have been the first African American to work at Geneva Foundry, on the lower part of Exchange Street near the rail yard.

The idea of employing African-American men in foundries may have arisen from still-popular ideas about the genetic capabilities of the respective races. Such ideas received an audience in Geneva at an 1881 emancipation celebration. There, African-American Frederick G. Stuart of neighboring Palmyra argued that the demonstrated usefulness of African Americans in the American economy established for them a higher claim to citizenship than such recent immigrants as the Chinese could make. "The negro belongs here," Stuart told some fifteen hundred persons who attended the celebration. ". . . He is the cotton picker, he is the sugar grower. He can labor where the white man cannot—in the warmest parts of the country." The *Gazette* reporter agreed. "The labor of the negro is indispensable in the cotton fields, and it has now lately been found that his labor is especially efficient in our iron foundries."[43]

African Americans had begun to find work in iron foundries whose unions permitted such hiring by the late 1870s.[44] By 1925, Local 109 of the Molders and Foundry Workers Union at the Geneva Foundry appears to have allowed black membership, and by the late 1930s, Eugene Linzy and John Kenney began working there (fig. 32). They may have been hired because they both caddied at Geneva Country Club for foundry owner William J. Brennan, Sr. Kenney described getting hired at the foundry and the work he did:

> I heard that they were hiring down there at sixty cents an hour, and here I was making thirty cents. And if you can get on, they said, as a machine man or a floor man that you would make good money. That was the highest wage there was around here then. Patent Cereals only paid forty, fifty cents an hour; Gordon worked there. Andes was the same; that was a strict union, a closed shop. They had to pay at least a dollar an hour for their journeymen. That's journeymen; that's ten, fifteen, twenty years, that's the most you made.
>
> . . . I started in the grinding room before I went to the actual foundry. And when they blew the whistle, if you worked in there and they wanted you out in the foundry to push the bowl—that's how come I ended up in the foundry—I'd push the bowl. [My boss] told me, "Go on, John; it pays ten cents more an hour," so, big fool, I got up there and boy, I tipped that thing down, it was just like pouring three hundred and fifty degrees at you. You get used to that. Well, it was hot for a while. And then after that I didn't like the grinding room, so I asked for a transfer, posted jobs. It didn't pay any more, but you could move around a little, see. So I went out in the foundry, shovel sand, helped around.
>
> . . . You picked iron up. They had a big ladle up there, they'd pour iron into what they called a bowl ladle that's on a track, and ran out here and ran there and ran over there. And that's what I

32. John Kenney (with shovel) at Geneva Foundry, about 1950.
Courtesy John W. Kenney.

did, and that's why I got burns all over me. This here came from
picking up what we call pigs, ingots of iron. The thing slid out and
it dropped down and a piece of that slit me in the face. I had about
eight stitches and Doc Snyder sewed it up, and my boss wanted
me to come back to work and he said, "You're going home, John."
So they wanted to dock me for the whole afternoon. That's when
the union stepped in. And I had joined. In fact I still got my card.

. . . My hands are quite steady, and I could set some of'the
most minute cores, and they'd call me to do that. And that's when
I went on the side floor. . . . I was a journeyman molder twelve
years, out of forty-seven. They don't give you that. I worked on a
machine on the side floor. I have pictures of myself on a big floor
and when I was on a side floor. They were assessing the—what
they do now when they say the atmosphere, the air is polluted—
they come in there and they told them, "Get that man out of there
or get a mask on 'em or so and so." I'm the only one that come out
of there without emphysema. I got this, though, and those. Then
after this man come in, this environmentalist, come in there and
told them what you should do and what you better do, they put
fans in the roof, driving the stuff out.

. . . It was a slave shop. They treated us all the same. . . .
When they started coming in, half of the force was black then,
because they used them on the night gangs, see. Those guys would
work so hard, that if they put a notice on the board that they
needed somebody to eat sand on the day shift, they'd sign up for
it. But they'd pay them twenty cents an hour more on the night
shift than they did on the day shift. So they missed that when they
come on the days, but then they were on days and they'd see these
guys on machines and side floors making twice as much as them
and they'd want to go for that. It was always grabbing higher and
higher.

Kenney appreciated the foundry work partly because it paid well
and partly because he often finished by early afternoon and used the
time to help at home and to coach Babe Ruth baseball, a league for
boys between the ages of thirteen and fifteen. But foundry work was
dirty, hot, stifling, and sometimes hazardous. It could be stunningly
monotonous, and not everyone could catch the unnerving rhythms
of mass production. Jim Richmond only worked at Geneva Foundry
for a month in the early 1950s.

The work didn't bother me, but somehow I just decided I would
walk out. I was on the night shift, went to work about two o'clock

in the evening and we finished about eleven o'clock at night. At
this time, you know, you had to rake the iron out of the coal, and I
got kind of stopped up with the smoke. I went to the door, and the
foreman came over, says, "Richmond," he says, "What are you
doing?" I says, "I got stopped up. I gotta get some air." He says,
"You can't do *that*." I says, "Oh yes I *can*," and I says, "You can
take this job. I'm all done." I went to the shower, and I left.

Gloria Peek's father also worked at Geneva Foundry.

I remember going to the foundry. And I remember the foundry just
being a horrible place, because it was all metal and steel and soot
and dirt. And dad would always come home, his clothes would be
black. You know, mom was always washing these black clothes,
trying to get them clean in these old washtub things. And I got a
chance to go in one day with mom to get dad. I just remember
gagging, and when I came out I started to sneeze and spit, it was
all black, and it really scared me, you know? And now that I think
about it, the fact that my father worked in there for so many years,
I'm convinced that that contributed to his heart attack and his decline in health. . . . Mom used to work at this big beet factory. . . .
Dad would work at the foundry and work at this place, too, to
bring money in, to make ends meet.

Industrial hazards and accidents were not uncommon. When
Peter Henry Harris died in February 1918 after working as a laborer
at the coke manufacturer Semet-Solvay Company for at least fifteen
years, his funeral record atttributed his death to "chronic bronchitis
duration 2 years, contributing poisoning coke works."[45] But industrial work was nonetheless the predominant occupation among the
few African-American men of working age in Geneva by 1925. Most
were probably laborers, but a few men were not: censuses listed
Ernest R. Moore as a stationary engineer at U.S. Lens Company
(later Shuron Optical Company) in 1915 and a machinist at American Can Company in 1925. Charles W. Kenney, who began work at
Shuron in 1919, was in charge of emery grinding at the company's
lens plant when he died in 1944.

Geneva's major mill, Patent Cereals, appears to have begun to
hire blacks by the late 1930s, although the common perception
among the city's African Americans was that the mill would not hire
them. The extreme shortage of white male labor during World War
II compelled many of the city's defense industries, including Patent

Cereals, to advertise for workers of both sexes. As one of only nine degerminating corn mills in the country permitted by the government to continue to grind corn "for critical purposes," Patent Cereals operated day and night shifts six-and-a-half days a week in 1943 and 1944. At the end of 1944, the company's president declared, "the manpower situation still remains extremely acute."[46] Perry Carter went to work for Patent Cereals in 1944.

> I went to Patent Cereal. They [other blacks] came in later; I was the first one to start working there. . . . I started working on the shipping gang. And there was an old fella there that worked there for a long time, and the jobs come up for bid, you know. The job came up for the meal sprout, and he told me to bid on it, and he said, "You'll get it." And I said I didn't think so because I wasn't that old. He said, "'Cause everybody think I'm gonna take it, and I'm not," he says. "So if you bid on it, you'll get it." So I did. So I went from there up to the second floor, and then I got to be second miller of the plant.
>   . . . [Not] many blacks worked at Patent Cereals because they didn't go there, see. When I went there and asked for the job, and they hired me, and then they called me in the office one day and asked me why none of 'em never come for a job. And I told 'em that probably somebody had told 'em that they wouldn't hire 'em. So then he told me to tell them.

African Americans also believed that American Can Company would only hire them to work as janitors, despite the fact that Ernest Moore was listed as a machinist there in 1925. Henry McDonald is commonly thought to have been the company's only black employee before the 1960s, and even in that decade black employees were scarce. James Henderson left a supervisory job at typecaster Hulse Manufacturing Company for better wages at American Can.

> I discovered that I could leave there and go to American Can and start off as a janitor, level one, working nights, they called the graveyard shift twelve to seven in the morning, and make the equivalent of thirty cents an hour more than I was making as a supervisor with a white shirt and a tie on. So needless to say, I left there and I worked at American Can, and I went from a grade one up to a grade twelve and was caught in I guess the largest layoff that they had.
>   . . . When I was working there, there was Noah Young, who was [earlier] stationed at Sampson Air Force Base, who married my

wife's cousin, Charlene Kenney, Charlie Kenney's daughter, and Noah worked there until that big layoff, and had an option of remaining there or going to a plant in Detroit. So he and his wife moved to Detroit. But there was myself, Noah—there was another gentleman there—it might have been three [blacks] out of about twelve or fourteen hundred. That's all.

American Can Company apparently offered African-American women their first industrial employment during World War II; afterward, canning factories and nursery packing houses became the primary employers of women in the labor force who did not do domestic work. Rosa Blue spent one season in the mid-1950s inspecting beets at a Waterloo factory and then became a food inspector at Nabisco's Dromedary plant in Lyons.

I went to Dromedary, where they had an evening shift. There I started as a food inspector; I probably worked there until 1966 or '67. Most times the evening shift was available, and it meant that I didn't have to hire someone to take care of the kids, especially in the summer. Working at Dromedary—it was not just a canning factory; they made all kinds of cake mixes, fruit cakes. And then they processed the fruits. They got the cherries from Wayne County, sweet cherries, and took all the good out of them and soaked them into brine or something, and then dyed them and sugared them down into what you see now as cherries for baking.
. . . They had quite a number of employees there. And I understand the only reason black folk got in there is with AFL-CIO. At that time there were refugees from other countries worked there, and they were guaranteed work. Most of us from the Geneva area—because most of the blacks that started there lived in Geneva and commuted—began around 1955, 1956.
Dates—that was one of their big products. They prepared dates for their own fruit cakes and also for the market. The work there was very fast. The work in the canning factory in Waterloo was slow. . . . The work at the National Biscuit Company, which was Dromedary, was different. You had to watch everything there.
. . . You could progress yourself somewhat from laborer to machine operator to line person or floor lady or a relief person, which meant that you had to learn all the jobs on the line so that you could relieve people for lunches and breaks. The jobs—they were not highly skilled positions. . . . The main thought on the supervisor level was quantity. The date line started with inspection of dates. Fellas would open up the big boxes that came from Iran

and Iraq. The dates had pits in them, so they'd first come through the line and there'd be several women sitting there pulling them apart, then they'd go through a machine that pitted them. Then they'd go down the line to the weighers; women would be sitting there with scales. And from there they had to go through a sterilizer process—they'd go in through the heat and on the other end come through a cooler. And from there they would go to be wrapped. That went through a machine also, and then finally they'd have to pack the boxes by hand.

The cake mixes came already prepared, and it would come down a big chute. It was dusty. I had asthma and I can't stand so much dust, so that was an area I didn't work in an awful lot. Even with the cherries that had to be soaked in brine, the brine sometime was so strong when it came into the factory that you had to open up the doors no matter how cold it was, and that was a cool area. I remember again that I quite often had to leave the building, because it would gag me so. The fruit mix quite often had to be so hot that when they packed it into jars that people would burn their hands. . . . But the main thing with Dromedary is that if you stayed there you had to be a good, quick, fast worker.

Leona Hardy James worked at Zotos International, which made solutions for home permanents.

They mixed up the batches and then you sent them down the assembly line, the bottles, they'd go in the capper; you'd pack them in boxes. I was doing everything. They had more than three hundred people. I was doing all right until I cut my finger, and some of that stuff got on me, and I broke out in a real bad rash. Itchy—oh, my goodness. It could have been the nerves, too, doing it. Anyway I had to quit, because I couldn't itch and work. They want production; you can't get behind in that. You mess up your whole line. It wound up I was paying the doctor more than what I was making, 'cause I had to go to the dermatologist. I never saw such rash. But it was *real* good money; in fact I started buying my storm windows. I said, "Gee, if I stay out here I can maybe get some siding on the house." But it was not to be.

War and Opportunity

With World War II and associated fair-employment regulations, opportunities for African Americans also emerged in clerical, retail, and civil service work. Marian Linzy, a granddaughter of Minor

Linzy who graduated from Geneva High School in 1931, was a domestic until she was hired at American Can Company in 1943. She remained there until 1946, when she became a stenographer/typist at Sampson Naval Training Station. A few years earlier, both military installations appear to have resisted hiring African Americans. HenryEtta McDonald Hughes, born in 1923, graduated from high school in 1942 and got work in the office at Sampson through an incidental conversation with a man who had come to Geneva to help organize the project.

When I got out of high school, most all the girls were going to the bank and getting jobs. And so I went to the National Bank down there on the corner of Seneca Street and Exchange, and I talked to the present banker, and he told me I didn't want to go work in a bank, there wasn't any money; my best bet was to work in a factory. But it didn't discourage me, because we had our mother; we had that type of mother that pushed us. So then I went over to Sampson.

We, Tony [Antoinette Foster] and I, went to call on Lillian Gant; she worked in a private family. So we were over in this kitchen, and this Mr. Clark came out. He stayed with this family on Pulteney Street. He was talking to us, and he had a cocktail in his hand. And you know from that day on I said, "Boy, when I get older and I get a job, I'll have a cocktail when I come home." Anyway, to make a long story short, he asked us, he said, "Well, what do you girls do?" We said, "We're seniors in high school." See, Tony went to Geneva High School, and I went to DeSales. So he says, "I'll tell you what—when you girls graduate and you want a job, we'll get you a job at Sampson." Well, Tony didn't make it but I did, but don't promise *me* nothing.

So Buzzy, that was Tony's boyfriend, he was out of the service, so he takes me over to Sampson at six o'clock in the morning. Mr. Price told me to fill out these papers. Mr. Price went in this office with Mr. Tindall, and he was talking with these papers, and they'd go in another office, and they'd come back out—this went on for almost an hour. So then he finally come over and he said, "I finally got you a job." So he says, "When do you want to start?" And I said, "Now." And I started right then. So I worked under the construction of Sampson. I worked in the office as a clerk. I was the only black one in there, too; that's why it was so hard to get me in.

So I worked there until they got the first survivors off the Wasp, and then they decided they wanted to give the jobs to their own men, to the sailors. See, the sailors were kind of taking over the base. So then I went over to Seneca Ordnance, and I got a job there. But before I got the job there, I went over, took a test—it was civil service, okay? And I kept driving over there for the job, and they'd tell me they didn't have anything. So this one particular day I went over, the gal told me they didn't have anything, so I went home. We got the papers around three o'clock in the afternoon, you know, early, the evening paper. So my mother says to me, "In the paper they said they want typists," she says; "you go right back there." This was quarter after four. And I did what my mother said and I went right back there and the gal says, "Oh, I was just getting your papers out of the file." Just like that. So I was hired.

Civil service hiring was governed by practices that appear to have worked against African Americans. Into the 1960s, there had never been an African-American police officer or firefighter in Geneva; by 1966, there was one black public works employee and one African American, Alvin Robinson, in the post office.

I worked in the post office for twenty-eight years and ten months. I'm the first black they ever hired and the only black they hired.

. . . I guess I was somewhat against the grain. When it became known that I had taken the post office exam and was going to pursue it, because everybody—mostly blacks, surprisingly enough—"They've never had a black working in that post office; they're not going to have any blacks"—you know, that was a challenge. First because, having made the second-highest score on the exam, I thought I was entitled to it; that was an indication that I was qualified for it. And that's the only merit by which I should have been measured. And to have someone pass me over because the civil service system allows you to hire from the top three people on the eligibility register—so if I'm one, you're two, and Joe Doaks is three, the employer can hire you and Joe Doaks, and all that does is keep me among the top three. So then he gets four, five and put them in that slot, I'm still in the top three, but I'm not being hired. And if you question it, it's legal. They say, "No, you're in the top three, but so-and-so has had some experience," and there's nothing you can do about it.

That happened to me; oh God, did it ever. I took the examination in June of 1947, and I think it took us thirty to sixty days to be notified as to what our qualifying scores were, and I went to work in the post office in October of '48. And the fallacy of it all was that I would go to the post office quite frequently and make inquiries as to whether there were openings, available openings, and of course no, there never was. And I would buy this. And you have to keep updating your eligibility; they send you a little card to ask you if you're still available for work. And if you get disgusted and say, "Well, no; take my name off the list"—beautiful, in my case; then they no longer have to deal with me. But I didn't do this, you know, I kept saying, "Yes, I'm available for work." Because all I was doing was working part-time work.

And I waited and waited and waited. And I think I would not have pursued it, possibly—I was good and ticked off about it, but I went one time and asked to see the postmaster, and I was given an audience with the postmaster, and I went in to see him, and he sort of threw me a curve by saying things like, "Well, I don't think you'd want to work here, because there's none of you working here." Well, that's an affront to me, you know; in the first place, I don't like being called one of *you*. And as I walked out of his office to go out of the building, I saw fellas who had taken the examination with me. And I wondered, "Well, how the hell were these people hired, you know, if there were no available openings? And how did these people get here above me?"

. . . So I came home and I gave it some thought and then I decided what I would do, I would give it one more shot. Because I had done this several times, meaning more than four or five. So I went down one more time and I filled out an availability slip and was informed that there were no openings. I said, "Okay; well and good." So I came home and I told my wife what had happened and I said, "I think I'm being given the run-around." And she said, "What are you going to do about it?" And I said, "I'm going to write the Civil Service Commission."

So I did. I sat down and wrote a letter to the Civil Service Commission, mailed it on a Monday, . . . on a Thursday of the same week, I received a TWX, a telegram from the Civil Service Commission saying that my case had been referred to the regional office in New York. That's on Thursday. On Friday I received a TWX from the regional office in New York saying, "Your case has been investigated. No further correspondence is necessary with this office." Saturday I got a call from the post office to come to work. Just like that.

The resistance to blacks in positions they historically had not occupied pervaded the occupational hierarchy. Elouise Kenney, who had a master's degree in education, was unable to find a teaching job in her home region in the 1930s; she ultimately went South to teach. Pauline Ray, daughter of domestic Elizabeth Ray, graduated from Cornell in 1913 and went on to teach languages in midwestern colleges (fig. 33). Trudy Kenney Spencer was unable to get a retail position at Geneva's premier department store in the 1960s, though she later got work at and eventually managed a local drugstore. As in Robinson's case, it took the intervention of outsiders to get James Richmond, who came to Geneva in 1951, office work at the local Firestone store.

> I walked into Firestone and I asked about a job, said I'd like to fill out an application. Fella said, "You worked pumping gas, or fixing tires before, worked on cars?" I said, "No. But I can learn." He says, "When can you start work?" And I said, "Right now." So I started pumping gas, and they taught me how to fix flat tires and stuff like that, and eventually they said, "We'll have somebody else pump gas, and you fix tires." I learned how to fix all kinds of tires, even the big tires, farm tractor tires, truck tires.
>
> . . . And then I said, "Well, I'd like to learn something else," and they said, "Okay, what would you like to learn?" They taught me a little mechanical work, brakes and front-end alignments and all that stuff, and I got pretty good at that. Then they said, "Tell you what, Jim; we will pay you (I think it was) a dollar a piece for every tire that you sell." And then I started selling tires, working in the shop. I was so happy when I'd receive an extra thirty dollars a month for selling tires. . . . That's how I saved my money for a down payment on my home.
>
> Then I talked to the manager and said, "I'd like to get a job inside the store," and he kept putting me off, and putting me off, and putting me off. I says, "I'm qualified; I have the education," but he kept putting me off. So one day the district manager came down from Syracuse, and he walked back and I was underneath fixing a car and I was clean-dressed, and the place was nice and clean. And he came back and says, "Gee, the place is real nice; everything is put away, Jim; it's looking good." Says, "How's everything doing?" I says, "Everything's fine, but I'd like to talk to you. Do you have time to talk to me?" And he says, "Sure. Come on; let's go in the office." So we went to our little office in the back and he says, "Well, what can I do for you?" So I gave him the story. I said, "I want to get ahead. I'm qualified to be a salesman inside the store." I says, "I'd like to get into that, and I'd like to get into office management." So when I finished talking to him, he says, "You going to lunch now?" And I says, "Yes." So he says, "I'll talk to you when you come back." So I came right home to lunch, with my coveralls on, which were clean, of course, sitting there having my lunch, and he called me up. He says, "Jim? Look,

CORNELL · VNIVERSITY

IRENE MAE QUIRIN, "Queenie", Olean, New York. Prepared at Olean High School. Age, twenty-one years. Agricultural course. Four years at Cornell. Irene, known to her most intimate friends as "Queenie", combines the pleasing qualities of the social butterfly with those of the true friend. Her studious hours have given her good results.

PAULINE ANGELINE RAY, "Paula", Geneva, New York. Prepared at Geneva High School. Age, twenty-two years. Arts course. Four years at Cornell. Paula comes from the small but renowned Geneva (N.Y.) and brings with her that "push" indigenous to all of Geneva's Great. Her four years were not spent idly, and we hope that some day, along with Geneva's celebrities, Calvin, Bonnivard, Rousseau, Amiel, and Marc Monnier will appear Pauline A. Ray.

RENA RICHARDSON, Ithaca, New York. Prepared at Ithaca High School. Age, twenty-two. Arts course. Four years at Cornell.

MARGARET LOUISE ROBINSON, "Peggy", Reading, Massachusetts. Prepared at Reading High School. Age, twenty-one years. Agricultural course. Four years at Cornell.

NINETEEN · HVNDRED · AND · THIRTEEN

33. Pauline Ray was one of four African-American graduates, and the only African-American New Yorker, among the 858 members of Cornell's class of 1913. Page from *Cornell Class Book 1913*. *Courtesy Rare and Manuscript Collections, Cornell University Library.*

I've gotta get back to Syracuse." He says, "Take off your old clothes and put on a nice shirt and tie and nice pants and come back." And that's when I got promoted from a mechanic or a tire changer to a budget man. And I was a budget man for about six months and I became a budget manager and then from there to office and credit manager, and then from there to manager. I worked there twenty-nine-and-a-half years.

From the beginning of their working lives in the North, African Americans had been encumbered by a set of beliefs that whites used to limit their economic participation. John Widner, overseer at Rose Hill for Robert Rose's slaves in 1815, later told a local historian that the workers "required constant watching and pushing ahead to keep them at work and to get anything done. . . . As a general thing, they cared but little for their master's property, were constantly guilty of petty thefts, and did no more work than they felt absolutely compelled to do." In *Allerton Parish*, John Nicholas Norton made a similar observation about Rose's bondsmen. "Those old Virginia negroes did not turn out well in their new homes," he wrote. "Too careless and improvident to take due thought for the morrow, their freedom was the occasion of their falling away into habits of idleness and intemperance; hardly any of the original company deriving the smallest advantage from the large pecuniary sacrifice which their benevolent masters had made."[47] The delegates to New York's constitutional convention in 1821 worried that immediate emancipation would throw thousands of African Americans onto the welfare rolls of cities and towns. "All are without the habits which would enable them to provide for their own subsistence," one delegate asserted; in the words of another, "These slaves turned loose would become strolling paupers, and would be willing to remain so if they could avoid labor."[48]

There is no doubt that African Americans were aware of these characterizations. In his novel *Clotel*, William Wells Brown described the exhortations of a white evangelist to a group of Mississippi plantation slaves unwillingly assembled to hear his sermon. The preacher urged them not to become "eye-servants . . . such as will work hard, and seem mighty diligent, while they think anybody is taking notice of them; but, when their masters' and mistresses' backs are turned they are idle, and neglect their business."[49] Brown described the slaves to have been profoundly uninterested in the message; some of them had fallen fast asleep, and others passed the time cracking and eating hazelnuts. In the 1930s, sociologist John Dollard described the behavior of blacks in the lowest socioeconomic brackets of Southern Town as "passive sabotage . . . that takes the form of slowness, awkwardness, and indecision about their work," and countless jokes and songs popular among African Americans in both centuries attest black awareness that their reputed laziness both rankled and rebuked those whites who expected so little of black labor.[50] The inattention and languor demonstrated by slaves in *Clotel* arguably protested the treatment they routinely received at the hands of whites in an economic system completely beyond their control. The appearance of indolence became one of the only means by which blacks could control their work situations and protest how whites thought about them, ideas principally formed in a context not of work but of use. Still, such protest fit neatly into the continued justification for paternalism, a system of labor management that circuitously applauded and perpetuated indolent behavior.[51]

Blacks had often met the labor requirements of labor-intensive, underdeveloped industries and were often the first to be let go when machinery was devised to reduce these high labor costs, a fact that partly accounts for the specific grievance with mechanization that the John Henry legend articulates.[52] Machines, like slaveowners, also controlled the pace of work. And when African Americans gathered so little profit from their labor, they found little justification for heeding those rhythms. In the 1820s, Frederick Douglass and his fellow Maryland field hands soon figured out that racing each other to produce a good day's work only stimulated overseers to require even more of them the next day. "This thought," he later wrote, "was enough to bring us to a dead halt when ever so much excited for the race."[53] Slave work songs might have attempted to exert some control over work by setting a pace that workers devised, as well as by establishing a clear boundary between workers and their overseers.[54]

Standing more directly behind white ideas about black laziness was also the thought that the right to relax was something only white people could earn by past faithful subscription to the culture's interest in industry. The nineteenth-century ascription of leisure to the lives and pursuits of middle- and upper-class white people coincided with racial ideas and came to define ever more sharply the boundary between white and black people generally. These associations help explain why so much of white caricature of blacks dwelled on laziness and why, in Geneva, whites so often recalled not the instances of black employment but of black idleness, not the times when domestics performed their jobs to perfection but the times that they failed to do so.

The consignment of African Americans to depreciated labor meant a life of work for most African Americans in Geneva. They began work earlier, sacrificing the higher grades of school and any thought of college. Their households often depended on more than one income. When Albert Arnold was a porter, his wife and one of his daughters were laundresses, another daughter Joanne cooked on a steamboat, and two of his sons were bellboys. After Sarah Prue's husband, John, a laborer, died, six of the children living with her were working as laborers or domestics. In Garrett Kenney's household of nine in 1870, eight people worked as laborers, domestics, or barbers; one seventeen-year-old daughter was "at home," presumably keeping house. Many lumped enterprise upon enterprise to make ends meet. Art Kenney shined shoes, blocked hats, cleaned banks, carried caskets, and served as a waiter and bartender at private parties. Devoe Linzy, who worked as cupola tender at U.S. Radiator, as a Hobart groundskeeper, and as a bowling alley janitor, also made and marketed fudge door to door; his wife and children shucked, cured, and cracked walnuts for the fudge on an old anvil, weighed and cut it, and packed it by the pound in hand-stamped boxes. The laundress Josephine Kenney baked hot-cross buns that her son Gordon sold all over Geneva. Working this way permitted subsistence but often very little else—least of all occupational mobility.

Inclusion and Exclusion

I always believed in questioning. I remember when Robert Kennedy made his speech and he said, "Some folks see things as they are and say, why? But I dream of things that never were and say, why not?" And I remember thinking, "God, that is *me*," because I'm always thinking of these things and saying, "Why not? Why *can't* it be this way?" You know, why does it have to be that way? . . . I was getting turned down for jobs that I was more than qualified to do, only because I didn't have that piece of paper, and it was like, boom, I began to learn that education is power, and I had to educate myself in order to free myself.

Born in 1951 of parents who could neither read nor write, Gloria Peek learned about the world outside Chartres Homes from television, her friends and family, and what she could read herself as a child. She aspired to professional work, medicine or law, but her school guidance counselors encouraged her to go to BOCES, an acronym for Board of Cooperative Educational Services and, in upstate New York, popularly understood to be a program that provides vocational training for those students not bound for college. Early on, Peek recalls having been labeled as a "problem kid; they put you in a corner, tell you to play with toys, and they go on about their business teaching everybody else." She had chronic spelling and reading problems as a consequence. Con-

34. Eighth-grade graduation, High Street School, 1914. The African-American student is Theresa Claggett, whose family lived on one of the original African-American lots on West Street. *Courtesy Geneva Historical Society.*

sistently advised to consider factory work instead of college, Peek dropped out of high school with a grade point average of 1.5. After she had spent a short time in jail and a few years in the navy, Peek came to her present philosophy. She went to college in the affirmative action years, even spending a year at Hobart, and received a bachelor's degree in recreational rehabilitation. She is now one of a handful of female boxing coaches in the United States.

Generations of African Americans before Gloria Peek subscribed to the credo that education is power, even in full view of the fact that education failed in many instances to deliver the promised reward. Frederick Douglass, William Wells Brown, and Austin Steward determined to learn to read and write largely because they perceived the value whites placed upon these skills, and the moment at which they grasped what Douglass called the "*mystery* of reading" became the critical turning point in the stories they told about their escapes, both literal and symbolic, from bondage. To

Douglass, learning to read was "the direct pathway from slavery to freedom."[1]

To these and other African Americans, the acquisition of literacy was the cornerstone of personal liberation, an idea that sprang naturally from the Enlightenment philosophies that supported the Revolution and seemed vindicated by its success. And if literacy was the great enabler of people and nations from the point of view of this inclusive ideology, the evangelical enthusiasm of the second Great Awakening was their moral bedrock. In the decades between the Revolution and Nat Turner's revolt, a philosophy that fused a belief in natural rights, literacy, and evangelical religious culture formed the first Bible and benevolent societies in Geneva, groups that embraced the village's black population among the beneficiaries of their missionary work. But racial exclusion in the churches began to unravel these threads, and Turner's revolt stirred the first real uncertainty about the uses to which literacy might be put. A series of schisms in church and debates in the public school system ensued. Segregation in both church and school became the rule until after the Civil War, when school integration became not only the law of the land but the only access African Americans had to the promises that literacy offered. And as the possibility of true and equal participation in secular spheres continued to recede in these postwar years, the spirit of egalitarianism and evangelicalism lived on in the idea (if not always the actuality) of the black church, the only place where a particular understanding of moral life might develop and flourish and where moral outrage might be safely expressed.

The Literacy Mission

Facing an enormous, swift-moving migration and an unprecedented population growth after 1800, few of the infant churches in the Genesee Country were uninfluenced by the messages and methods of religious enthusiasm. In a spate of revivals throughout western New York, itinerant Methodist and Baptist exhorters and New School Presbyterians spread the notion that anyone, not just the predestined few, could elect to be saved, that one's actions on earth could influence the possibilities of salvation. Universal salvation implied universal sinfulness to all but a few denominations; it was a message at once humbling, democratizing, and empowering. The medium of evangelical religion also made it truly popular. It was communicated orally in urban and village churches as well as in tented camp meetings in remote places.

Before the schisms of the 1830s, reforms to wash away all manner of sin—intemperance, gluttony, crime, poverty—were the natural sisters of religious enthusiasm, designed to prepare Americans for the millennium of which they, like no other people, were assured. The earliest flushes of evangelical fervor in the North were infused as well with a complementary dedication to abolitionism. Antislavery itself was a movement born in the meetings of Philadelphia Quakers after the American Revolution; William Lloyd Garrison, a Baptist editor, printer's apprentice, and temperance advocate, had been converted to the cause of immediate abolition by the *Genius of Universal Emancipation*, an antislavery journal founded in 1821 by the New Jersey Quaker Benjamin Lundy. The intersection of belief that merged abolitionism with evangelical religion was institutionalized at Cincinnati's Lane Theological Seminary, at Charles Grandison Finney's Oberlin College, and George W. Gale's Oneida Institute. It was a link compelling enough to effect the religious conversions of Lewis and Arthur Tappan in 1831 and Gerrit Smith in 1835. As late as 1852, when the sway of evangelical religion had weakened considerably, Harriet Beecher Stowe proclaimed her conviction that God, not she, had written *Uncle Tom's Cabin*.[2]

Because of its inclusive theology and its orality (widespread proscriptions against acquiring literacy in fact promoted the largely oral transmission of African-American culture), evangelical religion took equally strong hold of African Americans, particularly before the mid–1830s. Richard Allen, founder and first minister of the Bethel African Methodist Episcopal (AME) church in Philadelphia in 1794, was converted by itinerant Methodists as a seventeen-year-old slave in Delaware during the Revolution. A white Methodist preacher converted Frederick Douglass shortly after Nat Turner's 1831 uprising, and Garnet and Ward came under the influence of Gale's New School Presbyterianism at about this time. Jermain Wesley Loguen became a Methodist Bible reader after graduating from a Canadian Sabbath school in 1836.[3]

The generally inclusive tendencies of post-Revolutionary thought affected secular life as well: New York State's 1799 gradual manumission act, for example, stipulated that all owners must teach their slaves to read. But churches manifested these tendencies earlier, and more willingly, than did schools. In 1796, a year after New York State appropriated funds to create district schools, Geneva began its first public school. But it is unlikely that blacks—or many whites, for that matter—attended it. Village Episcopalians, by contrast, began to administer sacraments to "piously inclined" slaves whom their owners had sponsored for these rites by 1804, two years before Trinity Episcopal Church was formally established. Trinity continued to baptize African Americans until about 1816, and over the next two years, the village's Presbyterian church admitted African Americans to membership.[4] And it was these churches that provided blacks with their first formal, if highly selective, education.

Episcopalians and Presbyterians possessed much of the economic power and political influence in early Geneva and its region. Evangelical ideology had given this local oligarchy a domestic mission among those less well situated, a pressing sense of Christian responsibility to bring the impermanent, unsettled, and disadvantaged under the softening influence of institutionalized religious culture. Teaching the Bible to African Americans was an impulse born of this enthusiasm. The village's first benevolent society was organized in 1810 to provide aid and education to the "needy," an unspecified agglomeration of people that might have included African Americans. Though nondenominational, the Geneva Friendly Society was informally affiliated with Methodists in the village, who had also admitted African Americans to membership when the church incorporated in 1818. Within three years of the Friendly Society's creation, the established village churches began to supplement its missionary efforts. In 1813, John Nicholas's wife, Anne, a member of Trinity, founded the Female Bible Society to distribute Bibles among the needy; in 1816, Episcopalian and Presbyterian churchwomen formed the Female Benevolent Society "to gather in the colored people to be taught to read the Bible, and otherwise receive religious instruction."[5]

But the missionary zeal of this elite may have been driven less by an interest in improving the general lot of blacks than by an interest in preserving the time-honored social dynamic between superordinate and subordinate. Even if the idea of universal sinfulness affected them profoundly, early Episcopalian and Presbyterian churches did not embrace the antislavery sympathies of one wing of the evangelical movement. The Female Benevolent Society was initially under the charge of Misses Child, Cook, Axtell, and Fairchild; both Henry Axtell, Geneva's second Presbyterian minister, and David Cook, a surveyor related to Axtell by marriage, had free African-American girls younger than fourteen years old living in their homes in 1820. Sixteen of Trinity's nineteen communicants in 1814 and seven of its eight vestrymen in 1825 had slaves or free blacks in their households at some point between 1800 and 1830.

That less well-established denominations were active in Bible instruction suggests that the correspondence between political power and missionary effort in Geneva was not uniform. Yet there can be little doubt that those who held the reins of local politics and much of the real and personal wealth were unsettled by the democratizing, potentially radical tendencies of enthusiastic religion and the growing power of denominations such as the Methodists and Baptists, who, unlike the Episcopalians and Presbyterians, were organized from the bottom up. To distribute and provide instruction in religious texts was thus at once a Christian duty and a political imperative, a benevolence whose impulse to civilize was motivated largely by the need to control.

How long the Female Benevolent Society continued its ministry is unclear, but by the late 1820s the Presbyterian Church had assumed formal control of the missionary effort among local African Americans. One 1858 account stated that "both young and old, white and colored" had received Bible instruction in Geneva from 1815 to 1830, when the Presbyterian Church created "a separate school . . . exclusively for the colored people." Class rolls for the Presbyterian Church's colored Sunday school exist for 1829, 1830, and 1831. In the first two years, forty-six African Americans representing at least thirty-nine families—nearly two-thirds of the black households listed in the 1830 census—attended these classes. The sessions were taught by both men and women. In 1829, one class was in fact taught by a black woman, Mary Miller, who had been admitted as a member of the Presbyterian church in 1818.

The Presbyterian Church's African-American Sunday school evidently continued to operate through the 1850s. In 1858, D. L. Lum and Edwin Barnard, delegates to the state's third annual convention of Sunday school teachers, reported that the weekly school provided instruction—apparently the conventional pedagogy of listening to, memorizing, and learning to read Bible verses—for between fifty and sixty "scholars from the age of seven to *eighty* years." Lum reported to convention delegates:

> One of the little girls, on a recent occasion, recited seven hundred and nine verses from the Bible; and, during the last six months, the entire number of verses committed to memory by the school (not exceeding fifty scholars) was nearly ten thousand. Mr. L. gave these facts and figures as a commentary on the common argument that colored children should not be taught, on the ground that they have no capacity to learn.[6]

The "common argument" about the intellectual potential of African Americans had begun to emerge decades earlier as whites began to find the confluence of Bible instruction and literacy a difficult one to navigate. Teaching African Americans to read from the Bible had been stimulated by sympathies such as those expressed by Long Island slave Jupiter Hammon, whose *Address to the Negroes in the State of New-York* was published by both New York City and Philadelphia printers in 1786. Hammon's pamphlet included advice "to them who cannot read."

> I hope that those who can read, will take pity on them, and read what I have to say to them. . . . Let all the time you can get, be spent in trying to learn to read. Get those who can read, to learn you; but remember, that what you learn for, is to read the Bible. If there was no Bible, it would be no matter whether you could read or not. Reading other books would do you no good. But the Bible is the word of God, and tells you what you must do to please God; it tells you how you may escape misery, and be happy for ever.[7]

To Hammon as to at least some African-American ministers before the Civil War, slaves should learn to read only to discern "what the mind and will of God is"; the recognition of Christian duty impelled every slave "to obey our masters in all their lawful commands, and mind them, unless we are bid to do that which we know to be sin, or forbidden in God's word."[8] But it had become clear by the 1830s that not all African Americans responded to reading, even to reading the Bible, in predictable or desirable ways. Many were profoundly aware of how selective their exposure to biblical texts had been at the hands of whites. Charles Peyton Lucas wrote that his Virginia master, a Baptist minister, "never sent me to school, nor gave me any instruction from the Bible, excepting one passage of Scripture which he used to quote to me,—'He that knoweth his master's will, and doeth it not, shall be beaten with many stripes'. . . and after he had quoted the text, he would take me to the barn-yard and give me a practical explanation with raw hides."[9] In *Clotel*, William Wells Brown created a dialogue among the Mississippi plantation slaves assembled to hear the sermon of the white evangelist Snyder. "Dees white fokes," declared one, ". . . dey all de time tellin' dat de Lord made us for to work for dem, and I don't believe a word of it." Another responded, "Oh, 'thars more in de Bible den dat, only Snyder never reads any other part to us." Douglass took vehement issue with "many religious colored people, at the south, who are under the delusion that God requires them to submit to slavery, and to wear their chains with meekness and humility."[10]

Just how open to interpretation the Bible could be was vividly illustrated when Nat Turner used his reading of biblical scripture as a justification for open and armed revolt in 1831. Turner's insurrection proved to whites that learning how to read would make questions of determining what to read less tractable. For whites could see that African Americans found not only an invocation to submission in the Bible but also the prophecy of complete and revolutionary inversion. The sustained efforts of West Indians to achieve independence in the 1830s enhanced the suspicion among whites that even the Bible was not a safe text.

The recognition that acquiring literacy skills involved problems of social control had led other states to make teaching blacks to read and the possession among them of certain texts, including *Uncle Tom's Cabin*, punishable offenses.[11] And as both the region and evangelical religion matured in the 1830s, the churches of western New York split over the question of slavery, and a conservative wing of evangelicalism devoted itself increasingly to articulating the logic of white dominance and social stratification. Writing from England in the 1850s, Samuel Ward declared, "I know of more than one coloured person driven to the total denial of all religion, by the religious barbarism of white New Yorkers and other Northern champions of the slaveholder." The evangelical American Tract Society, Ward further observed, never published a single pamphlet on slavery and deleted all references to the institution in its reprints of British works; moreover, the American Bible Society would not distribute Bibles to slaves who, in nine of fifteen southern states, were legally banned from possessing them in any event. Ward held American religion in contemptuous regard for these and other contradictions.

> It is a matter of surprise to people in England that the Americans should profess so loudly the *Christian* religion, and insist so strong upon republicanism as the only proper form of government, and yet hold slaves and treat Negroes, as they do, in the directest possible opposition to republicanism and Christianity. . . . Some [religions] deny the sinfulness of slaveholding; others shelter themselves behind the faults of the abolitionists; others defend slave-

holding from the Bible; but I think their love of harmony is their chief alleged reason for their present attitude. Let it not be forgotten, however, that behind all this—and going very far, I think, to explain it—is the contempt they all alike maintain towards the Negro.[12]

The uncomfortable nexus between literacy, religion, and social control triggered a series of debates in Geneva in the 1830s about the role of Sunday school instruction and about the very entitlement of African-American people to education of any kind. By mid-decade, only white males had charge of Bible instruction for colored people, which suggests that the work had become too politically important to be entrusted to women.[13] Even with male teachers, the *Geneva Gazette* suspected that the efforts of the village's leading churches to educate African Americans to piety were not easy to manage. In 1836, the *Gazette* criticized New York City abolitionists for luring the African-American "shoe-black, the ostler, the waiter, the oysterman and clothes-scourer," whose work had given them "comfortable livings" and "the confidence of the whites," to abolition and equal rights meetings that developed in them "utterly false notions of equality and independence" and "an utter distaste for their former pursuits."[14]

The tendencies manifest in the local Sunday school for blacks carried, in the eyes of the newspaper's editors, identical threats. Also in 1836, "A Friend of Sunday Schools" covered the anniversary exhibition of the Presbyterian colored Sunday school for the *Gazette*. Certainly, the correspondent averred, Bible instruction could not fail to "correct their faults and vices, and better their entire character. It will promote a suitable, and check an excessive self-respect; it will make them modest and honest, and teach them gratitude to their benefactors, deference to their superiors, and obedience to their masters." But the writer was nonetheless concerned about the "qualifications of their teachers."

The blacks are ignorant and credulous; and receive with implicit confidence whatever is taught them as religious truth. They are incapable of forming opinions for themselves on doctrinal points, or on questions of duty requiring investigation and reflection. They of course adopt their opinions altogether at second-hand. It is therefore, highly important that their lessons should be confined to such portions of the Bible as their teachers are qualified to interpret, and they to comprehend. It is also important that the truth itself should be presented to their minds unmixed with questions of a foreign nature. It is no part of the business of a teacher in a sunday school for colored people, to give his class false notions on the subject of slavery, or excite their prejudice against institutions contrived by high benevolence, and aiming at the happiness of their race. . . . If . . . the object in view, with any of the teachers, should be to make their scholars *abolitionists* (in the restricted meaning of the term) we would suggest that the Bible has been selected for a text-book with singular infelicity, and that many modern publications might advantageously be substituted in its place.[15]

The report generated a rebuttal, published in the *Gazette* several weeks later, from "Amicus Justitiae," who defended the Sunday school teachers and argued that the Bible was not in fact designed to teach African Americans "obedience to a system of injustice and oppression."[16] But Bible instruction was still the only formal schooling available to the village's African-American population in 1836. New York legislators had authorized the organization of segregated schools in 1823, but fourteen years passed before Geneva educators felt compelled to create one for local African Americans. And blacks appear to have perceived that, in view of the proscription against secular schooling for members of their race, it would be more expedient to begin their first efforts to educate themselves in a Sunday school. This institution became known as the High Street Sabbath School, probably built in 1834 (fig. 35). According to one 1888 newspaper account of the school's history, African-American students had begun to meet on High Street in 1828 "in Aunt Amy Tompkin's house, and as the class increased they met under a spreading cherry tree in the yard just below, where now stands Joseph Condol's house." Tompkins evidently lived at the time in a dwelling she must have rented from white landlord William Tippetts. In 1829, Tippetts sold this property to Aaron Lucas, who in turn is said to have donated the land on which the church was built in 1834 (fig. 36). There is no record of this transaction, and one recorded deed shows that Lucas sold the land in 1831. Though no record shows that he repurchased it before 1834, his daughter Nancy Lucas Curlin later lived in the building and was declared its rightful heir in 1901 (fig. 37).

Local whites did not acknowledge the necessity to extend public schooling to African-American children even after a school had formally been established for them. An 1837 Ontario County school superintendent's report stated that seventy-two African-American children attended a district school located in the church on High

35. "Union Chapel, Colored, Interior, High St.," about 1865, photograph by James G. Vail. *Courtesy Geneva Historical Society.*

36. High Street Union Chapel, 1869–1884, photograph by James G. Vail. Aaron Lucas's daughter, Nancy Lucas Curlin, used the chapel as a home from the 1890s through at least 1901. *Courtesy Geneva Historical Society.*

Street, but a report on the status of local education published in the *Gazette* in November 1838 failed to mention the school's existence. A school district committee investigation in April that year found ten private and two public schools in the village with a total enrollment of 426 children. Of that total, 349 were between the ages of five and sixteen, which was just less than 40 percent of all children between those ages living in the village. The report stated,

> There are, then, 527 children in this village who do not attend school. . . . Of this number, we estimate that one-third are either learning trades, living out, or necessarily employed by their parents, and would not, unless a total change takes place in public opinion on the importance of education, attend school under any

37. Nancy T. P. Lucas Curlin, about 1880, photograph by James G. Vail. *Courtesy John W. Kenney.*

circumstances. There are, besides, between 40 and 50 colored children. Allowing for these there still remain more than 300 children
who are growing up in ignorance, idleness and vice, because we
neglect our duty.

If the language of this report did not intimate the fact plainly
enough, a simple computation makes clear that the "40 or 50" colored children were not included in the group of children that the
village felt obligated to educate. If one-third of 527 children were not
in, and would resist attending, school, 353 remained to be educated.
Subtracting 50 African-American children from 353 left the "more
than 300 children" whose absence from school so troubled the inves-
tigating committee.[17] The fact that New York lawmakers ultimately
declared in 1841 that all public schools in the state must be open to
all children of school age suggests that schools had heretofore been
closed to black children in many villages and towns. Despite the
existence of the segregated school on High Street, Geneva's whites
somehow felt disinclined to recognize it.

Hostility to educating African Americans was rampant throughout the North in the 1830s. Both Henry Highland Garnet and his
wife Julia, Genevans by 1849, had been victims of it. Julia Williams
Garnet had been a student in Quaker abolitionist Prudence Crandall's short-lived school for African-American girls in Canterbury,
Connecticut, which closed in 1834 after repeated stonings and an
unsuccessful effort to burn it down. In 1835, Garnet and Alexander
Crummell had attended Noyes Academy in Canaan, New Hampshire, rural and remote even today. Canaan townspeople were sufficiently alarmed by the school that they used ninety yoke of oxen to
pull it off its foundation.[18]

Increasingly exclusive tendencies in church and school were,
again, first evident in the churches. In 1831, African-American attendance in the Presbyterian Sunday school declined significantly;
many may have begun to attend Sunday school on High Street. And
well before the newspaper debates about the Presbyterian school
took place, what Christian fellowship had existed in earlier churches
had given way to increasing segregation of black communicants and
a more energetic insistence on hierarchy. African-American leaders
such as David Walker had been critical of northern churches from
the late 1820s. Colored people's conventions often debated what the
"true church" was, because they reasoned that it could not be the
"corrupt" body that failed to take a stand against slavery, that up-

held the institution of the "negro-pew," and that insisted upon seg-regated communion. Although some delegates argued that patient work within integrated churches was the only path to reforming them, to many others white churches were simply "past reforming." For African Americans to continue to worship in them was simply "slavery in another form, its very spirit."[19] To Ward, Walker, Doug-lass, Garnet, Crummell, and other African-American leaders before the Civil War, the contradiction between preaching and practice in most antebellum churches violated the Bible as surely as the civic subjugation of the race violated the Declaration of Independence.

The "indignities and hindrances in the simplest forms of reli-gious communion" that many African-American New Yorkers had confronted in white churches had, according to Austin Steward, led them to create "upwards of forty" segregated churches of Presby-terian, Episcopal, Methodist, and Baptist affiliation in New York State by 1840. Many had their own church buildings and settled, salaried pastors.[20] There were three such congregations in Geneva by that time. The first, "a place of Worship for the Colored people" reportedly in "a state of forwardness" in 1833, was apparently the High Street Sabbath School. The other two had separated from the village's Baptist and Methodist churches.

In 1830, the Baptist congregation was just four years old. It had taken shape during prayer meetings at the home of E. W. Martin, a former itinerant preacher whose circuit had included Geneva. Bap-tist congregants first met for communion in 1826, and, after a coun-tywide revival in 1830, the church's membership grew steadily. African-American Baptists had been admitted as members since 1827, but "recurring disputes" occurred between them and Martin from the earliest days. These disagreements appear to have centered on the issue of seating within the church. The matter was first ad-dressed in church meeting minutes on 31 July 1830, when the con-gregation voted "that the Back seat in the Gallary be reserved to the use of the Coloured people from this time forward." African-Ameri-can members promptly protested the vote by "absenting them-selves" from Sunday meeting, an action that caused the church to send a committee to meet with them "and counsel them."

Black parishioners objected not simply to sitting in the gallery, however. In October, the committee reported to the Baptist congre-gation that "an opinion exists among the coloured members that a wrong motive on the part of the other members was the cause of a partition being Errected in the meeting house as a separation be-

tween the coloured & remaining part of the congregation which motive is a bar to their fellowship." The partition was evidently so high
that it concealed the pastor.

The issue came to a head at the December covenant meeting, at
which the congregation considered whether Martin should be dismissed from the church. Ultimately, the meeting decided Martin
should stay "until present church difficulties be removed" and that
African-American congregants should publicly "state their differences with the other members." After they reiterated their disap-
proval of the partition, the meeting agreed "that said partition be
taken down to a level with the seats in the same House."

This resolution evidently did not satisfy Martin, who asked to be
dismissed on the grounds that "a certain member of this church has
exerted his influence to destroy my good character." Almost a year
passed under a new elder before the issue erupted again. In October
1831, the church decided to "reconsider all votes and resolutions
heretofore passed on the case in hand (viz) the difficulty between
the white and coloured brethren" by submitting the question to a
third party. This third party, an elder from a neighboring church,
declared that the partition should remain, a decision Geneva Baptists accepted.

Just before Christmas that year, the congregation offered African-American Baptists a compromise—"to give up the gallery of the
meeting house to the coloured people (exclusively) as their place to
set but they are to have the priviledge of free access to the stove at
all times to warm & to set in the lower part of the house on all
church meeting days communion seasons &c." This decision apparently served. Between April and July 1832, nine African-Americans
were baptized into the church, more than had been admitted any
year before.

But dissatisfaction persisted within the church. In June 1837,
Baptist meeting minutes state, "The colored Brethren requested to
be set apart as a branch of this church." The congregation assented
to the proposition but took no immediate action. During the next
month, the minutes allow that "the union of the church [is] not so
good as would be desirable," probably because African-American
congregants had boycotted Baptist communion. In July, the Baptist
elders appointed a committee "to visit the Colloured Brethren that
do not attend with us when the ordinance of the Lord's Supper his
[sic] administered." In November, the committee reported, "The reason they did not come to the Communion was because they were

dissatisfied with their seats on the Communion occasions. After mature deliberations," the minutes state, "the Church concluded that it was not expedient under existing circumstances to make any alterations" but resolved that "those of the Color'd & White Brn who Choose to sit together at Communion" be allowed to do so, as also would those white congregants who wished to sit by themselves, "with this proviso, that no slur be cast on either sides, if any one does to be dealt with accordingly."

African Americans continued to be admitted to membership in the Baptist church, but still the arrangement between black and white members was unsatisfactory. By December, a special church meeting granted the request of "our Color'd Brn" to form themselves into the Second Baptist Church and agreed as well to give them "the sum now due to this Church, from the Color'd Brn . . . when this Church is organized." Within three years, Anthony Freeman, Peter Lincoln, Aaron Lucas, John Bland, and Charles Kenney incorporated the Second Baptist Church, appointed themselves trustees, and bought the church and lot just vacated by the village's Methodist congregation for $642.50.[21]

Occupied by the Methodists since 1821, the new Second Baptist Church stood next to the Mechanics Society schoolhouse on Castle Street just north of its intersection with Main Street, an area that also had a small pocket of African-American residents. Local African Americans invited Samuel Ward, then minister to an all-white congregation in the Wayne County town of South Butler, to lecture on intemperance at their new sanctuary in November 1841.[22] When it was Methodist, the church had also had African-American members, including Philip Gillam, John and Mary Brown, Dinah Broadfoot, and Thomas and Matilda Waggoner, who joined in 1834 and 1835. But, apparently influenced by events in the Baptist church, these new members moved to change Methodist practice of serving communion. The racial dispute in the Methodist church seems to have been made more hostile by the attitude of ruling Methodists toward the nature of the claim for equal treatment, and by May 1839, all of the African-American Methodists who joined the church in the 1830s (except Broadfoot, who apparently left the village) had been expelled or had withdrawn.

The separation of African-American Baptists was just two months old when John Brown asked the Sunday meeting of the Methodist congregation to institute equal treatment at communion in the existing church. The minutes record that Brown was "allowed to deliver his communication which he did at some length, and from which it appeared that our *coloured* Brethren were dissatisfied with the distinction made between the white and coloured in administering the Sacrament and through Brother B. (their representative) begged they would be allowed the privilege of communing with their white brethren." The request was left to the white pastors Seth Mattison and Elijah Hebard to "arrange as they might think proper."

In May 1839, more than a year later, the question at last came before the Methodist trustees, who resolved to ask Brown's class leader, William Scritchell, to "examine said case and if necessary to bring said defendant to trial." It seems clear not only that Brown had repeated his request for integrated communion but that he might have done so in demonstrative ways that the trustees considered inappropriate. Twenty days after Scritchell was asked to investigate the "case," Brown was expelled, and his wife had voluntarily withdrawn. Within days, each Methodist class leader was asked to "see and converse with the col'd members of their respective classes and if possible to restore them to their right minds." Evidently, African-American Methodists would have none of this persuasion: by the first of July, they were permitted to withdraw, and by May 1844, they had incorporated as the First Wesleyan Methodist Church.

Brown and other African-American Methodists separated without financial support from the parent church, then in the process of building a new sanctuary at the head of Seneca Street. And rather than sell or lease their old Castle Street church to their own brethren, they sold it instead to African-American Baptists. The First Wesleyan Methodist Church must have been short-lived. By March 1840, Gillam had become a trustee of the Union Religious Society, apparently an interdenominational group of Geneva's African Americans that also included on its board John and James W. Duffin, Salaby Hardy, Samuel Condol, and Roswell Jeffrey. Other one-time Methodists may have followed Gillam's lead.

Such schisms demonstrate the presence of an ever-widening rift between the secular movement for equal rights and increasingly institutionalized evangelicalism. The Methodists' 1836 General Conference had condemned slavery and "modern abolitionism" in the same breath, and the Baptists remained officially neutral on the slavery issue until the 1840s. But the question whether American slaves should be emancipated immediately or gradually, whether African Americans were "ready" for freedom, roiled through the churches long before it was officially embraced. Laced through the conservative wing of the antislavery movement was the persistent metaphor of the slave as child, captured concretely and for all time in the form of Topsy in *Uncle Tom's Cabin*. Clerics such as Elmira's Thomas K. Beecher, Harriet Beecher Stowe's brother, preached sermons that at once condemned slavery and maintained the existence of a predestined earthly order in which the privileged and benevolent at the top of the social pyramid were bound as Christians to look after and guide the great mass of childlike, confused, easily misled people who composed the rest of society. To Beecher, the best society was, like a good slaveholder, paternalistic. Liberty was a "delusion," the Declaration of Independence a "lie," and those who sought the immediate abolition of slavery showed an excessive and dangerous obsession with worldly matters that only threatened to divide the peaceable kingdom that God had designed to reign on earth. After all, earthly existence was an ephemeral thing; Beecher believed one's duty on earth was to cleanse oneself of an interest in worldly matters and wait patiently for Jesus to guide one to a heavenly station.[23]

African Americans pointed out, however, that their example in the nation and the world provided ample justification for immediate abolition. In Auburn in August 1849, African Americans passed a resolution asserting that Great Britain's emancipation of the West Indies sixteen years earlier "prove[s] that while it is just, and righteous, that every bondsman should be immediately proclaimed a freeman, at the same time, it is perfectly safe and practicable."[24] By the 1850s, evangelical religion had split cleanly in two, one branch endeavoring to sustain its focus on the "other world" and its heavenly millennium, the other an increasingly secularized movement growing out of Charles Grandison Finney's original belief that salvation placed the saved in God's earthly kingdom, where they were bound to help their fellows.

Antebellum Segregation, Postwar Integration

Just as the churches attempted to steer African Americans to their place in the sacred order, the public schools sought to qualify and control the kind of education African Americans could receive. The very existence of segregated schools and the official state sanction of their existence indicate the unwillingness of white society to attach the same positive values to educating African Americans as were affixed to the rising literacy of white Americans. For African

Americans, the logical relationship between school and work was inverted. It was not that schooling helped one find one's appropriate place in the world of work and the means of getting there; it was that one's place in the economic order determined one's position, if any, in the school system.

As early as the 1850s, African Americans showed their awareness that black schooling did not deliver the same rewards, that, as Stephen Myers put it, "you cannot get your son, even with his collegiate education, placed above a porter." The stunning and persistent absence of correlation between years of schooling and increasing wage and opportunity among black Americans has led some analysts to suggest that it was the belief in the credo, not its historical reality, that actually empowered such leaders as Douglass and Brown, whose own successes led them to attribute the same importance to literacy that white American culture did.[25]

The relative merits of integrated and segregated schools, as well as of vocational and liberal education, were argued among blacks and whites since the 1830s and belied long-standing anxieties about control. At various historical moments, both whites and blacks have opposed integration, but their concerns were of fundamentally different character. State law permitted segregated schools in any New York school district in which the white majority deemed the presence of African-American children "offensive," a muted expression of the miscegenation arguments that were aired more openly in the antebellum workers' riots in New York and Philadelphia and, later, in the integration battles after the Civil War. But African Americans saw in integration deliberate and considered white control of the kinds of knowledge to which African Americans would be exposed, just as they had seen white churches attempt to manage their exposure to scripture. African Americans recognized the "indifferent or objectionable school culture" of the antebellum integrated school, the fact that "neither schools nor educators for the whites, at present, are in full sympathy" with African-American students. The 1853 colored national convention in fact recommended the creation of segregated schools so that an African-American youth might "catch up in the great race we are running; and hence, schools must be adapted to so train him; not that he himself is so widely different from the white youth, but that the state of things which he finds around him, and which he must be qualified to change, is so widely different."[26]

African Americans in the region saw Henry Highland Garnet's

school in Geneva as a model of the potential success of segregated education. After Noyes Academy had been closed, Garnet and Crummell, schoolmates since their years together at New York City's Mulberry Street African Free School, enrolled at Oneida Institute. Founded in 1830 by Charles Finney's mentor, the Presbyterian New School theologian George W. Gale, Oneida was financially supported in large measure by the New York City philanthropist Arthur Tappan, who had helped support Crandall's school as well.[27]

Garnet graduated from Oneida in 1839 and became minister of a newly organized African-American church in Troy, where he apparently stayed until 1847 or 1848. By December 1848, Douglass reported in the *North Star* that Garnet was a "late resident of Troy, but now of Peterboro," the central New York home of Gerrit Smith. By April 1849, Garnet was superintendent and teacher in Geneva's African-American school, and by the following January the American Missionary Association, whom Garnet served as a paid lecturer, assigned him as "home missionary" to the village's black church.

Garnet's school in Geneva attracted the attention of a number of well-known African-American antislavery lecturers, including Henry Bibb, Samuel Ward, and William C. Nell. The events of the 1830s had made Garnet well known among them, as well as among white abolitionists and quite possibly among others not affiliated with the antislavery movement. Turner's uprising and David Walker's radical writings had influenced his famous 1843 address proclaiming the voluntary submission of African Americans to slavery to be sinful and advising the use of violence in its overthrow.[28] Garnet's *Address to the Slaves*, opposed by Douglass and others who believed moral suasion was the only means to accomplish this end, made him a force to be reckoned with.

In April 1849, Nell, who had just moved to Rochester from Boston to assist Douglass with the *North Star*, came to Geneva to present an address at Garnet's school exhibition and reported on the event for Douglass's newspaper. The "elocutionary performances" at the exhibition addressed a range of subjects calculated both to appeal to and to jostle the sensibilities of the large number of people in the audience "not identified by complexion with the proscribed of this land," as Nell put it. Sprinkled in among the orations on "Hope; Things that I love; . . . Crucifixion; Good and Evil; Rainbow; Lying; Remember thy Creator; Spring; Punctuality; Liberty; Pleasures of the Grove" was one on American slavery and another obliquely titled "Triumph of perseverance." Nell noted that the exhibition gave whites the opportunity "of witnessing the mental capacity of those so commonly and unjustly termed an inferior class" and pointed out their essential superiority:

> The entire exhibition was one that Geneva may well be proud of, and moreover when it is known that of late similar exhibitions of seminaries among the whites in that place have been interrupted even to a discontinuance by a reckless demonstration of young men, the fact that Mr. Garnet successfully triumphed, free from any disturbances is one that should be remembered. There were also those in attendance, who had expressed their opinion that colored scholars could appreciate no higher mental exercise than a Juvenile Spelling Book, and yet the efforts of those same scholars at the exhibitions were most flatteringly commented upon by those same individuals, thus effecting a revolution in the minds of those preconceived against the colored man's capacity for improvement. These are just the triumphs desired by the intelligent Colored Americans. No favor does he crave at the hands of pro-slavery. Give him a fair field, and he welcomes the responsibility of proving his equality.[29]

Nell also reported that Garnet used the occasion to point out to the exhibition's racially mixed audience that Crummell, though not admitted as a clergyman in the Episcopal diocese in New York City, had been admitted to Cambridge College in England and that Charles L. Reason, then principal of a colored school in New York, had been appointed a professor at New York Central College in McGrawville, reorganized as a multiracial college by Gerrit Smith in 1849.[30]

Garnet's presence in Geneva surely influenced the eventual success of African Americans' efforts to have their children included more officially and formally in the local public schools. Organized into a district school a decade before Garnet came to the village, these children still had no school building in 1849. In 1841, the year state legislators declared public schools open to all children of school age, the village's African Americans had petitioned the school district to levy a tax that would fund schoolhouse construction. But the petition was tabled indefinitely, and debate on the issue did not occur again until 1849, when Garnet became superintendent. And not until 1853, two years after Garnet left the village for England, was the school actually built.[31] The African-American porter Roswell Jeffrey sold the lot diagonally across High Street from the church to the village school district trustees. His son Jason, also a porter, lived in a house on this lot; his grandson, also named Jason, taught at the school in 1862.

The High Street, or west branch district, School was one of three brick schools built in the village in 1853. Before the war, between fifty-four and sixty-eight black students attended classes at the west branch school, and probably only one teacher was assigned to the school at any time.[32] Most of the teachers in the school were probably white. Garnet, Jeffrey, Nathan Condol, and Nancy Lucas are the only African Americans known to have taught there. Two years after Condol left the village to prepare at Oberlin for a teaching assignment he hoped to secure in the South's new freedmen's schools, Presbyterian Sunday school records show that twenty-four-year-old Edgar B. VanHouten "left to teach in Col'd School." Now reassigned to whites, teaching at High Street School was also newly stimulated by a missionary impulse. In the midst of the ensuing integration struggles of the early 1870s, the Gazette feigned wonder at the fact that African Americans fought to admit their children to white schools when they had an "excellent male teacher, qualified to impart instruction in all branches from the alphabet up to civil engineering." But even in the Gazette's telling, African Americans were manifestly dissatisfied with the quality of instruction at High Street School. A jocular, pseudonymous piece written by "Ichabod Squigden," which appeared in the Gazette after one February 1872 school meeting, reported Albert Arnold's claim that the teacher at High Street School "would tell storys to the skollers, and play an old fiddle, and sing songs and sich. . . . He said that the skule hadn't advanced abit under him, but had seceded or suthin' like that—had been a disgrace to the skollers, to their parents and to their teachers. In fact, he thought the children needed a little less fiddlin' and more geografy." According to Squigden, George Bland agreed, stating that "the children didn't learn to speak the English language."[33]

By the Civil War, white children in Geneva's public schools were distributed into grades, each with its own teacher. But High Street School was still a single classroom, with one teacher teaching everyone between the ages of four and sixteen. The village had instituted secondary education for white students in 1839 when it created the Geneva Union School (later the Geneva Classical and Union School), but this school remained closed to blacks despite the 1841 state mandate for open classrooms. And the education African-American students received at High Street only prepared them for disappointment as they attempted to use postwar equal rights amendments to gain admission to the Classical and Union School. In 1870, a young African American whom the *Geneva Courier* referred to only as "a lad named Brown" (probably Albertus Brown, the twenty-one-year-old son of hackman William T. Brown) described how poorly his High Street School education had prepared him for the Classical and Union School's entrance examinations, administered by superintendent and principal William H. Vrooman.

> I had never been taught in the higher geography except one half term by Miss Chester; she taught the school one term and a half. Tuesday afternoon Mr. Vrooman gave me 14 questions in mathamatics [*sic*], and when I had answered these, he gave me 10 more, making 24 in all; I do not distinctly remember all of these questions, but I do recollect that there was one in "square root," and that the major portion were in branches I had not been taught in the high street school. I had studied Robinson's Practical Arithmetic but one-half term under Miss Chester's instruction. On Tuesday he gave me 24 questions in Grammar, consisting of a long sentence in which certain words were designated to be thoroughly parsed, giving the part of speech, person, number, gender, case, and the rules of syntax by which they were governed. I had never been instructed in this branch but one-half term by Miss Chester. She was the *only* teacher that ever attempted to teach these branches in the High street school that I know of.[34]

After the Civil War, the persistence of inequal educational opportunity had turned African Americans' earlier arguments in favor of segregation on their heads. Where some had felt creating segregated schools was the only way in which African-American scholars could avoid the reproach of whites and make educational progress, it became clear that white control of the school system had kept segregated schools from serving in this way, that segregation closed off access to those things—truly progressive education and enlarged opportunity—that American culture led African Americans to expect of schooling.

The inequities of public schooling were manifest in more visible ways as well. In New York City, one 1857 education society claimed that white children were schooled in "splendid, almost palatial edifices," while black children studied "pent up in filthy neighborhoods, in old and dilapidated buildings." The ratio of black to white children in the city was then one to forty, but the ratio of expenditure on black and white schools was one to sixteen hundred. Douglass had decried identical problems in Rochester's public school system in the 1840s, when he and other African Americans rejected the local school board's effort to put a colored school in the basement of the black Zion church, a *"cold, damp* and *gloomy"* space into which black children were herded at the behest, they charged, of "the pro-slavery Irish faction in the Board of Education." Little had evidently changed in Rochester by the mid-1850s.[35]

In December 1869, Geneva's African Americans turned once more to village school officials, this time to request that all children in the school district, regardless of "race or color," be accorded "the same educational advantages and privileges in any of the public schools of Geneva" and that any branch school student be admitted to the Classical and Union School "without distinction of race or color." The request was surely stimulated most directly by the passage of the Fifteenth Amendment, but Garnet's earlier activism may also have helped to persuade blacks that they might protest discrimination in the public school system and succeed. Moreover, the African-American community had mobilized itself to good effect during the war to raise money to send Nathan Condol to Oberlin College and then to the new southern freedmen's schools. By 1869, the fact that Condol had been teaching hundreds of African Americans in a school bearing his name in Aberdeen, Mississippi, might have inspired Geneva's blacks to press for equal educational opportunity in their own northern place.[36]

At the December 1869 meeting, Geneva school district officials agreed to admit black students to the classical department of the school "whenever they could pass an examination," a proviso that Brown would test and that his inferior High Street School training would cause him to fail within the year. Vrooman evidently used this resolution to examine Brown and one other African-American man but not to require the same of whites who also sought admission to the school. In the *Courier*, Vrooman was criticized for this action, as well as for sending the young men back to High Street School and not having tested them for the Classical and Union School's junior department. The inadequate instruction African-American students received at High Street School *"in itself,* is a violation of the law," the *Courier's* correspondent pointed out; the three postwar amendments had nullified the old state law permitting segregated schools, "whether the 'Professor' at the head of the public schools of school district No. 1, town of Seneca, is acquainted with the fact or not."[37]

District officials tabled the 1869 request for integrated schools indefinitely. At the first school meeting of the year in 1872, George Bland and others again presented their case for African-American admission to the Classical and Union School. This time, rather than argue simply that black students be admitted to the high school, African Americans proposed that the High Street School be disestablished for "maintaining an invidious distinction between the races," the *Gazette* reported, "contrary to the spirit of recent constitutional enactments and at variance with the progressive spirit of the age." The *Gazette*, very much against the proposition, reported that the issue had "been forced upon the attention of the people of this school district for the last three years, and although our colored population has met with adverse decisions, each defeat seems but to nerve them to increased persistency in pressing their claims to equal recognition with the whites in the premises." Just as the white Genevans had worried earlier that Sunday school teachers had brainwashed African Americans with abolitionist rhetoric, the *Gazette* deduced the African Americans' present claim to have arisen logically from the radical ideology of the Republican party.

> Bro. Bland insisted that the system of "equality" *they* had aided in enforcing upon the white people of the whole South, upon the cadets at West Point, and elsewhere, should be fairly and honestly recognized at home. The proposition is most assuredly a fair and legitimate deduction from the doctrines taught and inculcated by our radical friends. Some of them doubtless never imagined that this "chicken would come home to roost," but it *has*.

In this and later coverage of the school integration issue, the *Gazette* insisted upon deflecting readers' attention away from the issue of equal rights and toward the perils of Republicanism and miscegenation. So alarmed were the newspaper's editors about the commingling of black and white students that they sometimes followed stories about the school issue with articles about the alleged crimes of blacks against whites, just as they had done earlier in the century when the issue of colonization was current. The newspaper had probably cast its account of the February 1872 school meeting in the vernacular, rural-sounding English of the fictive bumpkin Ichabod Squigden to attempt to diminish the gravity of the integration issue, to make it seem, at least for a time, less perilous than the newspaper's editors clearly thought it was.

The *Gazette*'s editors believed that the issue was not equal educa-

tional opportunity; they argued that colored children already enjoyed "the highest advantages for education under our free school
system." Instead, they claimed, " It is plain enough their only desire
and aim is to force their children into the society and companionship
of white children, however averse the natural instincts of the latter
and their parents may be to such association. It will endanger good
order and discipline in the schools. . . . Some parents we know will
not send their children to our public schools if this policy of promis-
cuous association of black with white children be adopted." The *Gazette* concluded that the demands for equality in the school system
proceeded not from the appreciation of inequity but merely from
"the unwarrantable pride of a few persons of the black race among
us."[38]

In the *Geneva Courier*'s account of the integration issue, the correspondent "Fair Play" asked why B. F. Cleggett, who then lived on
Water (Exchange) Street "within twenty rods of the north-eastern
branch school," had to send his children a mile away to the High
Street School, as did George W. Allen, who lived on Elm Street,
close to the Lewis Street branch school. And why did the white residents of Catherine, High, William, and other streets near the High
Street School send their children "nearly to Hamilton Street, in mid-
winter, when there is one of the best of these schools within a few
minutes' walk from their homes?" In his *Gazette* account, Squigden
recorded Albert Arnold's consternation about the fact that African-
American children who lived on Water Street "had to go past three
skule'uses to go to their own skule, and that they ketched bad colds
in consekence."[39] The fact that the segregative impulses in the white-
controlled local school system persisted well into the twentieth century is attested by the presence of identical complaint before the
modified Princeton Plan came into existence in Geneva in 1967.

The petition that African Americans had presented to integrate
schools in 1869 did not come to a vote until 1872, and, one month
after an 1873 state law reiterated the intent of federal law guaranteeing equal rights to blacks, Vrooman evidently continued to resist the
efforts of black students to enter the Classical and Union School.[40]
After the state law passed, the *Gazette*'s opposition grew more stri-
dent.[41] The editors called integration "partial 'miscegenation' " that
was bound to "result in daily broils and collisions, a breaking down
of wholesome discipline, and a sad degree of demoralization in our
schools." They argued, "We don't believe in such *mixtures*, never
did, and never shall."

Throughout the 1800s, the *Gazette* had consistently refused to accept the principle of racial equality, but its impulses were never more vividly articulated than in its reporting of the 1870s integration struggle. The newspaper turned away from comparatively mild labels, such as "colored," and began to use instead "Negro" and "darkies," terms it rarely employed before or since. "Our darkies have at last gained possession of the magic *sesame* which opens up to them the door of every public school here as elsewhere," the editors lamented. ". . . If the result is *more* than bargained for by certain republicans—if their white children instinctively revolt at such associations as degrading—let them place responsibility for it where it belongs—upon the political demogogues who would have it so, despite of every direct vote of the people *adverse* to the doctrine of negro equality."[42]

Just as the 1838 school report had failed to mention the existence of the village's African-American school, school meeting minutes of the 1870s made no mention of the April 1873 state law prohibiting public school segregation nor of the ultimate integration of the local school system (fig. 38).[43] Some segregation may yet have occurred within classrooms long after 1873. But even those blacks who had felt the sharper sting of integrated schooling continued to support the idea of it, not only because it offered the only access to the promised rewards of education but because of the contact it established between whites and blacks. Much as Ward argued that blacks should live in integrated neighborhoods because whites "need to be taught even the first ideas of civilization, by being near to enlightened progressive coloured people," leaders such as Douglass and, later, Mary Church Terrell argued that the lengthy, continuous contact children have with one another in school was the only way to begin to break down the walls of caste that permitted each race to form its stereotypes about the other.[44]

Exclusion in the Churches

As the issue of integration came to the fore in village schools, the institutional religious life of Geneva's African Americans had also grown demoralizing. The three independent congregations that emerged in the schisms of the 1830s appear to have sustained themselves at least through the 1840s; the 1849 Dorcas (sewing) Society of the Union Religious Society had raised funds to support Garnet's Geneva ministry and perhaps even to build a church at the corner of

38. South Branch School, Madison Street, Geneva, about 1875, photograph by James G. Vail. By 1873, all district schools in the village were apparently integrated, though an 1874 county atlas map of Geneva still labeled the one on High Street "the African School." Two African-American girls, one on each side of the path, attended the south branch school. *Courtesy Geneva Historical Society.*

High and Grove Streets by 1856. The deed stated that the church to be built on the lot was for "the use of the whole colored people of Geneva," which suggests that the earlier black Methodist and Baptist congregations may no longer have existed by then.[45] By 1852, African-American Baptists no longer occupied the old Methodist church on Castle Street, but Rufus Derby was listed as their pastor in 1855.[46] By 1849, when he offered the prayer at the Christian Reform Convention in Geneva, Derby lived on High Street between Grove Street and the High Street church. Baptists might have moved their services to High Street (Garnet had ceased preaching there by 1850) after they left Castle Street.[47]

By the mid–1850s, nearly all churchgoing African Americans in the village probably worshipped in segregated churches. Only John Marshall's church may have been integrated. Marshall, an African-

American Baptist who had apparently come to Geneva from Santo Domingo in 1850, was also a peddler, selling fruit and nuts on the street during the week and preaching on Sundays at a second-story hall of worship that canallers and their families reached from an outside stairwell next to the canal towpath.[48] Garnet, Derby, Marshall, and John Thompson, who stayed in the village less than two years, are the only African-American Genevans known to have preached in the village until Frank Louis Brown (who lived in Rochester) became rector of St. Philip's Mission in 1929. By 1860, Garnet had been gone nearly a decade, Marshall had left Geneva, and Derby, then nearly seventy years old, was listed as a farm laborer in the federal census. For nearly a century, the clergy at St. Philip's, Garnet's old High Street church, and, eventually, the Union Religious Society church at High and Grove streets were probably white.

By 1860, denominational affiliation may have become far less important to the village's African Americans than the presence of sympathetic feeling in any pulpit. Between 1853 and 1868, perhaps only the Episcopal church offered as much. Probably in some attenuated form, integration had persisted at Trinity until William Henry Augustus Bissell became rector there in the late 1840s. In April 1853, Bissell created the African-American St. Philip's Mission and began to hold services at the newly constructed High Street district school. In his diocesan report that year, Bissell reported that the "weekly service for the benefit of the colored people in the village . . . so far has been very acceptable, and promises to become the means of a great blessing to them." James Duffin's family moved from the Union Religious Society to St. Philip's Mission in that year, a switch that seems puzzling in view of Duffin's energetic support of abolitionism and equal suffrage and the Episcopal church's decidedly noncommittal stance on the slavery issue. But Bissell himself may have opposed slavery and may have preached against it to his mission. When he left Geneva in 1868 to become Bishop of Vermont, his native state, Bissell's farewell address to the High Street parishioners moved the group to pass a resolution in his honor and to publish it in the *Geneva Gazette*. "The finger of God is made visible in his promotion," the resolution stated, "giving a foretaste of the rewards that are in store for him who is a friend to the needy and preaches deliverance to the captives." That Bissell preached against slavery is also intimated in other *Gazette* articles published at the time of his departure. "The Bishop elect differs politically from the majority of this community—if we mistake not, from the majority of his parishioners," the newspaper observed; "but his 'influence' has not been 'marred' thereby, because among Churchmen of the Empire State the utmost freedom of political opinion is recognized."[49]

Whatever tied Bissell to his African-American congregants, it appears that at least some of the longstanding family relationships with Trinity Church may have dated from his twenty-year service in Geneva. In 1868, Salaby Hardy did work under contract for the church, and Anthony Jupiter sold Trinity a load of "Greens," perhaps for Christmas, in 1867. Jupiter's funeral took place at Trinity five years later, and his daughter's family, the Fosters, were lifelong members of the church. The Cleggett and Duffin families remained Episcopalian for generations, as did the Kenneys, Gillams, Hacketts, Johnsons, and Linzys. Parts of the Hardy family appear to have been Presbyterians in the 1880s and 1890s, but by the 1930s they too had affiliated with Trinity. The Condol and Hawkins families appear to have begun attending St. Philip's Mission by the turn of the century.

Persistent discrimination in the village's white churches might have enhanced the appeal of attending St. Philip's. At least one diarist noted discrimination in the local Baptist Church in the 1860s, and in 1859 Douglass took the First Presbyterian Church to task for refusing to allow the three thousand African Americans who came to Geneva for the annual West Indian emancipation celebration to use the church in case it rained. In the 5 August *Frederick Douglass' Paper*, he wrote,

> The celebration at Geneva, while it met with much kindness and cordiality from the Water Cure Establishment, and the citizens generally, met at the hands of the pro-slavery Presbyterian Church of that place a piece of flagrant inhospitality and characteristic meanness. . . . Very much to the annoyance of some of our audience, we took occasion, in our humble speech, to characterize the conduct of the Presbyterian church in a manner befitting its enormity. We had rather join the Water Cure to save our body, than such a church to save our soul.[50]

During and immediately after the war, the Presbyterian church began to admit its first African-American members since 1821, and by 1895 the church taught Sunday school classes for the Union Religious Society of Colored People. In 1891, nearly fifty years after it had purchased the lot, the society was able to build its chapel at High and Grove Streets, perhaps motivated by Nancy Curlin's decision to occupy the High Street chapel as a dwelling (fig. 39). But the dwindling numbers of African Americans in Geneva apparently made it difficult to sustain the new church, and in 1933 the society sold the property to local Freewill Baptists.

By this time, joining St. Philip's may have been influenced more by the felt need to be part of an African-American congregation with an African-American minister than by any particular characteristic of Episcopalianism. Brown, a Jamaican and a graduate of the Philadelphia Divinity School of the Episcopal Church, was assigned to "assist" Trinity rector Samuel Edsall with St. Philip's Mission in 1929. John Kenney talked about Trinity and the place of St. Philip's within it.

> All the old blacks that lived in Geneva . . . all of those people were not all Episcopalians; they were Methodists, Baptists, and so on. *But* they all came to St. Philip's Mission; they all came to the church.
>
> . . . Now we had, at our service, all these that are on that list, which wouldn't fill the chapel. The rest of the people came to hear the choir. We had a good choir. We had my cousin George Hardy, sang a beautiful bass, Harry Kenney, Herb Kenney sang bass, Charlie sang bass, Art was a tenor, I was a tenor—he wanted me to be a tenor—Lawrence [Kenney] was a tenor, Harry Derby, he was a good bass. And there was a man who was Cappy Whitaker's brother, Perk Derby, who lived in Auburn and was my wife's first cousin, he used to come, when he was in Geneva, he used to come to our service.
>
> Trinity . . . was segregated in a way. You see, our church, we had Sunday school every Sunday, but church only came every other week. A minister by the name of Father Brown came down from Rochester, and that was our only association. . . . We had our own church, what's now the Lillian Franklin Room; we had a dias, viridas, we had our own altar, we had our own organ, we had our own choir pews, and our seats. . . . Edsall wouldn't even come out of his back door to acknowledge the fact that Father Brown was there, and he was a staunch religion, very tall, very religious; he was also West Indian. No, it wasn't that it was segregated; it was certain people didn't like to sit near you or you, or you and you. It was all right if you went there and sat next to him and him, but to go and sit next to you and you—there was a lot of money in that church then, awful lot.

Three years after Brown's assignment to St. Philip's, a spectacular fire virtually destroyed Trinity Church. St. Philip's Mission was the first to pay in full its pledge to help restore Trinity after the fire.

39. The church at High and Grove streets, about 1915. *Courtesy Dorothy Scott Cooke.*

The pledge was made despite a bitter argument between Edsall and Herman Kenney, an active member of the mission and teacher of its afternoon African-American Sunday school, over what would become of the mission while the church was rebuilt and afterward. John Kenney told what he knew of the conflict.

When the church burnt down, where were we going to go? Back up on High Street? . . . Where were *they* going to go? What was going to happen? So my father as much as said, "You put your arm up here and I'll put my arm up there, and if I rub my arm against you, I don't *think* it's going to rub off." It's an old cliché. Edsall couldn't believe it, he got mad, my father got hot, he was hot-tempered, and they got into it. "Well, we don't have to stay here."

. . . As I remember, they went to St. Peter's for a while. They reclaimed part of the old parish house where we were, the Lillian Franklin Room; they moved us out and moved them in. And they held services there, there and St. Peter's. Their services were in the morning, ours were in the evening. So we had Evensong and that's what a lot of people liked. So we used the same as they did; that's where the disruption and my father came in.

They reconciled directly after he [Edsall] found out that they had to have church together; there was no place else for them to go.

Kenney's brother Charles remembered that the controversy revived the historic issue of communion.

You've never experienced it, but we *know* what Geneva used to be like. So let's say I'm seventeen years old; I wouldn't think of going to the Seneca Hotel to get a drink, because I know that I'm uncomfortable about doing it. Even church-wise. My father got in the biggest argument with Father Edsall over whether or not they were gonna serve black people communion at Trinity Church. This was when they were talking about doing away with St. Philip's Mission, see. And there were those in the church—well, I think I mentioned it one time, how Professor Boswell said, "You're sitting in my pew," one of those things.

Leona Hardy, George Hardy's daughter, talked about going to Trinity in the 1930s and remembered the nature of the controversy still differently.

I went to Trinity, when I went. In my younger days, I was [a regular churchgoer]. When I was going, they held St. Philip's in the chapel, a building to the side, little chapel. Father Brown didn't like us meeting there, so he told Reverend Edsall that he wanted us to be in the big church. He [Edsall] had to go through, because Father Brown was a priest. Edsall didn't like it because they had to use extra heat. . . . Trinity Church was mostly southerners; that's why they didn't like colored up there. They wanted it separate.

At Trinity, the caste system that had long ordered life in Geneva seemed to express itself ritually from time to time in the twentieth century. By midcentury, Trinity had become an anachronistic micro-cosm of the social structure that had struck industrial and civic leaders of the late 1800s as eminently sensible, appropriate, virtually foreordained. Even as Geneva city government was more often in the hands of Irish and Italian Americans, the central pews at Trinity were occupied by white persons whose ancestors had, with promi-nent Presbyterians, once possessed most of the capital, industrial power, and civic responsibility in the village. When integration came and St. Philip's Mission was brought under Trinity's roof, some of the church's white parishioners resisted. One of them was Theodore James Smith, son of an English immigrant who, with his brother, had founded one of Geneva's most prosperous nurseries. Theodore Smith's son Warren Hunting Smith, born in 1905, talked about the place of African Americans within the church.

> In 1884, they decided to have a parish house at Trinity church and have a chapel for the colored people to have their services there, and their services were usually in the evening. They had a little choir, and those services were separate. They were welcome to come to the other services, but when they did, they came sort of as visitors and usually sat in pews at the sides of the church and not at the middle. And I remember my father once, when a lawyer in town, descended from the Rose family, had a Sunday school class of colored boys and he brought them to his own pew, which was in the middle of the church, and my father afterwards rebuked him and said, "That really isn't quite the thing to do. Of course we're glad to have them there, but they shouldn't be sitting right among ladies in the middle of the church." . . . [My father] liked black people; he just felt that there were certain usages that should be kept up, but he felt that way about other people, too.
> . . . There was quite a bad time at Trinity Church once, be-cause one of the members of the [black] congregation was waiting on table at a dinner party at the Chew's house on Main Street. The

Chew family were bankers for a couple of generations, and Hilly Chew, as they called him, was, shall we say, *most* undemocratic. He used to say, "I *hate* gum-chewing democracy." And he happened to remark to somebody that he really didn't like seeing all those black people in Trinity Church, he didn't think it was right, and that was overheard, and the entire little black congregation rebelled, and the rector had an awful time calming them down and getting them back again.

By the 1940s, the persistence of a caste system was most visibly expressed when the mission's weekday services were moved to Bethlehem Chapel in the basement of the church. Alvin Robinson recalled his reaction when he first visited Trinity with members of the "established" families in the mid–1940s.

You walk into this big beautiful church and there was a high nave and all this sort of stuff, and all of the sudden all the black people are going downstairs to St. Philip's. That was a one-time visit for me. It was—I guess it was a sort of a throwback to me, because I thought how satisfied these people are, and yet, without the signs, they're undergoing the same thing southern blacks are undergoing. They're segregated, you know, but they're made to appreciate it and enjoy it by being given the thing that, "We're doing this because you're such good people."

Even without the association of St. Philip's with Bethlehem Chapel, Trinity, to some, manifested a singularly exclusive attitude that was born not only of prejudice but also of the conflation of social class and Episcopalian practice. Dorothy Cooke went to Trinity briefly in the 1920s but during her high school years chose the city's Methodist church, where she was the only black congregant. When she returned to Geneva from Rochester in the 1970s, she joined Trinity.

I have always thought it [Trinity] was a very cold church, and it still is, but once they get to know you—see, I've been there just long enough and am involved enough, and I'm just active there. Once they get to know you up there you're all right. But if they don't know you they just put you in a way of speaking in a corner by your*self*. And you could just stay there from now until the end of time. I just think it's the way the people are. Now, 'course, Trinity Church was nothing but wealthy, old families, you see, and they just moved in a certain circle, and you just didn't break into that circle.

After the war, Geneva's small African-American population could not support an independent black church of the sort the village had known in the 1840s and that then thrived in such places as Auburn, Elmira, Ithaca, and Rochester. These churches supported a lively social system in which the egalitarianism and evangelicalism of the early antebellum period lived on. Unlike schools, churches required no public financial commitment, which may explain why whites tolerated the presence of black churches in their midst. But the African-American church also thrived because blacks faced utterly distinct moral issues that could not be aired from the pulpits or pews of white churches. These concerns were articulated in an elaborate, allegorical network of meanings layered onto received "knowledge," arguably a spontaneous response to the attempt of whites to control access to knowledge in both church and state. Antebellum African-American spirituals focusing on the idea of heavenly salvation pivoted on an allegorical understanding of the Bible, a feature that made them a perfect medium by which Harriet Tubman could communicate escape plans and Frederick Douglass could first conceive the idea of fleeing and then express hope as he neared the moment of his "pilgrimage toward a free state."[51]

African-American folklore, humor, religious practice, and music represent a stock of understandings fashioned and owned solely by African Americans, a cultural system of practice and belief not available to whites. This very inaccessibility stimulated the creative, lively, and prolific investment of African Americans in these parts of their culture; their comparative richness must have developed in part because this belief system, often orally transmitted, was one of the few areas of American life they were left free to develop and cultivate. And it helps to explain the survival of emotional religion in the black churches of the North, though not in Geneva until World War II.

Integration and Control

The integration of Geneva's classrooms took place at a time when African-American children made up less than 3 percent of the local school-age population. Through 1925, as the city's population grew and the number of African-American residents shrank, the number of African-American children in the schools grew slimmer still, and economic exigency appears to have pulled some who were of school age into the work force. In 1915, nearly one-third of all African Americans between the ages of five and eighteen were no longer in school: Charles Whitaker was a fifteen-year-old laborer, Joseph C. Gillam a deliveryman at age seventeen, and Florence Derby was a sixteen-year-old domestic. With so few African-American children in the school system, integration had a twisted effect: instead of being the primary—if not the only—means of racial advancement and interracial harmony, it made African-American students more noticeable and therefore more marginal. Still, integration seemed inclusive. The broad wash of ideas, values, and cultural beliefs that the schools were charged with inculcating seemed to touch students irrespective of race, and the belief persisted that schooling would open the doors to enhanced income and new occupational opportunities. For many, racial distinctions did not emerge until dating forced them to surface in junior high school and high school. But the white majority's control of the system subtly channeled the participation of black students within it and limited their access to its rewards. Such constraints, coupled with the isolation that attached to black students as a statistical and racial minority, made school a bittersweet experience (fig. 40). Dorothy Cooke was a student in Geneva schools in the 1920s and 1930s.

> When we grew up years ago, you weren't conscious that you were colored. There weren't that many colored people in Geneva, and everybody was respected for who you were. [But] at school they had their own friends, I mean, they stuck together, and I was always a lonely child because I had no brothers and sisters, for one thing, and I didn't make friends easily. I had a few friends, but not really buddy-buddy like I would like to have, but I just wasn't that type of a person. I suppose nowadays the term is a loner. That's certainly what I was. I knew the colored kids that were around, and the families that were here, and even with them I wasn't close.
>   . . . I went to Lewis Street School; I went over there kindergarten to sixth grade. To my knowledge, I went there, Charles and his brothers went there; I don't think there was anybody else.

Mildred Mathis graduated from Geneva High School in 1936, two years after Dorothy Cooke.

40. High Street School classroom, 26 April 1910. The identity of the African-American student in this view is not known. *Courtesy Geneva Historical Society.*

Well, you know, in those days it was a good school. It was a happy place. You didn't have things going on in school back then that you have today. And so that was where the activity was, where you enjoyed the school dances and so forth, you know . . . little ten-cent Saturday night dances, you know, at the high school. We didn't [dance with white boys] in those days. We had enough boys of our own to dance with, you know. There was the Kenney boys and the Moore and Fosters.

    . . . I always felt it [a color line] because, well, they didn't dance with you, I didn't get invited to their parties. When I was a little, little child and in the neighborhood if somebody had a birthday I might be asked to maybe one or two. In the neighborhood when I was born and was coming up we all socialized together, you know. You didn't realize it then but when you got older, maybe a teenager and you was ready to socialize more. See, little children, they don't feel it so much because they play together, black and white and so forth, but when it gets up to the time when you're supposed to start dating, then you become conscious of it.

. . . My mother couldn't, didn't prepare me, you know, for it, but I prepared my children for it when they started to get ready to go to kindergarten. I wanted to be the one to tell them so they wouldn't get hurt. And so I said to them, "Now you're going to school, they're going to have plays and different little functions and I don't want you to feel bad if you don't get chosen 'cause white people don't think there's black kings or queens or angels or whatever they have in their little school plays, so you don't get chosen to be in it." And so they coped with it.

The settlement of new families in Geneva in the late 1940s and 1950s caused not only an African-American population explosion in the Geneva school system but a disjuncture of backgrounds between urbanized northerners and rural southern newcomers (fig. 41). These events may have brought issues of control more consciously to the fore, but there was little apparent alteration in the methods the school system used to constrict the place of African-American students within it. Gloria Peek, born in Geneva several years after her parents migrated north from Florida, was a student in Geneva schools in the 1960s.

I was always conscious of a division. I experienced a lot of discrimination. I guess some people would say, "Na, that's favoritism," but I remember in elementary school it seemed like any of the best activities, any of the nicest activities, that all the white kids got them, okay, any special programs that came up where you could— let's say you could travel, you know, if you did a science project or anything. The white kids' projects were the ones that were selected, and they always got to go, and they got to do this, and they got to do that, and it was always expected that you either weren't going to do it, or you weren't going to do it well. Or you just weren't capable, so you just got overlooked.

At base, children of old families felt little less marginal. Beth Kenney Henderson went through school in the 1950s.

When people talk to me about prejudice, and did I grow up in prejudice, I have to be honest and say no, not in my area that I

41. Prospect Avenue School second-grade class, 1962–1963. A fast-growing population and residential concentration among African Americans combined to give Cortland Street School the highest proportion of black students by the 1960s. *Courtesy Rosa Akins Blue.*

grew up in. But when I went to school I did, in grade school, and then it was just a subtle prejudice through school. In grade school kids would just be point blank and call me nigger.

. . . When I graduated I was the only black girl in my high school class. Johnny Sales and Wilmer Alexander were the other two black guys. Wilmer did not graduate, so I was the girl, and Johnny Sales was the guy, and that was it in our class. And it was very difficult. . . . We were good friends, we would talk, but it was that typical— "Well, Beth, you know, you're black, and Johnny's black; you two should be together." Well, I didn't like Johnny; he wasn't my type, and he was the all-around basketball, football player, but it just was not for me. And that was very difficult, and if a white guy even traced that he liked me, it was like we can have friendship and this and that, but God forbid if the parents ever knew. It was very secretive. And I really never had a boyfriend all through school; I really didn't. I had nobody to really, besides my own brothers, that I could sit down and talk to and say how I felt. . . . Because girls could talk about who they went out on a date with, who they went to the movies with, and my mother would say, "Your time will come."

Edith Jackson Harling, who graduated five years later when the children of new families made African-American students a more visible presence in the school system, recalled a willed segregation that kept racial conflict to a minimum.

There was quite a few black kids at the high school. Everybody seemed to get on well with everybody when I was there. Maybe I was blind and didn't see, you know, anything that was going on. We—I don't know—we segregated ourselves. You know, blacks ate with blacks, and we had our own table, and things like that. Maybe because we were all friends, all in a group; that's the way it was. We played in all the sports; there was no prejudice there— they didn't care what color we were, we played sports. You know, I don't understand why was there prejudice there, because I did not see it. Maybe somebody else could say, yes, there was, and they seen it. I didn't. We had a few white friends.

Isolation was not the only problem for African-American students in the school system; their presence continually revived the historic debate over vocational education. The question whether African Americans would benefit more from vocational or liberal education predated the controversy between Booker T. Washington and W. E. B. Du Bois over Tuskegee Institute by at least half a century and was formulated as much by the limiting expectations of whites as by the obstacles these expectations placed on the ability of blacks to achieve progress through education. As early as 1847, African Americans recognized that the education to which they were exposed was "cribbed" and "narrow," and that no rational arguments could be advanced to deny them access to liberal education.[52] Colored people's conventions often advocated creating colleges based on a manual labor plan so that blacks might learn the skills that would not only allow them to escape menial labor—training the workplace systematically withheld—but would help them pay room and board and make these schools independent of the need of white financial support.

Advocacy of skill training also stemmed from an almost Darwinian idea that African Americans had to pass through the occupational hierarchy in stages in order to enable the race to partipate in professions. Douglass told Harriet Beecher Stowe that his people would have to progress through and succeed at "the intermediate gradations of agriculture and the mechanic arts" before they could "reach that of *Ministers, Lawyers, Doctors, Editors, Merchants, &c."* Moreover, skills training would turn African Americans into producers. It would keep them from becoming superfluous to the American economy, an idea that would receive its most elaborate expression from Booker T. Washington. "Schools are only valuable in their teachings, as they assist in making both thinker and worker," committee delegates at the 1853 national colored convention argued. "They may saturate men with the learning of every age—yet, except they strive to make them something more than literary flowers, they sin greatly against the individual and humanity also." Douglass reasoned, "To live here as we ought, we must fasten ourselves to our countrymen through their every day and cardinal wants. We must not only be able to *black* boots, but to *make* them."[53]

Despite such arguments and various specific plans for creating a mechanical arts school for African-American youth, no such college was created until Tuskegee Normal and Industrial Institute was founded in 1881. Tuskegee's creation revived the debate about vocational education.[54] But by then, the continuing narrowness of opportunity for African Americans and the blatant outrages of Jim Crow legislation and practices in the South prompted many to lose patience with the idea that blacks might, or should, make themselves indispensable to whites by such means. W. E. B. Du Bois charged that Washington's program was nothing but a "Gospel of Work and Money," the same ideology that inspired white Social Darwinists and capitalists of his era, the very system whose profits depended upon devaluing manual effort, the precise set of beliefs that had kept African Americans marginal both in the economy and in society.[55]

The cultural value attached to liberal education remained so strong in any event that no African-American graduate of Geneva High School who aspired to go to college between 1931 and 1952 indicated a desire to attend Tuskegee. Some, including Dorothy

Cooke, Margaret McDonald, Robert LeVerne Miller, Charles Adelbert Hardy, and Leona Hardy, listed such black colleges as Howard University and Hampton Institute as their first choice; others listed prestigious white colleges in the area, including Colgate and Cornell, from which Pauline Ray graduated in 1913. Yet, regardless of aspiration, the tendency to steer African-American students toward vocational training was evident throughout the twentieth century. Beth Kenney Henderson graduated from Geneva High School in 1961.

> I never thought of myself as a college person, so I never took the Regents—I did take Regents English, but I really took business courses pretty much all the way through. My dream was to be a black model on an Ebony or Jet magazine. As long as I can remember, that's what I always wanted to be. That was my biggest fantasy. And when I decided like in my senior year . . . my guidance counselor did tell me that no, that was nothing for me. Naturally homemaking, that was probably all that she thought I could do, and where I did I think I was going to go? And she would not assist me, help me at all at even a modeling school. Not one. Debby [her daughter] went to Barbizon's in Rochester, and I mean that's been going on since the day one, even when I was in high school. That could have been—well, if this is something that you really want to pursue, here's Barbizon School in Rochester or Syracuse—but she never would do that for me.

Edith Jackson Harling, who graduated from Geneva High School in 1966, recalled the same sort of steering to have been manifest in junior high school.

> There was only one teacher at the junior high school, we felt that she was prejudiced, because she wanted all the black girls to take home economics, you know, and the boys were only supposed to take shop. And my friend Lillian, she's a straight-A student, and this teacher told her that's all she could do is take home economics. She said that I couldn't go to college because I didn't have enough—she didn't say brains, but aptitude—my grades were kind of bad, because I had problems at home, and when I told her that I had problems at home she wanted to get into my business, and my mother's very close-mouthed, and if she heard me talking, she'd have probably bopped me up the side of my head, talking about our business on the street, you know. So she

told me that I couldn't go. I wanted to go to the LPN school at
Geneva, but what can you do when your guidance counselor tells
you that? So I took home economics like everybody else did.

The steering of African-American students toward vocations was
evident too in the fact that African-American teachers were absent in
the Geneva school system until the 1960s. In the 1920s and 1930s,
Dorothy Cooke observed, "You didn't even acknowledge that there
were colored teachers even in existence." Charles Kenney recalled
how his sister, who had a master's degree in teaching, could not
find a teaching job in upstate New York.

> My oldest sister Elouise, she did some domestic work for the Clark
> family, who have a real prominent name here in Geneva. She grad-
> uated from Geneseo Normal and she got her masters in Buffalo U.
> She was a school teacher. They give her a job paying fifteen bucks
> a week down in North Carolina up in the hills or something; kids
> come to school with no shoes, and, you know, she couldn't take it.
> They wouldn't think of it [giving her a teaching job up here], no—
> are you kidding, black teacher?—no.

McKinley Flowers, who moved to Geneva from Coatesville,
Pennsylvania, in 1972, picketed Geneva schools as a member of the
local chapter of the National Association for the Advancement of
Colored People to force the hiring of African-American administra-
tors and teachers.

> I see it now as a very conservative, if not reactionary, atmosphere.
> We picketed the schools because of the absence of black teachers
> and administrators, pointing out that the lesson learned by black
> students when they see no black teachers, no black administrators,
> is that somehow blacks are less than qualified. And an equally neg-
> ative lesson is taught to white students, that somehow if you syl-
> logize the condition your conclusion is that all teachers must
> be white because I don't see any blacks. . . . Of course denial
> was always the conclusion and promises that we're going to try to
> get black teachers, and most of all no black teachers apply—that
> routine.

James Henderson attested to the effect African-American role
models had on him during his high school years in Philadelphia. He
told his guidance counselor that he wanted to be a social worker

because "the only one that seemed to come into my neighborhood with a college education was a social worker, checking on people that were on welfare to see whether they were working or not." The counselor told him there were not many black social workers, and that he would be better advised, he recalled, to "go into a commercial track, or take up sheet metal or something like that." But his family's belief in the value of education persisted.

> College wasn't something that was really planned as much as graduating [from high school]. . . . In my family, I was the first to graduate from high school, and that's all I heard from my grandmother, grandfather and my mother was that you couldn't even drive a sanitary truck, a garbage truck, unless you had a high school diploma.

Rosa Blue, who used to help her illiterate grandfather with tobacco processing by reading him the cooking instructions, graduated from high school in Florida before moving north.

> When I was coming up, my mother, although we lived on the farm, used to supplement her income doing washing sometime, and she helped do that to get me through school. . . . So when I would be scrubbing and doing domestic work, I would say to myself, "Why, that's not what I went to school for." . . . My ambition as a young person was to become a math teacher, junior high math, that's how crazy I was. Even in high school, sometimes if a teacher was sick I got to sub, as some of the seniors did, and we got paid for that. But then I got married so young and I kind of lost my ambition, but I transferred it to my children. I said, "Well, there's no way I can go to college and complete my education," so I said to them at an early age, "Now, *you* can. If I have to scrub, I'll do it, for you to go." And that's one of the reasons I did continue to work some, because I wanted to be able to help the kids get their college degrees. And every one of them went to college, with the exception of the youngest.

Dorothy Cooke had planned to go to Howard until her uncle's death foreclosed the opportunity, but she took college-level courses in Rochester, where she worked from about 1940.

> I went to RIT, I went to U of R, I went to Monroe Community, but all those colleges I didn't take courses preparatory to work; I took

courses to continue that liberal education that I started, and I'm *still* going to finish it. I think I've got about half the credits that I need. . . . [One daughter] went a year to Brockport; she works at the Experiment Station. Now my other daughter, the one in Washington, is a programs systems analyst for the government. She graduated from Howard University, and my granddaughter graduated from Howard, and my daughter took her to law school in Ohio just two weeks ago. . . . I don't feel you are really rounded unless you have that college education.

The increasing residential segregation of newer families in the flat below Main Street kept segregation alive in the Geneva school system and brought racial issues generally into sharper relief. In 1967, one study found that the sixth-ward Prospect Avenue School was 56 percent nonwhite and that reading and math test scores were consistently lower there than they were in the city's three other elementary schools. The school had no library, no principal, and inadequate classroom space. In 1968, in what the newspaper called "a surprise move," the Geneva Board of Education implemented what was known as the "modified Princeton Plan," which shattered the historic relationship between schools and neighborhoods in an effort to improve the racial balance throughout the elementary system. The plan withstood a court challenge by a local citizens' group, which charged that Prospect Avenue School was "inadequate, unsafe and unsuitable" and should no longer be used, and that the modified Princeton Plan should not in any event be implemented. Like challenges to busing and school redistricting elsewhere throughout the 1960s and 1970s, the plan to improve racial balance in Geneva was not an easily won objective, hardly less of a struggle in the late twentieth century than it had been for Genevans almost a century earlier.

The Reemergence of Black Churches

By the Second World War, integrated churches showed as unpromising a future for most African Americans in Geneva as did integrated schools. But for decades African-American churches in the larger cities of upstate New York had exemplified the vitality of the segregated church and the survival of extemporaneous, emotional, congregational forms of religious practice that made the black church a different social world.[56] Charles Kenney discussed the difference between the music he grew up with as a member of St. Philip's choir and what he learned at his wife's Pentecostal church in Rochester.

> She belonged to the Church of God and Saints in Christ, who had a storefront place up on Kelly Street in Rochester. I did a lot of singing up there. . . . I used to go over there and learn their songs and their rhythms and everything. [At St. Philip's], we sang stuff out of the book.

Such differences in religious practice and philosophy became more clear after the settlement of new families. Clarence Day described the differences between his religious background and Geneva's integrated First Baptist Church, which he and his wife eventually joined after they moved to Geneva in 1957.

> The service, it's different, because I was from Baltimore, and I used to sing in a chorus, on a male chorus, we had forty-six men, all men, male. And we sung a little different music than what they sings. I was thinking about that the other week here. Now, they sing strictly by the music. Music is beautiful, but some songs you can soften it a little sometimes. But it's good, it's good. It's just different. You just don't get, you don't get the feeling sometimes.

James Henderson grew up in an African Methodist Episcopal (AME) Zion church in Philadelphia and described the differences between the service there and at Trinity, where his wife had attended all her life.

> Black ministers . . . are very emotional, dramatic. I had to go to church [every Sunday] when I was young, and I was in the choir, and I mean it was all those thing, you know. And I can remember—I wouldn't stand up and shout and holler, but it was like the minister would start off, and it would like build to a crescendo, and you could feel it. And I came here, and I was looking for something like that. And I think we visited every church in Geneva, even went to some meetings with the Bahai faith right there on North Main Street. . . . I was looking for something that was not available in Geneva.

Beth Henderson described the services in the new black churches she and her husband visited from the point of view of a woman who had grown up on Episcopalian doctrine and practice.

> The sermons were much livelier, and I really felt it. And I could go out and I could leave that church and I could remember what they said. And it meant something to me—seriously, it really did. And I could remember the songs, the music, the gospels, and everything was put to what the sermon was for. And what always impressed me to this day—and I'm probably the one that goes to church and prays to God and does this whole thing, but I couldn't tell you where to find half the stuff in the Bible—I feel so proud, because I can't do that, to go into a church and see little kids open up a Bible, a prayer book, and know exactly what it's saying, and they could tell you a text and tell you where to find it that's telling you it's different from that, and the people tell you the same thing, and I think, "My God, the folks here in this church really know their Bible." And I said, "I'd be lost." I would honestly be lost.

The practice of northern churches followed the canon not only of liturgy but also of respectability. It was sedate, rule-bound, scheduled, and analytical. Richard Wright recalled being told at one Methodist church, "This is a new day. We don't holler and moan in church no more."[57] But for many southern-born African Americans, church and church-related activities had been an all-Sunday, every-Sunday affair that was as important socially as it was spiritually. Essie Tucker described going to church in Florida in the 1920s.

> I went to Rockaville Missionary Baptist Church. I wanted to go. Out in the country you be glad to get out. We went up until eleven or twelve o'clock at night. You had breaks between that. You went to Sunday school, and after Sunday school you got your morning service; after morning service if you're close enough, go home, come back to come to BYPU and training for the young folks. Then after six o'clock we had preaching service again.

Cora Burke had a similar Sunday pattern.

> I went to First Methodist Church in Sanford, Florida. Sunday school, too. I would go to Sunday school if I didn't eat. You didn't *eat.* You get up and go to Sunday school and come back and eat. My mother say, "Come back and eat." We go to Sunday school

nine o'clock in the morning, get out of Sunday school, then church at eleven o'clock, then after church, then they have some afternoon church all day, you know, then after that, six o'clock, you go to BYPU—oh my, I'm telling you. I went to church *every* Sunday. You gonna get out of there and go to church. That's right.

In the 1940s, as older African-American congregations disintegrated, the first new black churches in more than a century emerged. In 1942, with the death of Herman Kenney, the African-American Sunday school at Trinity ceased to have a black superintendent; three years later, Father Brown retired, and St. Philip's Mission lost its first and only African-American pastor. By the early 1950s, the mission had merged with the white Trinity congregation (fig. 42).[58] Though their history is less clear, the churches in the High Street neighborhood had also died by that time. But new churches sprang up in the industrial "butt end" of the city, the first apparently being St. Paul Negro Missionary Baptist Church, which was evidently built for servicemen at Sampson in 1943. First located near the company housing for Andes Range and Furnace Corporation at 67 Andes Avenue, the church moved often until by 1958 it settled on East North Street and changed its name to St. Paul Community Baptist Church.

Late in 1944, Mount Calvary Church of God in Christ became Geneva's first black Pentecostal church (fig. 43). Also a mission, Mount Calvary was created by Phillip P. Handy of Syracuse to provide a place of worship for African Americans on migrant farms. Handy's wife, Rosetta Brown Handy, born on a farm in Clay, New York, in 1899, told how he became involved with Geneva's black people.

I met my husband in Syracuse. We used to go to this Methodist church, and I met him there. He worked in a garage. He was from South Carolina, but he moved up to Syracuse and got work there. He was a member of this AME Zion Church. He was faithful in Sunday school and faithful in the services. And then he studied the ministry. After he got along in years he felt like he was called to the ministry. . . . He used to go out on farms to minister. Our people was migrating up from the Southland, and they wanted to stay over. They didn't want to go back South. Some of them had bought homes in Geneva.

. . . He said that he felt that the Lord was working on him to start work in Geneva. So he went to Geneva and found a few peo-

42. Girls' junior choir, Trinity Episcopal Church, 1952. Margaret Kenney and Carol Linzy are in the third row; Charlene Kenney and Beth Kenney are in the top row. Rev. Samuel Edsall stands at left. *Courtesy Charles H. Kenney.*

ple who'd come up from the Southland, and they had no church. So he opened up a little mission there. He started a Holiness church. [There was] the Methodist church and the Baptist church, but the Holiness church was a deeper work of grace, and people came from the Southland and opened these Holiness churches not only to be converted but they went on farther in spirit and received the baptism of the Holy Ghost. Now they call them Pentecostal churches. Anybody who wanted to be saved could come to this little mission. Some of them went to the white Pentecostal church, but the Lord give it to him to start a Holiness church for the colored people in 1945.

Handy commuted to his Geneva ministry, sometimes bringing Syracuse people with him, every Sunday for nine years. Mount Calvary began in an African-American home and then moved to a storefront at 14–16 Tillman Street, one of few buildings in which

43. Mount Calvary Church choir, about 1953. *Courtesy Mildred Smith.*

African Americans could then find housing. The church relocated again to a storefront on Wadsworth Street. Anne Russ, a Florida native who had come to Geneva from a migrant farm in Wolcott in 1941, had helped start Mount Calvary; her grandson, Harry Gramling, separated from his grandmother's church to form his own pastorate, First Love Church of God in Christ, in 1980. By 1959, a schism at St. Paul Baptist Church had created Mount Olive Missionary Baptist Church. Both had occupied Dee's Hall, a second-floor room above Dee's Tire Service on Exchange Street. In 1960, Mount Olive members built their own church on Clark Street, adjacent to Chartres Homes. In the same decade, Willie Golden, another Syracuse minister, created the Church of God by Faith, located first at 686 South Exchange Street and then in Border City.

The new African-American churches were also exclusive in the sense that they were perceived to be emphatically for the new families. Beth Henderson, who had spent her life in Trinity, described how it felt to attend them.

> There was still enough turmoil among the blacks in their own black churches, that who was running the church, and that's where you found out a handful started going over to the Clark Street church, then you got your North Street church and you still had your Mt. Calvary. And it was still "Who do you know?" and "I'm running the church; you gotta do this and that."
> . . . Even when we walked into the church, they'd look at Jim and I like, "What are you doing in our church?" That's the feeling I got. It was a shock. "You don't belong on this side of Geneva." And even though I probably knew I was going to stay at Trinity anyway . . . . I felt guilty [going around to other churches in Geneva], because I was leaving my home. It was more or less like I didn't belong, and I just didn't want to deal with that. . . . It's like, you know, you should be up there with those folks.

Still, the contradictions between preaching and practice that had inflamed Douglass and others in the decades before the Civil War continued to affect African Americans in the twentieth century. Mildred Linzy Mathis, who attended Trinity as a child, stopped going to church regularly by the time she was an adult because she questioned, like others before her, whether there was a "true church."

> That's what's sad when people say they don't like one another. That's too bad. That's why church, it makes me so mad, because all these people that say they don't like someone or anything, boy, they sit up in church and they, to me, it's hypocrisy, because church is supposed to teach you different. I belong to Trinity Church. At that time [when she was a child] it was the only place really where you had to socialize. But I grew away from church because of the fact that I become disillusioned about church, you know. People do so many mean things, unkind things, then going to church—I could never see it. Because whether I went to church or not, I was always going to try to be kind to people and do what I could for people. I *know* what I'm supposed to do. I don't go very often [now]; because first of all, to me, there should only be one church, because there's only one God. And I believe in all religions

and I don't criticize religions. And I can't see a Methodist criticizing a Catholic; it used to be one time a Catholic wouldn't go inside any other church but their own church—all that sort of stuff, and I don't go for that. I just have faith in everything that's right and good. That's the way I believe. And I don't hold no malice. I get hurt more than to hold malice.

But for many newer families, the African-American churches formed the core of a cohesive and sensible social universe. And just as the spirituals had taught an allegory of moral redemption in the nineteenth century, the gospel music and the spiritual message in twentieth-century churches spread a philosophy of Christ-inspired accommodation that helped some adjust to the inequity and limitation that so characterized African-American secular life. Harry Gramling's grandmother, Anne Russ, experienced a conversion that helped to explain her commitment to the infant Mount Calvary Church of God in Christ.

My grandmother was totally a church woman. . . . Her whole life, daily, was God. She says she was a pretty mean lady and everybody feared her in Florida—the stories that she'd tell about herself, if you walked past her, you'd come to attention like a soldier. But somebody led her to the Lord. And it changed her whole outlook on people. She became one of the most beautiful women around. And her whole life changed.

Virginia Peek described a similar release from anger.[59]

I took so much in my young days, and I'm gonna tell you the truth. I used to hate white people's gut until I learned better, until I went to going to church and listened at the preacher and then listen at the Bible and knowed you cannot hate if you want to try and make it with God. And I have changed a lot, a *whole* lot, you understand? And so this is the reason why I'm trying now, too. I not just, what you say, completely over it, but I just thank God I'm over it a whole lot. I thank God for it, you know, because a white person couldn't tell me nothin' because they have done me so bad.

The first struggles of a new civil rights movement in their native South had given Geneva's new African-American residents ideas about society and equity that the disappointing reality of northern life had only amplified. In the churches, these ideas could be expressed both allegorically and, as civil rights became a national is-sue, directly.[60] In Geneva's modern-day black churches, songs such as "The Lord Will Make a Way Somehow" express comment on pres-ent-day, secular political reality as much as they express what Du Bois once called "faith in the ultimate justice of things":

> Like a ship that's tossed and driven,
> Battered by an angry sea,
> When the storms of life are raging,
> And their fury fall on me,
> Oh, I wonder what I've done
> That makes this race so hard to run,
> Then I say to my soul, be patient,
> For the Lord will make a way somehow.
>
> Try to do my best in service,
> I try to live the best that I can.
> When I choose to do the right thing,
> Evil turns up on every hand.
> So many nights I toss in pain,
> Wondering what the day will bring,
> Then I say to my soul, take courage,
> For the Lord will make a way somehow.
>
> I'm often misunderstood,
> Out of all the good I try to do.
> I go to my friends for consolation,
> And find them complaining too.
> I look up and wonder why,
> Good fortune always passes me by,
> Then I say to my soul, don't you worry,
> For the Lord will make a way somehow.

Historians have often interpreted African-American churches North and South as polities, places in which blacks could govern themselves, build civic capacity, and organize efforts to help the larger community of which the church was part.[61] Political leader-ship indeed emerged in the post–World War II churches, just as it had in black churches before the Civil War. But perhaps more im-portantly, the churches were moral centers, the only places in which African Americans could safely express their long-term moral griev-ance with American society. DuBois called the church "peculiarly the expression of the inner ethical life of a people in a sense seldom true elsewhere," a people for whom the biblical prophecy that the meek should inherit the earth had a genuine secular meaning. Church was the place where the prophecy could be ritually enacted, the place where blacks in fact could express and share a sense, virtually everlasting, of moral superiority over whites. Emancipation celebrations and school exhibitions permitted the occasional articulation of such sentiment, but only in church could such notions be expressed regularly. And even if it should never be possible to earn their rightful share of a society they helped to build, at least African Americans should have the spiritual certainty of knowing and affirming in church the validity of their claim—a certainty they might believe whites would be eternally denied, both in this world and in any other.

Accommodation and Action

The battles over integrated churches and schools formed one particular, local expression of an overarching preoccupation with the question whether, as the Quaker William Thornton put it in 1786, there could be "sincere union between the whites and the Negroes."[1] Between the Revolution and the Civil War, the question took shape in the debates about slavery and suffrage, on the one hand, and colonization on the other. Originally a movement that embraced a broad spectrum of racial attitudes, colonization ultimately became the conservative position of those who believed integration neither desirable nor possible.

The efforts of those who opposed slavery and supported integration diverged on a fundamental point—whether black Americans had immediate right and claim to citizenship or somehow had to be prepared for it. The Union victory and ensuing equal rights amendments made integration the law of the land, suppressed the colonizationist impulse, and erased the ostensible need for black political organization. But white reaction to the real possibilities of integration stiffened existing social and economic constraints on the lives of blacks, who had been virtually bereft of national leadership in the postwar years. In Geneva, as blacks witnessed the decline in their numbers and unprecedented white hostility and resistance to school integration, their political life was reduced to the sporadic emancipation celebration.

In the 1890s, even that tradition fell away, and in the twentieth century the disappointing and sometimes grisly consequences of legal integration gave rise to new expressions of old questions. Booker T. Washington revived the gradualist argument as the grip of Jim

Crow tightened on the South and white terrorism was on the rise. The same events generated two anti-gradualist movements. Colonization now emerged as black nationalism, the radical advocacy of willed segregation articulated by Marcus Garvey's United Negro Improvement Association. The integrationist National Association for the Advancement of Colored People renewed the claims for immediate and total enfranchisement of blacks in America. But if Geneva's African Americans took positions on these issues, there remains no record of them, and their relationship to white benevolence gradually changed from cooperative to dependent in the early decades of the century.

Yet accommodation probably signified not so much the slavishly passive subscription to white ideals as the deliberate and considered assessment of the possibilities of action in any given local situation. The question whether African-American dedication to white values was genuine is impossible to answer on the basis of historical evidence; there is, in fact, much evidence that suggests that it was not.[2] Accommodation may have been little more than a recognition of the necessity to demonstrate shared values in order to make progress in larger ways. James W. Duffin was well aware of Gerrit Smith's interest in temperance when he complained to him about intemperance in western New York. Jason Jeffrey knew it was imprudent for Charles Lenox Remond, an African-American lecturer employed by the Western New York Anti-Slavery Society in 1848, to be spending his time dancing rather than lecturing; he wrote Henry Bush, a white stove dealer and antislavery activist in Rochester, to complain of Remond's "triping the 'light fantastic toe'" when "he had ought to teach better things."[3] It cannot be known whether Duffin and Jeffrey were actually opposed to such frivolities as drinking and dancing; it is only clear that they professed to oppose them before whites who favored political causes of larger significance to African Americans generally.

At different historical moments, Geneva's African Americans contemplated their local situation and took its measure. They continually assessed and reassessed how open or closed local white society was, when it would allow them to take direct political action on their own behalf and when it would not. And when it did not, accommodation became a strategy, not a mindset—a means to an end, not a hapless end in itself. As a racial and statistical minority, for African Americans it was always a question of how much accommodation was necessary in order to live a stable life. At some times, local circumstances and the political climate of the region and the country made action to improve the quality and opportunities of life for themselves and their children seem possible. Some sought broader improvement for their neighbors and their race generally. At other times, direct political action seemed only to promise to encumber them further, to heap liability upon fundamental disadvantage, and accommodation then seemed to be the only logical route to security. These issues cycled through the lives of individuals as they did through the history of the local population and of the country.

James W. Duffin and Antebellum Activism

Before the Civil War, James W. Duffin struggled with the uncomfortable intersection of race and nationality, and his political life revealed the odd combination of optimism and desperation that characterized antebellum African-American political activity generally. Duffin knew and worked with nearly every African American who fought for equal rights before the Civil War; the presence of him and others like him in Geneva probably attracted antebellum African-American leaders, all of whom are today better known than he, to the village (fig. 44). Like many of these men and women, he either did not know or deliberately concealed the date and place of his birth.[4] He was probably one of two sons of John and Susannah Duffin, who had come to Geneva from Canada by 1829. Living in James's High Street home in 1855, Susannah Duffin claimed her birthplace as Maryland; it is possible that the Duffins were American fugitives.

By 1829, John Duffin lived on High Street next door to the fugitive slave Aaron Lucas, and James was among the students in the First Presbyterian Church's African-American Sunday school. In 1840, John and James Duffin had both become incorporators of the Union Religious Society. In that year, too, James Duffin signed a call for a statewide convention of African Americans in Albany (the first such convention ever held in the United States), and he was one of ten—and one of only two from communities west of Utica—appointed to the convention's business committee. Duffin was also a subscription agent for the New York City newspaper *Colored American* and was probably a member of the Geneva Colored Anti-Slavery Society, of which no local record exists.[5]

In the 1840s, Duffin's main political interest was equal suffrage. He was undoubtedly responsible for having convened the first free

STATE
OF
STEUBEN,
And So Forth.
A Two Days'
MASS MEETING
Will be holden at
PRATTSBURG, on
Tuesday & Wednesday,
29th & 30th inst., com-
mencing at 10, A. M.,
on the 29th.
Another at **BATH**,
on *Friday & Saturday,*
June 1st & 2nd, and
at **CORNING**, on
Monday & Tuesday, 3d
and 4th of June.
And at **ELMIRA**,
*Wednesday & Thurs-
day*, 5th & 6th of June.
**H. H. GARNET, S.
R. WARD**, and others
will attend.

44. "A Two Days' Mass Meeting," advertisement in *Impartial Citizen*, 23 May 1849. Ward and Garnet were cousins, fugitives, and, for a time, Genevans. In December 1843, a disease "of the uvula and tonsils" threatened Ward's effectiveness, and he moved to Geneva from South Butler to be treated and to study medicine with "Doctors William and Bell." While there, he sometimes spoke "to a small church in Geneva" and then, in 1844, began lecturing in support of Gerrit Smith's Liberty Party. *Reproduction courtesy American Antiquarian Society, Worcester, Mass.*

suffrage meeting of New York's African Americans at Geneva on 8 September 1845; he served as secretary to this convention, as he had for the national colored people's convention at Buffalo two years earlier.[6] In 1849, he sat on the committee that nominated candidates for state offices on Gerrit Smith's antislavery Liberty party ticket. At the 1853 national convention in Rochester, Duffin was appointed to the eight-man New York State Council of Colored People; with Jermain W. Loguen of Syracuse, he was one of two delegates from the vast region west of Albany. In 1855, Duffin was one of a group of black New Yorkers who organized the New York State Suffrage Association and was one of five appointed to the association's board of managers at its September meeting in Troy.[7]

Even after the passage of the Fugitive Slave Law, Duffin seemed optimistic about the possibilities for African-American advancement in the region. At the 1855 National Council of Colored People meeting in New York City, Duffin argued with Douglass about whether blacks in western New York needed or could afford a trade school. He asserted that the "failure" of the manual labor system established at Oberlin and the Whitesboro (Utica) schools resulted not from "the attempt to blend mechanics with the classics" but from the "admission of a sort of *lily*-fingered aristocracy, which degraded the labor whence income should be derived, and drove the poorer and more substantial students hence." And he recognized that the political climate of his own region had changed for the worse. His observation that in Ontario County, "the pro-slavery county of New York[,] the Abolitionists have abandoned our ground to the heathen," perhaps referred to the fact that county voters in 1846 had overwhelmingly defeated an effort to remove the property qualification for black suffrage.[8]

Duffin's position on suffrage no doubt led to his long involvement with Gerrit Smith, whose Liberty party he continued to support when other blacks had turned to the Republicans.[9] The 1846 referendum had grown out of the state constitutional convention that year, and the tendency of the convention probably inspired one of Smith's greatest philanthropic gestures. Smith had inherited thousands of acres in New York State from his father, a fur trader and speculator who had been partners with John Jacob Astor. In an August 1846 letter to Charles B. Ray (former editor of the *Colored American*), James McCune Smith, and the Reverend Theodore S. Wright, all of whom lived in New York City, Smith announced his intention to make three thousand deeds, each from forty to sixty acres, of land "acquired principally by my father" to unpropertied African-American men in the populous urban area in and around New York City. After long deliberation about whether to give the deeds to "the meritorious poor generally" or to "the meritorious colored poor," Smith chose in the end to give the land to blacks, even though he abhorred on principle putting "a bounty on color." The state's black Americans were, he wrote, "the poorest of the poor, and the most deeply wronged class of our citizens," and he acknowledged that their "mean and wicked exclusion" from the rolls of eligible voters "has had no little effect in producing my preference, in this case."[10]

Smith asked Ray, McCune Smith, and Wright to provide the names of 1985 African Americans between the ages of twenty-one and sixty who lived in twelve downstate counties, who were not property owners or "in easy circumstances as to property," and who were not "drunkards." But intemperate behavior and the patent unwillingness of many to leave their urban homes kept the men from reaching Smith's quota, at which point he extended the land offer to African Americans in other parts of the state through such leaders as Samuel Ward, who had just moved to Cortland from Geneva. Ward appointed Duffin to determine who in Ontario, Yates, Seneca, and Livingston counties deserved to receive the deeds.[11]

Early in September 1846, Duffin sent Smith a list of western New Yorkers, including forty-one names from Ontario County. Austin Steward, then a resident of Canandaigua, was among them, as was William Wells Brown, then living in Farmington between Canandaigua and Geneva. Several days after sending the list, Duffin wrote again to explain why he had not included the name of Henry N. Baker, a blacksmith who had evidently complained to Smith of his exclusion, and to assure Smith that he and his African-American neighbors were genuinely devoted to the temperance movement.

> I should have ben glad to have sent his [name] and others were it nor for thier love of strong drink previous to recieveing Brother Wards letter informing me of my apointment we had got in fine opperation a division of the Philantropic Order of the Sons of Temperance numbering some 20 members in the place and some 8 or 10 in adjoining Countys in edeavering to enlist all of our people here in the temperance cause we had conversations with all of our people so that we obtained thier views with regard to Temperance before we heard anything of your noble gift amongst our strongest opponents was this H. N. Baker and a few others that are urgeing

him on. I know that as I set myself about this work that I should
call down upon my head the curses and misrepresentations of all
that were not qualified to be reported to you instead of chargeing
thier loss to thier evil propensities they charge it to partiality and a
desire to crush the poor &c.

Duffin claimed that organized temperance activity accounted for
his success in delivering the requested number of names only from
Ontario County and not from the others he had been asked to can-
vass. He explained how the names of the twenty-eight Genevans on
the list had been selected.

we drew the names in the presence of a room full of our most
respectable citizens contained in the list are the names of 5 or 6
men that have each of them a house and lot but upon each there
are mortgages varying from $200.00 to $500.00 dollars I suposed
that such could not be considered in easy circumstances. . . . I
cannot express to you Sir the gratitude that our people feel towards
you for this very Benevolent gift. You have confered upon us a
temperal blessing which will never no never be forgotten.[12]

All of the Geneva men, including Duffin, were granted lots in
the towns of Totten and Crossfield in Hamilton County, part of the
still lightly settled Adirondack Park wilderness.[13] But the 1850 and
1860 Hamilton County censuses show none of the African-American
grantees from Geneva as residents; in fact, only Duffin is known to
have taken Smith's offer of settlement seriously. In March 1847, he
wrote to tell Smith that his wife had just had "a fine little son,"
whom they chose to name Gerrit Smith Duffin, and to ask that his
son's name be substituted for his own on the deed Smith had earlier
sent him.[14] And, after Smith announced his intention to transfer a
different parcel to Duffin in 1849, Duffin wrote, "I thank you kindly
for the interest you have taken in my behalf, having made up my
mind to go upon my land I feel very grateful for the exchange."
Several weeks later, he asked Smith to deed to him the lot intended
for Elder William Thompson, who by that time had left Geneva. "If
the lot intended for Elder Thompson lies next to mine you may put
it to me and when I sell out here I will pay you for it it will be just
about enough for me and my five little boys," Duffin wrote.[15]

In the end, even Duffin chose not to settle his Hamilton County
land. In 1850, he was one of the three largest African-American

property holders in Geneva, and he operated a barber shop in the first building north of the Franklin House, then the village's most fashionable and trafficked hotel. His sons Theodore, James, and Henry were barbers as well, two of them still contributing their incomes to the High Street household. After W. H. A. Bissell started St. Philip's Mission at the High Street district school, Duffin and his family became Episcopalians, and they continued to be active in black politics. While Duffin attended suffrage meetings and colored people's conventions, his wife was one of four African-American women representing Geneva on a committee formed to raise funds in support of Ward's Syracuse newspaper *Impartial Citizen* at both the 1849 Auburn emancipation celebration and the New York State Fair that year.[16]

Before the Civil War, the Duffins were only one part of a thriving group of African Americans in the village that supported its own pastors, churches, schools, benevolent societies, and political activists. Noah Polk and Jason Jeffrey, a porter at Rochester's Eagle Tavern who had moved to Geneva in 1840, also attended the 1843 national convention at Buffalo. Polk, a drayman born in Delaware, is said to have written a letter to a newspaper, probably between 1845 and 1849, disavowing any relationship with the Democratic President James Knox Polk. Jeffrey was a subscription agent for the *North Star* in 1848, and he served on the executive committee of the Western New York Anti-Slavery Society in the same year. His wife, Mary Ann, served with Duffin's wife, Charlotte, Charles Peyton Lucas's wife, Catherine, and Julia Condol on the *Impartial Citizen* fundraising committee in 1849; in 1853, MaryAnn Jeffrey was the only female delegate to the national colored people's convention at Rochester, an event sufficiently novel that Frederick Douglass mentioned it in a letter to Gerrit Smith a week after the July meeting. Julia Condol's father, William, was also a subscription agent for Douglass's newspapers. Condol, James Duffin, and his son Theodore were contributors to Douglass's periodicals; and in her biographical sketch in Geneva historian George Conover's 1893 county history, George J. Bland's wife, Mary Jane, was described as "a coworker with Frederick Douglass in the anti-slavery cause, and . . . much interested in the elevation of her people, the colored race."[17]

But the events of the 1850s took their toll on African Americans in Geneva and the region. Henry Highland Garnet, his wife, and other Genevans (perhaps including Aaron Lucas and his daughter, Nancy) left Geneva, bound eventually for Jamaica. In the 1840s,

Duffin had decried "any system of general emigration offered to our people, as calculated to throw us into a state of restlessness, to break up all those settled habits which would otherwise attach us to the soil, and to furnish our enemies with arguments to urge our removal from the land of our birth."[18] But by the mid–1850s, he was one among many who had begun to look favorably on colonization, and by 1861 he announced his intention to emigrate to Haiti.

Duffin's life bore personal evidence of the pushes and pulls of the issue of colonization, which had preoccupied every colored people's convention before the Civil War. Thornton asserted in fact that "sincere union" between whites and blacks was not possible, and this conviction had given birth to a diffuse coalition of interests that aimed to colonize blacks in Africa or in an unsettled part of the North American continent. Before 1815, blacks in Boston, Providence, New Bedford, Philadelphia, and other cities supported and participated in efforts to interest American blacks in African repatriation. In 1816, the American Colonization Society was founded to raise funds to compensate slaveowners for the loss of slaves then sent to Africa. In 1821, the society founded Liberia, the country in which it aimed to resettle American blacks.[19]

The American Colonization Society was founded on contrasting impulses, and by the 1830s it had lost the support of most blacks and many whites. Originally, its membership had included such men as Gerrit Smith; the Quaker Benjamin Lundy, whose *Genius of Universal Emancipation* had inspired William Lloyd Garrison's *Liberator*; and Theodore Weld, who had been converted by Charles Grandison Finney and whose explication of the British debates about slavery and West Indian emancipation influenced many American philanthropists. But it also included Henry Clay, a Kentucky slaveholder who at the society's first meeting characterized blacks as "a dangerous and useless part of the community." As Clay and other southerners gained control of the society, its initial association with benevolence was severed, and African Americans regarded the society with patent disdain. In a speech to the British and Foreign Anti-Slavery Society in the 1850s, Garnet commented upon the irony of the name "Liberia" and charged that benevolence was merely a cloak under which the society concealed its real aims:

> May we estimate the American Colonisation scheme by its president and officers? Who are its chief supporters? Slaveholders and their apologists. Who is its president and great supporter? A slave-

holder! and the most consistent hater of the black race in all the land. Yes, and more, the advocate of the late Fugitive Bill—Henry Clay of Kentucky. This man is the popular president of the American Colonization Society. This Society has encouraged outrage and oppression toward the coloured people, and in their affliction they deceitfully come up, and with smiles say, "Now had you not better go to Africa?" And when the coloured man replied that he would rather remain in his native country, they would urge the matter more persuasively, saying, "But don't you see that the laws are against you, and therefore you had better go?" Why, who made these laws? The very men who would be first to transport them! The Daniel Websters, and Henry Clays, and such-like men, slave-owners, with their hundreds of slaves—these were the men who made the laws, and would then transport the black man that he might be freed from their operation![20]

At least since the 1840s, African Americans had recognized that while the American Colonization Society might have been "established upon pure motives, . . . its subsequent operations show that it has been fostered and sustained by the *murderous spirit of slavery* and prejudice." The 1843 convention registered a vote of no confidence in the society and vowed that "neither persuasion, intrigue or physical force" could drive free blacks from the United States. In Geneva, African Americans had made their own symbolic claim by asking that the name of Liberia Street be changed to Bland Street.[21]

A sense of obligation to blacks still in bondage also fueled African-American resistance to colonization, and the necessity to fight against slavery continued to motivate such leaders as Douglass, even when others had come to view colonization as the only path to full freedom.[22] Like Garnet, Ward, Crummell, Brown, and Martin Delany had left the United States by the early 1850s, and Delany had written and circulated a pamphlet advocating the establishment of a black stronghold in the Caribbean. The Haitian government and African-American leaders had by then renewed an earlier campaign to interest American blacks in settling the island nation.[23] Within months of the publication of Delany's pamphlet, Garnet and his family settled in Jamaica, and by the following June he published his own call for seventy black emigrants to Jamaica in both the *New York Tribune* and *Frederick Douglass' Paper*. By the end of 1853, Garnet was reported to have started two day schools and a female industrial school run by his wife, Julia, and a "Mrs. Lucas," possibly Nancy Lucas, whose biographical sketch in an 1893 county history notes that she taught two years with Garnet and another twenty-five years in the West Indies before returning to the United States in 1878.[24]

In the 1850s, new arguments in support of colonization may have helped turn the tide of African-American opinion on the subject, even among those who continued to feel an obligation, as Douglass did, "to labor and suffer with the oppressed in my native land."[25] James M. Redpath, the white general agent of emigration for the Haitian government in 1859, argued that African Americans should settle in Haiti not only to prove their ability to govern themselves but also to compete economically with the American South.

> Would you fight Virginia with a weapon that she will fear as much as she dreaded the rifles of John Brown? Grow tobacco in Haiti then, and fight her with it on the Liverpool exchanges. Would you retaliate on the Carolinas? . . . The way is open. Tar and cotton them in England. Haiti could produce enough sugar to drive Louisiana out of every market in the world, could raise cotton enough to corrupt the morals of a hundred generations of American politicians, could raise rice enough to bury Wilmington, Charleston and Savannah out of sight.[26]

Arguments like Redpath's were influential. The national colored people's convention in Cleveland in 1854 endorsed Delany's pamphlet and thus became the first convention to advocate colonization, although at least one earlier convention had attempted to raise money to support a fugitive slave colony in Canada. African Americans organized the first National Emigration Convention, which took place in Cleveland in the same year. Garnet returned to the United States in 1856 and lectured all over upstate New York—including to a group of seven to eight thousand assembled at Clifton Springs—in support of emigration to both Haiti and Africa. Douglass, still opposed in principle to colonization, wrote in 1858 that those blacks who felt they must leave ought to choose Haiti because of its proximity to the United States; by 1861, his frustration with Lincoln's reluctance to support abolition over union and the Republican party's failure to take a stand against slavery moved him ultimately to endorse the Haitian emigration movement.[27]

Duffin was among the 1,573 African Americans who emigrated to Haiti between 1858 and mid-1862. In November 1861, he wrote Gerrit Smith from St. Mark about his new situation.

You will recolect that when you called on me in Geneva last spring I told you that I was a going to Hayti, acordingly through the good providence of God I arrived here on the second inst.

I am much pleased with the country it is emphaticaly the "land of the free and the home of the brave" its soil is rich and productive, its inhabitants kind hearted polite and sociable. the country here seems to be one vast wilderness and needs thousands of emigrants here to till the soil they are coming from the States and Canadas very fast, three vessels with about four hundred emigrants came over at the same time that we did and I think a larger number will come in the next embarkation.

The Haytien Government however is a slow "coach" and do not facilatate things fast enough to suit the emigrants and many become disatisfied and impatient before they get thier lands. with right management however I think the movement will result in great good both to the government and to our people.

We sacraficed evry thing in getting here and are comparitavely destitute until we get on our lands and get a crop. Should you feel it in your heart to aid a poor emigrant in this Foreign land, I will tell you what I most need. viz. Flour (I lost a barrell on the way) an old one horse wagon and harness and a small plough, flour here is eight cents pr pound and the other things are not to be had if we had money to buy them.

Duffin and Curlin were evidently not the only Genevans to abandon the United States before the Civil War. Sarah H. Bradford, Harriet Tubman's biographer, wrote in her 1862 history of Geneva that "the rage for emigration has . . . seized upon the little hamlet known as the 'Colored Settlement'. . . . a number have already left for Hayti; while others are making preparations to leave for Liberia."[28] But by May of that year, only one-third of those who had emigrated to Haiti remained on the island.[29] Like many others, Duffin had fallen ill in the hot climate, and by June 1863 he wrote from New York City to William H. Seward, the Auburn attorney who befriended Tubman and was then Lincoln's Secretary of State.

Dear Sir
I think it very probale that you will not recolect me when you see my name but sufice it to say that I am an old friend and [illegible] of yours.

I went to the Island of Hayti two years ago; to raise cotton was taken sick with the fever laid sick for several months lost my first crop and evry thing that I had and returned to this country poor and peniless.

My objet in writing to you is to see if you will not get me a situation in some office under the government in Washington. Col. C. A. Seward tells me that there are several colored men employed there in good situations. I can give you the best of recommendations from Gentlemen in Geneva my former home and birth place and also Gentlemen in this city. I can do any kind of work that will pay well.[30]

The benevolent impulses that had helped found the American Colonization Society seemed to reemerge, albeit in a more conservative form, in the 1850s and 1860s colonization movement. Harriet Beecher Stowe and Abraham Lincoln supported colonization, and a committee of the House of Representatives had proclaimed in 1862 that "the retention of the Negro among us with half privileges is but a bitter mockery to him, and . . . our duty is to find for him a congenial home and country." Still, African-American leaders continued to question the motives of white colonizationists; the 1862 colored people's convention in Boston officially resolved "that when we wish to leave the United States we can find and pay for that territory which shall suit us best. Resolved, that when we are ready to leave, we shall be able to pay our own expenses of travel. Resolved, that we don't want to go now. Resolved, that if anybody else wants us to go, they must compel us."[31]

B. F. Cleggett and the Rise of White Patronage

After 1863, Duffin's whereabouts are unknown, and as his example grew obscure to local African Americans, Benjamin F. Cleggett's arose in its place. Cleggett was connected to the political life of the antebellum black community both by predilection and by his marriage to the sister of black abolitionist William C. Nell. But his later career relied heavily on his reputation among and contacts with influential white people, and his life encapsulates the shifting political life of black Americans in the region during and after the Civil War. A barber like Duffin, Cleggett was born in 1828 in Dutchess County, New York, and settled in Rochester as a child. The family went to Canada in 1836 but returned to Rochester in 1847. Cleggett moved to Geneva in 1858, and as war came upon the country he was the village's chief African-American proponent of raising black regiments. Lincoln had abandoned his support of colonization only as the lengthening war persuaded him of the greater necessity to use African Americans to supplement Union forces and unsettle the Confederacy, and upon the heels of the Emancipation Proclamation black leaders mobilized to recruit troops throughout the Northeast for Massachusetts's Fifty-fourth and Fifty-fifth Colored Regiments.

Cleggett was Douglass's Geneva contact in this effort. In March or April 1863, immediately after Douglass had come to the village to urge blacks to enlist, Cleggett enrolled seventeen potential recruits, none of whom actually were mustered into either regiment.[32] But eventually, after repeated pleas from African-American New Yorkers had created federal colored regiments in New York over the opposition of Democratic Governor Horatio Seymour, half of the African-American men eligible for service in Geneva did join the Union forces.[33] In September 1864, Cleggett, then thirty-five and the father of five children, joined the Union navy, which had always accepted free blacks into service despite at least one federal order prohibiting the practice. He served as a landsman (that is, not a sailor) on five Union vessels and was discharged in October 1865. Acknowledging Cleggett's return, the *Gazette* noted that "a host of friends, his former customers," would quickly rebuild his barbering trade at "the old stand."

The activism that characterized the African-American community in Geneva before the war existed afterward, but not in the same form, and not for long. The ratification of the equal rights amendments after the war seemed to remove the justification for the colored people's convention movement, and, of all the leaders of African-American political life in upstate New York before the war, only Douglass still lived in the area. Clearly, the region was no longer a political center. Population shifts literally moved idealism westward, and urbanization relocated political activity in large cities. Their political leaders gone and their political crusades ostensibly won, the African Americans of upstate New York faced a society changed for the worse by the Civil War. Their political rights guaranteed, their social claims faced more rigid resistance.

There is no evidence that Cleggett took part in the battles over school integration in the early 1870s, but he was active in the Ontario Debating Club and the annual emancipation celebrations, the only other signs of postwar political vitality among Geneva's African Americans (fig. 45). From 1840, two years after the first such celebration took place in Utica, through 1892, Geneva played host to at

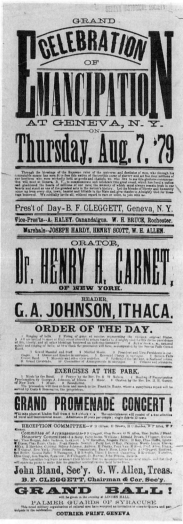

45. "Grand Celebration of Emancipation at Geneva, N.Y.," 1879. Illness prevented Garnet from attending the 1879 celebration, whose honorary committee included Lockport's Theodore Morgan, who married Arabella, daughter of Geneva hackman William T. Brown, and Benjamin F. Cleggett's son, who lived in Boston. *Courtesy Geneva Historical Society.*

least eight of these huge regional meetings. They usually took place in early August, and they were always a ritual protest of the Fourth of July, an independence day for whites but not, blacks pointed out, for them.[34] The celebrations continued to commemorate West Indian emancipation even after the American emancipation took place partly because the absence of complete freedom among American blacks also survived the 1860s.

The emancipation celebrations usually contained overt political protest, but the white community seemed to read them in ways that effectively sanctioned them. As Douglass recognized before the war, they were the indulgence that white New Yorkers permitted their black brethren, much as plantation owners permitted slaves a Christmas season of luxury and indolence that temporarily inverted the normal course of penury and unrewarded labor. In 1827, the year of New York State manumission, African Americans in Ithaca hosted a parade and celebration on 5 July, a day when, according to the *Ithaca Chronicle*, "every man must be his own servant for the day; and many fair hands are constrained to engage in culinary and household matters."[35] Douglass described the 1859 celebration in Geneva.

> The great good nature and boisterous merriment of the colored people, as they passed to and fro, or stood in groups about the streets, shaking hands, laughing and talking, though at times not over regardful of good taste, seemed to awaken in the white people a good deal of mirth, but it was mirth without malice. The little extravagances into which a few of our people are apt to fall on such occasions, are much more painful to the judicious among ourselves than to the white people who may witness them. To many of us the first of August is like the white man's 4th of July—a day of freedom from ordinary restraints, when every man may seek his happiness in his own way, and without any marked concern for the ordinary rules of decorum. There were a few at Geneva who carried this 4th of Julyism a little too far, but they were the exceptions. The masses conducted themselves with propriety as well as freedom.[36]

Nine years before, "Achilles," a correspondent to the *Impartial Citizen*, worried similarly that African Americans played into the hands of a pessimistic and venal white majority on emancipation days. Instead of traveling to celebrations at which they tended "to copy the vice instead of the virtue of their oppressors," he advised blacks to keep their money out of the pockets of white stage lines, railroads, hotels, and restaurants and celebrate instead "in their own localities, and in a national manner."[37] But the meaning of these large regional gatherings justified for most the expense associated with attending them. They were social events featuring "all the paraphernalia of a well-regulated celebration," such as food stands, dances, and lake excursions.[38] But they were also political events, the only occasions at which African Americans throughout the region could discover not only how numerous they were but how their experiences differed from community to community as well. They featured pointed political addresses by the best-known and most eloquent African Americans of their time.

Emancipation celebrations were probably the single most meaningful annual event for black Americans, far outweighing the colored people's conventions in popularity. At the 1859 celebration in Geneva, a local African-American minstrel group sang antislavery songs, Jason Jeffrey read the act by which England had freed West Indians, and Douglass presented an address that, among other things, lambasted local Presbyterians for denying celebrants use of the church in case of rain. In 1860, when Geneva again hosted the August celebration, Douglass spoke for nearly three hours. He reprinted the entire text of his address in the September 1860 *Douglass' Monthly*, but none of Geneva's 1860 newspapers even mentioned the fact that the emancipation celebration had taken place. White newspapers almost never recorded the content of emancipation day orations, and when they did it tended only to be in the service of their own political sympathies. In 1868, when Douglass again presented the major address in Geneva, the *Gazette* described the oration as "at times . . . quite bitter, at others jovial," noted Douglass's distrust of President Andrew Johnson and suspicions about the political leanings of Chief Justice Salmon P. Chase, and then observed that Douglass "expressed great confidence in the friendship of Grant towards the black race, and wound up by expressing hope in his election next fall—all which will be properly blasted." The only time the *Gazette* ever quoted an African American's oration directly was in 1881, when Frederick Stuart expressed his views about the usefulness of African Americans in cotton fields and foundries, and his belief that "the mission of the American republic is to raise up . . . dark types" such as the Chinese, the American Indian, and the African.[39]

White newspapers like the *Gazette* were much more likely to regard emancipation celebrations as displays, almost as theater. White people were literal spectators as thousands of black people gathered for services, parades, lectures, and dances. In 1859, three thousand African Americans converged on Geneva, then a village of only forty-eight hundred people. In 1881, the *Gazette* reported that the village was "quite full of colored people and strangers." In the face of the overwhelming presence of such large numbers of African-American people, statistically and socially negligible in everyday village life, whites perhaps found it untenable to think of these gatherings as anything else but theater. After all, a stage was set, actors populated it, several acts transpired. In 1864, the *Gazette* editors were invited to the celebration's evening ball and sat on the stage at Linden Hall, "where a good view of the situation could be had without the aid of field glasses."[40] No matter that these celebrations sometimes lasted several days; like a play, they did end.

By turning these events into drama, whites defused their political content—indeed, their reality. The language that the editors of the short-lived *Geneva Ledger* used in announcing the 1859 celebration revealed their inclination to think of the event in terms of its performance value. "The colored folks expect to have a 'gay' time on Monday next, in Geneva," they reported. "Excursions, Promenades, Orations, Dances, Eating and Drinking, will be the order of the day and evening. A steam-boat will convey persons too [*sic*] and from the head of Seneca Lake at half fare."[41] White people were not listening to political addresses. They were audiences at staged "orations" where they attended as much to the style of presentation as to its content, much as they did at school exhibitions. They watched blacks "promenade" and parade; even "eating and drinking" were spectacles, as though the celebrants, like Ethiopian minstrels, played roles and used props specifically for the enjoyment of white people.

Even so, blacks realized, whites stood witness when Douglass, Garnet, and Sojourner Truth spoke. In Geneva in 1860, in his first public appearance since he returned from England only months before, Douglass extolled the beneficence of Great Britain, which had emancipated the British West Indies. "How striking and humiliating is the contrast in respect to slavery, between England and America, the mother and the daughter!" Douglass proclaimed. "If the merits of republican institutions, as against those of a monarchy, were made to depend upon the character and history of the American Republic, monarchical institutions would most certainly bear off the palm. . . . The American Government is worse than winking at the slave trade, and slavers are fitted out in sight of our business men's prayer meetings." Douglass continued to criticize the United States before a crowd of thousands, both black and white, and he closed his three-hour address with a final slap at the Dred Scott decision and a tribute to John Brown, hanged seven months earlier for his armed raid at Harper's Ferry.[42]

African Americans had long recognized that because whites regarded the emancipation celebrations and school exhibitions as curiosities, they could use them as a forum to demonstrate the error of white ways of thinking. In 1849, Garnet had used the High Street school exhibition to point out the accomplishments of other African-American leaders, and Nell touted the more dignified manner in which the event had transpired compared to white school exhibitions in the same village. In 1873, William Kenney formally invited the village council to attend that year's celebration, surely so that they might witness Cleggett's ritual recital of the civil rights legislation New York State had passed only months before and George J. Bland's excoriating address about blacks' failed attempt to integrate the Classical and Union School.[43] Teaching in Aberdeen, Mississippi, in 1866, Nathan Condol described, with some skepticism, how local white leaders reacted to an exhibition at his freedmen's school.

> Several of the distinguished Gentlemen of the City were present . . . all of whom spoke encouragingly to the gathering, which numbered, perhaps, 800, or more. They expressed themselves to be greatly surprised, yet highly pleased with the progress the scholars had made during so short a period (three months) and also remarked, that even now, *our* school would compare favorably with any school in the state, white or black, *some* informed me that *they* went for the purpose of having *fun*, but I assure you their *fun* was of a different character, than they expected.[44]

For the white community, the "free day" that the West Indian emancipation celebrations symbolized was permissible because it was ephemeral, and they distanced themselves from their political meaning by ogling their social aspects. The *Geneva Advertiser* forewarned Genevans that the 1881 celebration would be a "grand 'blow-out'"; afterwards, the *Gazette* reported the "amusements" during the day—excursions on Seneca Lake, carriage rides "in the suburbs," a concert of "colored native and foreign talent" at Linden Hall. There was also "a street promenade," and at ten o'clock celebrants gathered at Linden Hall for a dance that the *Gazette* described in detail. The *Advertiser* reported later, "The colored people didn't begin to 'grow tired' until Friday afternoon, when the natural element broke loose and they made the streets resound with their musical demonstrations—all in perfect peace, however."[45]

Other white accounts of the efforts of Geneva's African Americans to build and express political solidarity were similarly patronizing. The equal rights amendments inspired the *Gazette* to make tongue-in-cheek references to black Americans by using the old antislavery term "man and brother," and to refer to the members of the Ontario Debating Club as "our 'feller-citizens'." It satirized the "grave and important" nature of the resolution it had chosen for its public debate against Penn Yan, and those parts of the debate it endeavored to quote appeared in dialect—*wid* for *with*, *ob* for *of*, *nuffin* for *nothing*. When the African-American debating club had first formed in 1853, the year the High Street district school finally opened and Bissell began St. Philip's Mission, the New York City weekly *Brother Jonathan* wrote similarly: "In the lonely village of Geneva, New York, the 'cullerd pussons,' in emulation of their white brethren, recently formed a Debating Society for the purpose of improving their minds by the discussion of instructive and entertaining topics," among them whether the layer or hatcher of a chicken's egg was the real mother of the chicken.[46]

But Cleggett's debating club minutes of the 1870s establish that African Americans quite often argued issues of political immediacy and importance; usually, they simply chose not to air these questions before crowds of whites. In 1871, they took the stage in the wake of equal rights amendments that evidently caused local whites much anxiety and that inspired both the school integration effort and its hostile reception. Club members must have surmised (probably from reading the village's leading newspaper) that Geneva's leading whites were not in the frame of mind for additional displays of the "unwarrantable pride" of black citizens. African Americans stood by as the *Gazette* took every opportunity to disparage African-American life. After the war, the newspaper called the only business block in which blacks predominated "the Freedman's Bureau." In 1872, the editors criticized "the black Douglas's speech" at Linden Hall that year, though they had frequently failed to report his many earlier visits to the village. Speaking before a "respectable audience . . . made up more than one half of *ladies*," Douglass's address contained "nothing new," the *Gazette* observed; it was in fact "threadbare trash."[47] In 1865, the newspaper insisted in an article on

African-American suffrage that "the people of America . . . will ever hold themselves as superior to the black race" and that the "laws of this country were framed for men—*white men*—and they alone should and will be the ones to see these laws carried out." It cannot have struck black or white readers as coincidental that the *Gazette* chose to precede this article with one entitled, "Diabolical Outrage at Evansville, Ind.—A White Woman Violated by Negroes—They Attempt to Murder Her."[48] In the *Gazette*'s view, just as school integration threatened chaos and miscegenation, the freedom suffrage wrought was merely license for sexual corruption and mayhem.

After the war, protest was increasingly confined to symbolic occasions. Cleggett and George J. Bland tried to take up the mantle thrown off by Duffin when he emigrated to Haiti by keeping the emancipation celebration alive in Geneva, at least for a time. Two days after the Fifteenth Amendment was ratified in 1870, Cleggett wrote to ask Gerrit Smith to serve as president of the day at a "celebration commemorative of Ratification of 15 Amendment to take place on the 5th of May next in Geneva. . . . It be a great pleasure to us to have an old tried and trusted friend." On 11 May, the day before the rescheduled celebration was to take place, the village trustees met in a special meeting to appoint "an extra police force to assist in preserving order during the celebration of the colored inhabitants which is advertised to take place in Geneva to morrow/ Thursday May 12th 1870."[49] There is no record of the village having felt compelled to increase police protection at any other emancipation celebration; perhaps the prospect of a large regional celebration so soon after African Americans had been guaranteed equal suffrage was unnerving. The *Gazette* in fact noted in a one-paragraph account of the event that "our 'cullud brethren' had possession of the town yesterday," a turn of phrase that belies concern that blacks had, however temporarily, stepped in threatening ways beyond their normal territorial confines in the village.[50]

Geneva's African Americans sponsored only five more emancipation celebrations, the last apparently in 1892. Cleggett was president of the day in 1879, the only celebration planned for central and western New York that year. In 1881, he organized another one. In January of the next year he left for Washington to work as a messenger (classified as a laborer) in Charles J. Folger's treasury department (by November, Cleggett had resigned, claiming in a letter to Folger that the position "was no longer compatible with my interest").[51] Like others in the postwar years, Cleggett appears to have turned off the antebellum path of self-reliance and toward a life strategy that relied on white patronage. By the time he returned to Geneva, most of the people who had led the equal rights movement earlier in the century were dead or had left the region. Even Douglass and his family had moved to Washington in 1872. Between 1865 and 1884, Jermain Wesley Loguen, William Henry Seward, Austin Steward, James McCune Smith, Samuel Ward, Charles Lenox Remond, Gerrit Smith, James W. Duffin, William Lloyd Garrison, Garnet, Folger, and William Wells Brown all died. Between these men and Booker T. Washington, no leader of national or regional significance emerged. No one continued to stress the importance of self-reliance the way antebellum leaders had.

Village newspapers focused increasingly on aspects of African Americans' "little culture"—the May balls, the masquerades, the sculling contests, the fund-raising concerts performed by the High Street Chapel and St. Philip's Mission choirs. Such events were often covered, probably because they threatened nothing in the order of things. In 1872, the *Gazette* announced the coming concert of the Jubilee Singers from Fisk University, whose selection of "religious, sentimental and comic, embracing old plantation melodies" were designed to demonstrate the progress that the American Missionary Association had made among southern freed people. Now more than ever, African-American people were virtually exhibited, and the presentation of their life was increasingly romanticized. To sustain themselves, Geneva's own struggling African-American organizations appear to have seen little option but to use these popular formats (figs. 46, 47). In 1876, the St. Philip's Mission choir presented a concert at Linden Hall of "the Jubilee and Moody and Sankey spiritual songs." Like the music of the Fisk Jubilee Singers, the gospel songs that American evangelists Dwight Moody and Ira Sankey assembled had been compiled specifically for white Protestant audiences after the Civil War and described a plantation culture from which all cruelty had been excised and of which all vestiges had disappeared, or so most northern whites believed. That same month, the High Street Sunday school choir sang selections from "the Hamden [sic] collection of plantation melodies and refrains, all of a religious character, quaint in language, but exceedingly beautiful in harmony" to raise money for the High Street School library.[52]

But blacks were evidently uninterested in the message of these songs and in the postwar evangelical revival in general. A "colored Chautauqua" scheduled to take place in Loomis Grove north of the

ST. PHILLIP'S MISSION

EXHIBITION.

LINDEN HALL, GENEVA,
Wednesday Evening, April 11, '77.

Programme--Part First.

1. OPENING CHORUS—"Ring dem Charming Bells,".....Sunday School
2. SONG AND CHORUS—"Still I Love thee,"............Wm. Proctor
3. SOLO AND CHORUS—"I've been Listening,".........Julia Lewis
4. DUETT—"Leaf and the Fountain,".....Miss Whitmore & B. Cleggett
5. DECLAMATION,................................George Lincoln
6. SONG—Selected,............................Little Charlie Seals
7. DECLAMATION,..................................Artie Clark

TABLEAU--HOMELESS.

8. RECITATION,......................................Hattie Bias
9. SONG—"Drunkard's Lone Child,"................Little Ida Ray
10. GUITAR SOLO—Pease's Nocturn,................Prof. D. H. Ray
11. DIALOGUE,.....................Misses Cleggett and Seals
12. BALLAD—"Love's Request,"...................Miss Whitmore
13. SONG AND CHORUS—"Moon Behind the Hill,".........Mrs. James

Part Second.

1. DUETT AND CHORUS—"Waneta,".....Misses Cleggett & Duffin
2. SONG AND CHORUS—"God Bless the dear ones at Home,"
                                              Geo. Holland
3. RECITATION,..............................Fannie Cleggett

Tableau--Hiawatha and Minnehaha.

4. RECITATION,................................Maggie Kinney
5. SONG—"Little Footsteps,"......................Ada Ray
6. GUITAR SOLO—Selected Airs....................Professor Ray
7. SONG—"Lovely Rose,"........................Four Little Girls
8. SONG—Slavery Days,................Wm. Allen and Wm. Proctor
9. DIALOGUE—Little Tramp,............Allen, Brown and Kinney
10. SONG of Blanche Alpine,........................Lillie Bland

Grand Camp Meeting Scene,

With songs "Jesus said He wouldn't die no more," "Book of Revelations,"
Daniel in the Lion's Den," &c.
THE CHORUSES WILL BE LED BY Mrs. JOHN BLAND.

THE LADY MANAGERS WILL GIVE A FESTIVAL AT THE CLOSE OF THESE EXER-
CISES, TO WHICH ALL ARE INVITED.

Doors open at 7; to commence at 8 o'clock.
Admission, 25 Cents. - - - - - Reserved Seats, 35 Cents.
Children under 12 years of age, 25 Cents.

46. Broadside for St. Philip's Mission exhibition, 11 April 1877.
Courtesy Trinity Episcopal Church, Geneva.

47. Lewis and Laura Scott with gospel singers at Lake Bluff, Lake Ontario, about 1900. Lewis Scott was a member of a Wolcott (Wayne County) family that organized itself into the Scott Brothers Orchestra and played largely at white barn dances, house parties, and weddings throughout the region into the 1940s. Originally, Lewis and his wife Laura Linzy sang gospel in an integrated choral group. Two of Scott's brothers married two of Linzy's sisters. *Courtesy Dorothy Scott Cooke.*

village in August 1894 failed because too few people attended to cover its expenses.[53] In schools, churches, and other social settings, blacks looked on silently as whites appropriated and misinterpreted their culture and attempted to construct a black mainstream that emulated, from a distance, white postwar society. Plantation owners and white northern teachers often commented at the time on how difficult it was to "decipher" black Americans; Mary Chesnut wrote, "People talk before them as if they were chairs and tables, and they make no sign. Are they stolidly stupid, or wiser than we are, silent and strong, biding their time." The African-American schoolteacher

Emma Brown described how the black teachers in one Georgetown school exhibition stood in silent witness as a white preacher rhetorically polled the audience on whether black students were as teachable and honest as whites. "The colored teachers as though they had known of this ridiculous performance beforehand and had together resolved on their course, declined taking any part in the debate," she wrote in 1867. "None of us voted. All looked just what they thought."[54]

Arthur Kenney and the Triumph of Patronage

As the size of the local African-American population reached its nadir in the first four decades of the twentieth century, its political activity virtually ceased. There were still friends of the race in Geneva, principally Gerrit Smith's daughter Elizabeth Smith Miller, a Genevan since 1869, and her daughter Anne Fitzhugh Miller. Both women were active in state and county suffrage associations, whose attention by then had turned toward women. In 1911, two years before her death, Harriet Tubman joined a Geneva suffrage association, probably the Geneva Political Equality Club, which Elizabeth Miller founded in 1897. Miller corresponded with Frederick Douglass, and she played hostess to Mary Church Terrell in 1908 when she attended the sixtieth anniversary of the Seneca Falls women's rights convention. But there were no independent African-American churches, no more emancipation celebrations, no organized sign of interest in the programs advanced by Garvey, Du Bois, and Washington. Between the Ontario Debating Club and the Geneva Social Club of the 1940s, African Americans new to the village formed associations, but they were short-lived, and no evidence exists that identifies the nature of their activity (fig. 48). By the 1930s, their visible presence seemed reduced to their participation on baseball teams, in choral groups, and at occasional dances and cake walks (fig. 49). One 1939 newspaper account of a pageant on the history of the city's schools related how the eighth scene, played by local African-American children, presented the story of the colored school with the intent to depict "how civilization has gained through the music and rhythm of the negro race."[55]

More than ever, African-American life in Geneva hinged critically on the number and status of whites one knew and how one could work these associations to secure at least a modicum of comfort and stability. By the turn of the century, the community's musi-

48. Genevans, about 1914. The dress of these young men and women suggests that they had gathered for some formal occasion, but no record exists of an African-American club in Geneva in the teens. Standing second from left is Theresa Claggett, whose father was a member of the short-lived African-American "Monrovia Society" in 1894. Next to her is Maude Whitaker, and sitting at the right is Maude's brother James. *Courtesy Frances Craven.*

cal tradition and the tendency to use it both as a credential and as a means of support had passed to Arthur W. Kenney, Benjamin Cleggett's son-in-law and his partner in business in his waning years on Seneca Street. By 1922, Kenney had moved from his father-in-law's old shop to South Exchange Street, where he remained until shortly before his death in 1968. He was a leading member of the St. Philip's Mission choir, often serving as its instructor, and he was a faithful and lifelong Trinity congregant. By 1910, when he was thirty, he, his brother Herman, Theodore Derby (a cook, and grandson of Baptist

49. Joyce Kelly, June Hardy, and Robert Hardy in St. Philip's Mission nativity pageant, Christmas 1949. *Courtesy Trinity Episcopal Church, Geneva.*

minister Rufus Derby), and one other African-American man had organized themselves into the Colored Boys' Quartet, which sang throughout the region at various picnics, parties, and fraternity outings (fig. 50).[56] Kenney and Derby were also among the nine members of the Colored Athletic Association's Geneva team in 1900. By the 1940s, Kenney began to sing with whites who came to harmonize at his South Exchange Street shoeshine parlor on Saturday afternoons. He taught the men songs he had sung in the Colored Boys' Quartet, a repertoire of sentimental tunes from the World War I era and humorous songs stereotyping rural blacks, such as "Hambone Am Good" and "Jasper Johnson, Shame on You," whose lyrics repeated the often-told fable of the black preacher who stole chickens from his parishioners. When Kenney and his barbershop quartet sang publicly at parties and Hobart football rallies, he instructed them to substitute "country preacher" for "colored preacher" in this latter song. R. George Chase, a quartet member born in 1908 in Geneva, talked about Kenney.

> I'd say I was a very close friend of Art Kenney, who was the famous black shoeshine—we called him the mayor of South Ex-

50. "Forget-It-Not Outing at Highlands on Seneca, Aug. 11, 1909." In the formal portrait of Geneva's Forget-It-Not club, the three African-American men might be taken for club members, but the companion image of the club's dinner shows them cooking and waiting table. They were probably hired to sing at the outing as well. Lewis Scott is standing with the guitar; Theodore Derby is standing third from left. Both were probably members of the Colored Boys' Quartet. The identity of the third man is not known. *Courtesy Geneva Historical Society.*

change Street. We were brought together principally because we both loved harmony. Art was a great booster of athletics at Hobart. . . . And Art was always called on to lead the cheers, which he did in a magnificent manner.

Now the harmony epic in this little story is that Art had his own shoeshine shop at South Exchange, just right next to what is now the Chase bank. And his shop was not a glittering jewel, but he kept everything clean and neat. He had two chairs for shoeshine clients, and he got not only college students and business men but he got ladies that'd come in for a shine, and for their convenience

Art had a great big curtain from ceiling to floor which he could maneuver and pull right around the front of the shop, which would isolate the possible racket in the back, where some of the boys might be crooning a tune, or something to that effect.

Back in that era, there was very little trouble of any sort and not a great deal of thought given to it [race relations]. . . . It wouldn't be quite right to say that blacks knew their place, but they were smart enough not to attempt things that perhaps could be a black mark against them. . . . For instance, Art wouldn't be liable to call me up and say, "Can I come down? Let's get together." But I could call him up, and he'd welcome it. That's just a small incident, but today I think it's quite different.

Like his brother Herman, to whom Hobart seniors dedicated their 1902 yearbook, Kenney was a Hobart institution. Kenney began making speeches at Hobart pep rallies in 1918 and claimed to have missed only one home game in sixty years. He cashed checks for Hobart boys, retrieved hazed freshmen in his truck, let William Smith students smoke cigarettes in his shoeshine parlor, put on a white waiter's jacket and served punch at the college's many teas for visiting dignitaries (fig. 51), and once stated his intention to leave five hundred dollars and his High Street home to the college. In 1955, more than one hundred Hobart alumni invited Kenney to be guest of honor at their annual Christmas luncheon at Toots Shor's in New York City, and a portrait of him wearing his Hobart scarf hangs in the college gymnasium. He was "The Most Unforgettable Character I've Met" in the eyes of Hobart alumnus Thomas Johnson, whose article about him appeared in a 1961 *Reader's Digest*.

Kenney was also a Geneva booster. He had received a commendation from the city for helping fight the fire at the downtown Wilson Block in 1916, and he was chosen to lead the parade at Geneva's 1957 sesquicentennial. In his shop, Kenney posted the thousands of letters he received from Geneva soldiers serving overseas, and he kept scrapbooks in which departing and returned servicemen from twentieth-century wars signed their names. In his own hand, Kenney indicated their service records next to their names and remarked on their character if they had been killed in action. On a piano donated to him by a local music store, he played carols to entertain Christmas shoppers passing by his South Exchange Street store. He collected and displayed photographs and postcards of the Geneva he knew as a boy, when it was in its glory days, steamboats carrying freight and excursionists up and down the lake, industries

51. Art Kenney and Father Donald Labigan at a cocktail party, 28 March 1953. *Courtesy Geneva Historical Society.*

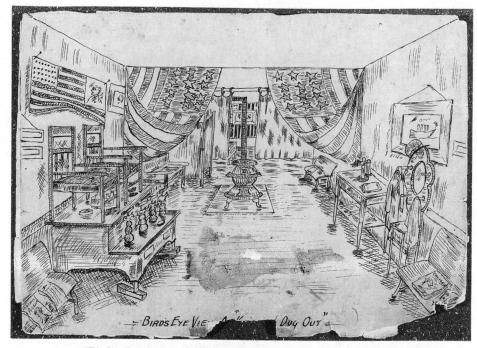

52. "Bird's Eye View of Kenney's Dug Out," Seneca Street, about
1910, drawing by Jim Malone, Geneva. Kenney's Exchange Street
shop also had a portiere that he sometimes drew to shield women
customers from activity in the back. *Courtesy Geneva Historical
Society.*

and businesses booming (fig. 52). He wrote to local historian Arch
Merrill in 1959, "Many times in my life I would have a job as a paid
pallbearer in the morning, would serve punch at a tea dance in the
afternoon and at a senior dance at Cox Hall in the evenings. In those
days it was my job to turn out the lights at 5 a.m. They would dance
until 6 a.m. The last number was always 'Home Sweet Home.' I
have seen a great many tears at the last dance and much laughter."[57]

Although many Genevans remember Kenney, it is not surpris-
ing that whites seem to remember him better. The livings he and his
wife built were based on serving the city's white community. In her
will, his wife left him money and her High Street house, and after
her death in 1939 he lived on that bequest and the income he was

able to put together shining shoes, blocking hats, carrying coffins, cleaning local banks, serving at Hobart functions, and tending bar at South Main Street parties. For many white Genevans, Arthur Kenney epitomized the black person who understood and accepted his place in white society; for some blacks, he epitomized Uncle Tom. There is no evidence that Kenney was ever politically active in African-American affairs, and it is not known where he stood in the dispute his brother Herman had with Trinity rector Samuel Edsall after the 1932 fire. He once stated, "Discrimination? Segregation? Those are things I read about, but don't experience. I guess life is what you make it—or unmake it. You do the right thing by life, life'll do the right thing by you."

Arguably, Kenney did know his place in the sense that he knew what his native town was like and how he could best live there. He was evidently never interested in industrial work, but he never registered complaint that factory and service jobs were the only ones available to him and most other African Americans in Geneva. Kenney liked to sing, he liked sports, he liked church. He was remarkably social. And he knew how to get the kind of work that would allow him to pursue his interests. The implications of fitting so neatly into white stereotypes of how black people behaved and should behave perhaps mattered little to him, for that fit is precisely what brought enough work his way for a living.

Henry McDonald also "knew his place" in this sense. As Kenney was the mayor of South Exchange Street, McDonald was called the "dean of Finger Lakes Sportsmen." A native of Haiti, he had been brought to Canandaigua by a fruit importer and excelled in high school sports there and in Rochester. In 1911, he became a halfback on the Rochester Jeffersons, one of the teams in the league that was predecessor to the American Football League, and he played for at least four other teams through the mid–1920s. In 1973, McDonald was inducted into the Black Hall of Fame as the first African-American professional football player.

But football probably brought McDonald less money than Art Kenney earned shining shoes. He was once quoted to state, "In all that time I never once took home more than fifteen dollars for one day of football. And I had to play two games to get that much." By 1916, he had married and built a house in Geneva next door to Art Kenney on High Street. Between 1919 and 1929, McDonald worked as a trainer for Hobart's football and lacrosse teams (fig. 53); then, when he was forty years old, he turned to professional baseball. He

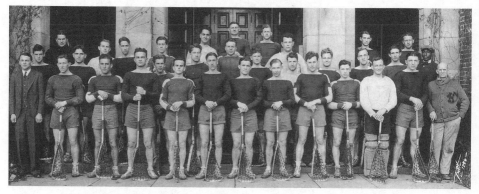

53. Henry McDonald with the Hobart College lacrosse team, 1929,
photograph by H. B. Tuttle. *Courtesy Geneva Historical Society.*

played outfield for several colored baseball teams and for Geneva's
semiprofessional club. In the late 1930s, then working as a janitor at
American Can Company, McDonald volunteered to coach football at
St. Francis DeSales, Geneva's Catholic high school, which his three
younger children attended. He supplied the team each year with
Hobart's cast-off equipment. At DeSales, McDonald taught football
to many of the men who would become city officials, and he was
well known for having played against Jim Thorpe and for having
tried to recruit Paul Robeson for the Rochester Jeffersons.[58]

McDonald frequently spoke at sports events in the region and
was the former president of the Rochester Stadium Club. His son
Edward recalled his father's work at DeSales and his later days in
and about Geneva.

> At one time my sister and my brother and I were the only
> blacks in school, outside of my father. In Geneva, my father was
> the coach, and he was loved by all the kids, which were all white
> except my brother and I, my sister, and all the time that I grew up
> in Geneva, I never had been called a name, not either one of us, all
> the time we were there. . . . When my father died, the funeral
> parlor was right in the proximity of the high school, and they said
> prayers for my father over the loudspeaker in each room. And then
> they came up to the funeral parlor, and each one said a prayer at
> the casket. The line must have been a mile long. It took almost all
> afternoon.
> . . . Every day my father [after retirement] would go down to

the high school and go in—now, the only person who could do that was the principal or the bishop—and he'd go to any one of the classes at random, and the teachers would stop the class, and my father would talk to them for ten or fifteen minutes, then he would go from there to Hobart and watch whatever games they were playing, lacrosse, or football, and check that out, then go home. But before that he would meet with the city manager, and the mayor, and two or three other city officials. I guess they talked over whatever was going to happen that day, every morning down at the cafeteria they'd have coffee and all of 'em would sit in a big circle and talk, then my father would go visit the school, then up to Hobart, then go home, and read, or watch tv. And he did that every single day.

My father didn't hang around many black people. He knew them good, but for some reason all the males seemed to be like this [spreads his fingers apart]. See, they had nothing in common with my father. My father was strictly sports, and he was up on everything. And he had many, many friends. Most of them were city officials or sports people, or somebody from the colleges or up at the high school.

Henry McDonald relied upon his extensive network of friends to improve the lot of his family whenever he needed to. After his wife died in 1960, he "went to see his friend" to engineer a transfer for his daughter Paula from a King's County Veterans' Administration Hospital to the facility in Canandaigua so that she could take care of him and the Geneva house. After his son Edward graduated from Howard University and finished his military service, McDonald and his wife helped him get a job in his field.

I came home out of the service, and I was working in a dry cleaning plant, and the fellow wanted to send me to school in Baltimore to become a plant manager. And he says, "If you take the job, I don't want you to press, because pressers are standing all the time." And I really didn't care for the job; I was just working, you know, to make extra money. And then my mother said, "They're hiring soils engineers in Rochester. Why don't you have your father take you up and see if you can get a job?" My father took me up, and the regional engineer hired me right then. I've been at the same job since.

. . . When I first came to Rochester, my father gave me the chief of police's name, the fire chief, and three or four detectives, and all these different names. Oh, he had a couple of judges.

"Anything goes wrong," he says, "call so and so." Two or three times I had to do that, too. It got straightened out immediately.

Many members of the older African-American families in Geneva determined that their relationships with whites presented the only means by which they could respond to discrimination when it arose. Charles and Lillie Kenney relied upon white associates several times on behalf of their teenage children.

LILLIE: Marge had a bad run-in in the school system.

CHARLES: Oh, we had our battles.

LILLIE: One of the teachers—she [Marge] wrote an article, and she said, "I'd like to be a private secretary." And the teacher over there said, "Marge, I gotta tell you something. You should write about being a housekeeper. Nobody black is a private secretary."

CHARLES: She graduated in '59, so it had to have been just prior to that.

LILLIE: And she walked out, and he went over to school—

CHARLES: I raised particular hell over there. And that same girl was a cheerleader one year, so their instructor, after I think she was cheerleader for two years, then this instructor says, "Well, we have too many girls; you'll have to go." . . . You know where it ended up? In Albany. Yeah, it did. I went to see Senator Metcalf. We worked in Auburn.

LILLIE: And my son had all these swimming trophies, and he was in college, and he applied for a job as being a lifeguard. And the guy down at the employment agency said to another guy, "He's a good swimmer, he's got all his licenses; I can't see a nigger sitting up there." So when Charles came home, the guy went to the bathroom and he called Charles, he said, "You're going to tell your son he can't have the job." Well, the guy told Charles that, and Charles called Rochester, New York, all over. See, they close it right up quick. He got the job. And they loved him. This is down at Seneca Lake.

CHARLES: And my daughter went back to cheerleading, too. Oh, man, the Senator, George Metcalf, a good friend of mine—

LILLIE: He was one of his general foremen [at Columbian Rope in Auburn]—

CHARLES: He referred it to the Human Rights Commission, state, and they had an office in Auburn, and we were friendly with the guy—

LILLIE: And she came over once, and that was it. Even the principal. My son flunked out. He got girls and cars, he was kind of a good-looking kid, athlete, you know. So he flunked his English, so he wasn't going to college. So we talked to Carlton Roberts, the judge here, and the judge said, "Charles, I'll get him a job in Canandaigua, in an office." Charles said, "I don't want him in an office; I want him to get a college degree. If he gets a good job like that, that's where he's going to end up." So he said, "I'll tell you what. I'll put him on the back of a truck." In wintertime, years ago, they had to shovel salt and sand, so Charles [Junior] had that job. Well the principal, God rest his soul, he saw Charles one day, Charles was playing basketball with some kids, and he comes up and he says, "Charles"—he was getting ready to go to prep school, he went to prep school for a year, and he came out with three scholarships—"Charles, why would you want another job? That's a nice job you got." You know? And Charles just looked at him. And I was at a meeting with that man one day and he said to me, "Lillie, what makes your kids so haughty? They all walk with their heads up in the air like they're somebody." I said, "'Cause they *are* somebody." But this is something that's inbred in people—it's ignorance, but you have to accept it, and you have to just kind of educate them, that's all.

But even members of the "older families," such as HenryEtta McDonald Hughes, were conscious of the implications of having to depend on people one knows.

I can remember when my brother came home from the service, and they wanted to go down to Isemans' or Peters' to see the old gang, you know, that's where we used to hang out. And so they went to Isemans' and they didn't see anybody, so they went over to Peters' and they didn't see anybody, so they figured they'd sit down and have an ice cream soda, and Mr. Peters wouldn't serve them. So they came home and they told our father. And Henry—of course, I wouldn't say that if I weren't so old—he got on that phone and he called up Mr. Peters, and he said, "What do you mean not serving my boys?" He said, "Henry, I didn't know those were your boys." And my father said, "What the hell does it make a difference *whose* boys they were?" And these were the little incidents. . . . The ones that seemed to progress were the ones that seemed—you can't just approach and say, "My name's Hanky; you got something for me?" But, "I'm Henry McDonald's daughter"—"Oooh, come on in." You know, you always seemed to be riding on somebody.

By the end of World War II, when African-American veterans returned to the city, it was no longer a small society of "old families." The population explosion stimulated by the two nearby military installations and the agricultural migration had brought to the city new families with vastly different political attitudes. They settled in Geneva as racial hostility again affected the nation—the violent Detroit and Harlem race riots of 1943; the United States Supreme Court's segregation ruling, Emmett Till's lynching, and Rosa Parks's refusal to leave her seat on a Montgomery bus. Martin Luther King's successful nonviolent boycott of the Montgomery bus system in 1955 and 1956 suggested a strategy that became popular among African Americans who were relatively new to the region. Not until 1969 did Geneva have its own NAACP chapter, but Geneva's blacks organized boycotts and marches from the early 1960s. These tactics seemed useless to many members of old families, who had worked long and hard to establish networks that operated on an individual and nondemonstrative principle. Charles Kenney described the differences in their political approaches.

> There are those that march the streets or something like that, but we know people in good standing that can do things for you. You ever see a black man or a white man, I don't care who, hold their fists up in the air like this? They ain't got a damn thing in their fists. But I got something up here that we can use. We know people in places that you can use to do things.

Dorothy Eldridge described her perception of the political differences between old and new families as they crystallized around a proposed boycott of the local A&P, part of a nationwide black boycott of the grocery chain in the early 1960s.

> We were what you considered old families, 1940. We watched other people come. So the newer families to me are different. They bring their attitudes with them, and they don't understand why we don't have the same attitudes as they do. Because they were raised up in a different environment than we were. For instance, when we weren't supposed to go to the stores, you know, to the A & P and stuff like that. And I said, "I'm *going* to the A & P; it's the closest store."
> . . . Often you're called an Uncle Tom if you don't participate in what they do. But I was raising children; I don't have time to participate in it. I'm a person, and to me people just have different ways and things about them, but we're all people. . . . Like I said,

I'll march if they'll say some good man is going to get up . . . but if he's not going to do it, I've got to go to work.

For African Americans who came from the South during and after World War II, it was all the more disappointing to find discrimination in the North when one had grown up believing that it did not exist there. Alvin Robinson discussed the institutionalized discrimination of the South and the less systemic racism he encountered in the North.

Most of my life in the South I considered myself to be very fortunate because I was never really thrown into any situation of outright prejudice directed at me. Now, there were general standards that were observed. There were places you didn't go. I mean, for instance, the places that had white and colored, you of course went to the colored, you know; I mean this was just a matter of course. So, other than the general segregation attitudes, I was never really exposed to any cause to feel different. I think that in the philosophy of the southern blacks, it was a way of life. They accepted it. There were those who possibly hated it, wanted to do something about it, but were limited in what they could do.

And those who found it unbearable left and came North looking for utopia, you know, which you run into the same damn thing; it's just lack of signs, that's all. And this turned out to be rather frustrating to a lot of blacks who moved North, you know, thinking this is where you can be free, you can do this, you can do that, and all that sort of stuff. . . . Until you actually went somewhere that you weren't supposed to be, you didn't know that you weren't supposed to *be* there.

But. . . . I've never been a blockbluster. I never set out to create any dissension in that regard. I more or less adopted an attitude of, "Well, if you don't want me here, then I don't want to *be* here." And until I ran into situations that were just a blatant display of prejudice, I guess I did what most blacks did—you know, sort of roll with the punches.

Virginia Peek described the difference in similar terms.

In Florida you know what you can do and what you can't do. You know whether you can go—because in Florida, you couldn't go, like in a bus station, you had the back door to go to . . . in Florida you don't walk right on in the store like some people, you know, looking to be waited on before the white because, you know, down there's Jim Crow and you know what you got to do. So you stay in your place because you know that what it's like, understand?

But then you have say, up, well, up North it's not prejudiced, you know, it's OK, it's this and that and the other; but *they lie*. It is a lot of prejudice in the North; I mean a whole lot of it. . . . Like you can go, like when they had the five and dime ten-cent stores and thing in Geneva. You can go in there and you can stand there to be waited on, okay? And you stand there and wait and it could be a white person come up, stand right by you and, long as you been standing there, they'll come up and ask that person what they want and wait on them and you still standing. And that's the same way with the clerks. They'll wait on the white person quicker than they would wait on you. Oh, it was a lot of Jim Crow, a lot of it, but, hey, you go along with it because what could you do, you know? You couldn't do that much about it.

The presence of vastly more African-American people and of an active USO in Geneva dramatically altered social life among blacks in the city during the war. The number of African-American service-men called for the creation of a USO specifically for them; dances there, at the local Moose Hall, and at Sampson were popular events for African-American civilians throughout the region (fig. 54). After the war, the composition of the local black population was altered permanently by new families, some of them originally drawn by the bases and some as migrant workers. Some members of old families, discouraged by two decades of withering contempt expressed most pointedly in the Trinity dispute and the rise of Ku Klux Klan in the North (fig. 55), dissociated themselves from new families and con-tinued to socialize house to house with other old families and in the older African-American lodges and churches in larger cities.[59] Among them, being a member of an old family was a hard-won label, the only basis for local security, a caste in itself. The percep-tual differences between the hill and the flat were enhanced in the eyes of some old families and many whites by the emergence of a small, largely black, district of bars, hotels, tenements, and apart-ment buildings around the intersection of Exchange, Tillman, and Canal streets. What had been William B. Dunning's New York Cen-tral Iron Works had become Linkner's Hotel and by 1957 the Central Hotel, owned by Geneva Foundry molder Eugene Linzy. Charles Kenney recalled that the area's tawdry reputation was enhanced by the fact that Geneva police tended to avoid it.

54. Scene from a dance for African-American servicemen at the Geneva USO, April 1944, photograph by P. B. Oakley. *Courtesy Geneva Historical Society.*

The Central Hotel was the wild spot. You take it like it is. There's so many things happened down there, ordinarily the cops would have closed the place, but they ain't gonna close it because this is a place where black people congregate and they ain't gonna bother it, you know. There was another place right around the corner from there that was run by an Italian guy, Sam's Bar and Grill. That was another place where the blacks *and* the whites—the intellectual whites from Hobart College—oh, what a mixture, I'm telling you. It was something else. Black people went to black places because— I don't think they were ever *stopped* from going to any other place, but they wouldn't have been comfortable. When something happened there at Club 86 for blacks, that's all that was there. When we came back here to live, Club 86 had the best entertainers in the country there, sure—you got money, pay, you go.

55. Ku Klux Klan gathering west of Geneva, October 1925, photograph by P. B. Oakley. Evidently invited to Geneva by some local
whites, the Klan had planned a large rally outside the city and a
parade through Geneva streets. But a freak snowstorm and high
winds discouraged attendance and forced the Klan to cancel its
plans. *Courtesy Geneva Historical Society.*

By the time James Henderson came to the Seneca Army Depot
in the early 1960s, he was told the Central was the only place in
Geneva that blacks frequented.

People in the service when they're stationed somewhere quite
quickly find out what sources of recreation, entertainment, and social life exist off the base. And I very quickly became familiar with
Geneva my first weekend pass. And it's really ironic. Some of the
guys in the service took me into Geneva, and they were black, and
they took me in on Lake Street and came around after they crossed
the railroad tracks to the back of the Central Hotel. And when I
went in there, my God, it reminded me of some of the places in the
South—very run down, all right? And they told me that was the
only thing that was for blacks here in Geneva. I was so disap-

56. Lionel Hampton at Club 86, 1948–1950. *Courtesy James Legott.*

pointed I said, "Well, where else can we go?" And they said, well, Ithaca wasn't far away. And we were there in Geneva for about an hour and immediately went over to Ithaca. There was an American Legion which was predominantly black in Ithaca, and they had a dance. I later found out that there was more for blacks than just the Central Hotel. Club 86 was very popular at the time, and they had a very popular group that was playing once a week Thursday nights, Wilmer Alexander and the Dukes. They were local, and it was there that I met my wife-to-be.

Club 86 symbolized a coming together of some of the old and new families, and it became the favorite site of benefits sponsored by those groups who, beginning in the 1940s, tried to integrate the African-American population and provide assistance to needier people (fig. 56). The Geneva Social Club, begun as an African-American women's club whose membership included newer residents by

57. Geneva Social Club at the USO, about 1945. *Standing, from left:*
Katherine (Mrs. Lawrence) Kenney, unidentified, John W. Kenney,
Herman F. Kenney Jr., unidentified, Harry and Dixie Bray, Beulah
(Mrs. Herman Jr.) Kenney, Alvin Kenney, Capitola Whitaker, and
T. Everett Johnson, "negro director" of the Geneva USO. *Seated,
from left:* Rose (Mrs. John W.) Kenney, Josephine (Mrs. Herman Sr.)
Kenney, Nancy Yancey Hogan, Mildred (Mrs. Clyde) Mathis, Ruth
(Mrs. Eugene) Linzy. *Courtesy Charles H. Kenney.*

the 1950s, sponsored fashion shows, dances, picnics, and raffles to
support sick and needy people and to provide assistance to college-
bound black students (fig. 57). Charles Kenney stated that the Geneva Men's Club had similar goals.

> My brother John and I and a fella by the name of Al Robinson and
> Clyde Mathis, we decided this community needed something that
> was going to do not only us older guys some good but the kids
> coming up, see if we couldn't do something here to ease the ten-
> sions in the community and do something worthwhile for those
> that would follow us. So we formed the Geneva Men's Club. It was
> all black. This was during the war, and some of these people Rosa

Blue says come up from the South, we thought here's the time where we can get these people who are almost strangers in this area with kids, and we can help them in a whole lot of different avenues.

You think we could get them to join this thing? Didn't want any part of it. They just wouldn't attend meetings; they didn't want to have nothing to do with it. But who did want to have something to do with it was the service people, the transients. And I don't know what their idea of joining something like this, except we had a lot of good times, raising money, we put on dances, had card parties, anything to raise money so we could help the younger generation. We sent kids to camp and depending on their marks and this and that and this and that. And it was good. We even left a bank account downtown. Well, it got so bad I was president and my brother was treasurer and somebody else was—I said the hell with it. It was funny the way it ended up. I imagine the state had a big party on what we left in the bank.

I would say maybe five or six years [it existed]. We put on dances, for adults, at Club 86. Yeah, we put on big dances, hired the best bands in the area, black bands—this here again was an opportunity where people from all around—they used to come from Elmira, Ithaca, Syracuse, Rochester, they'd come down. Had a big time. But the thing behind it all was raising money, so we could send kids to camp or establish a scholarship, you know, something like that. But I can name some of the black people here who were raising kids at the time and struggling along in life doing menial work and that. What we were trying to do was to help them. . . . But it just seemed like the younger married, they didn't—here you got a community that's filled with servicemen, this means big time, lots of girls and young people floating around. I can understand why they weren't interested in a social organization; too many other things to do.

Perry Carter remembered being too busy even to meet people when he first came to the city in 1942.

There were the Kenneys, the Jackson, and Linzy—I think there were two separate families of Linzys, weren't there?—not that many. . . . You see, when you were working then you didn't get a chance to meet many people because you were working seven days a week, and you go to work in the morning seven o'clock and they only had the one way in all the way or out, you know, like 5 and 20 coming into Geneva and went on out to Canandaigua, Buffalo, and Rochester. So you had to get up early in the morning to catch the bus to be on time. You go to work at seven o'clock so you had to get up by five o'clock, go down and catch the bus. So you knock off sometimes five-thirty, six o'clock, and sometime it'd be seven o'clock before you get back in, the traffic was so heavy. So you didn't get a chance to meet many people, only on the job where you work at.

Clarence Day, one-time treasurer of the local NAACP chapter and president of the current Geneva African-American Men's Association, described the faltering social cohesion of Geneva's African Americans.

We done had a couple of NAACPs. They break 'em up, they break 'em up, they break 'em up. I don't know. I'd say they had them for the last ten years. I was in the NAACP in Baltimore, so I joined the branch here. They stay a while, and they quit.
. . . Charles, John, his brother; I been knowing them for years. We used to have a club together, me and Charles did. I don't know if John used to belong to our club or not. Charles did, I know Charles did. That was a long time ago, we used to have men's club, five or six of them used to have a club together. Robby Robinson, me and Robby, Charles, who else was in that club? I don't know. We used to give dances at Club 86. We never was able to give a scholarship, and that's like the men's club this time. . . . We don't give nothing. It's hard to give anything and make any money. Don't laugh, but tell you the truth we got five [men in the club now]. So we ain't doing nothing. Can't do nothing with just five. Can't do nothing. Can't even sell tickets to buy something and try to raffle it off. We have had more [men], but this here's the worst place in the world I ever seen in my life where men don't want to work together. They just don't want to work together.

Clarence Day was one who believed in marching to make a point or press a cause. He participated in every march related to African-American issues since Geneva's first in 1965 (fig. 58), and in 1970 he and his wife also helped establish the Center of Concern, which gives away food, sells clothing and household goods at low prices to disadvantaged people of all racial and ethnic backgrounds, and helps needy people generally cope with everyday life. As Club 86 did socially, the Center of Concern tended to bring together parts of the older and newer African-American populations in benevolent work. Geneva native Beth Kenney Henderson described her participation in the Center.

58. March in support of southern civil rights movement, Geneva, 20 March 1965. *Courtesy Geneva Historical Society.*

I try to stay involved with the Center of Concern because although it [discrimination] hasn't happened to me as often as it does to the poor, minority, and disadvantaged that we try to gear in to, I try to help to see that that does *not* happen, and that if they can't read or don't understand something, we try to be there to help them out, at least guide them in the right way. Because I know it *could* happen.

The late Margaret Carter, who moved to Geneva during the war, worked at the Center of Concern for eighteen years.

If you want to talk, I'll listen. You know you be talking a lot. You know that. But you afraid the one that you would turn away would be the one that needs you the most. So that way you aid them all.
. . . Why do I do it? When I was a young girl, my mother used

to take in a lot of girls. And I used to ask the question why. And she said, "I don't know. They may not do anything for me, but if they do something for you or one of your children, I've got my reward." So when my daughter went to college in Raleigh, North Carolina, and she was driving up to New York City, and she was stranded, and somebody helped her. What I do at the Center pays for that.

The civil rights movement promoted a broadly humanistic view that places such as the Center of Concern articulated locally. For some African Americans in Geneva, the face-to-face community still exists; Day, who mans the ticket booth every summer at Seneca Lake State Park, and "Robby" Robinson, a longtime mail carrier, are still known by many whom they don't know, and often only by their first names. But for others, the demographic changes that occurred with World War II made it no longer possible to "ride on somebody," and political changes have made it no longer desirable. Beth Henderson described Geneva today and her place within it.

I feel—and I've looked at all of this in many ways—there's not that many old Genevans anymore. There's a lot of people who don't know me. He's no longer Beth Kenney's husband. I'm Jim Henderson's wife. It's been a complete role reverse of "I know Jim, but I really don't know you. I don't really know your family." I didn't know anybody out at the Girl Scouts. People are coming from outside in. They could give a heck who you were. It's not the same. So you've got to carry your own weight.

Epilogue

Once in Geneva, for a time in the 1850s, there lived an African-American man named Sam Thornton. On the scale of how well the city's black people have been remembered, Thornton is near the bottom. Hundreds of others rest beneath him, all of the African Americans who were in Geneva too short a time to be recorded in a census or a city directory, all of those who lived out of sight of enumerators, all of those who, because their names escaped, are permanently unknowable (fig. 59).

Unlike Harriet Bias and Margaret Douglass, of whom photographs have survived, no likeness of Thornton is known to exist. He was never counted a Genevan in any official source. But because he was ostensibly the stuff of legend, whites wrote tales of Sam Thornton in letters and newspapers. One man who remembered him claimed he had been a slave until the 1827 emancipation. Thornton worked in the 1850s as a "scavenger" in the Colt's Hill neighborhood, the precipitous slope between the bluff of South Main Street and the flat of South Exchange Street. Past the landscaped gardens behind the water-side South Main Street homes, Colt's Hill was a network of winding and increasingly tawdry alleys, of sheds, clothes poles, and tenements, a pocket of working-class, and, increasingly, black domestic life verging on the industrial acreage of Herendeen Manufacturing Company, the Coursey flour mill, and the shacks of people who built and rented out boats at Long Pier. Several steps below a gardener or a whitewasher in prestige, Thornton appears to have done the dirtier work in the backyards of South Main Street homes—picking up rubbish, collecting and selling junk, cleaning wells—and is said to have disposed of "dissected objects" for Geneva Medical College.

59. Unidentified man with Miss Kaiser's horse, Lochland Road, Geneva, 1869–1880, photograph by James G. Vail. *Courtesy Geneva Historical Society.*

Boys and grown men who passed Thornton on the streets of Geneva would taunt him regularly. "He would chase a dozen boys all over town on the cry 'Dog-in-the-well' or 'Butter in the hat,'" one *Gazette* columnist wrote in 1910, "and woe betide the boy if old Sammy laid hands on him." Another former Genevan, writing a letter to his niece in 1933, remembered, "Most of the uptown people sported a cane in those days. As they passed Sam, they would hit him a whack and then light out. That made him very mad and he could not run very fast; so if there were any loose stones or bricks he would let fly. He was about 4 1/2 feet tall and crooked legs and feet."

The *Gazette* columnist pointed out that older readers of the newspaper would probably not recall Thornton by his real name but instead by one of the nicknames ascribed to him. He was called Sambo Dog-in-Well, or Sammy Dog-in-the-Well, or Bushnell's, Boots, or Butter-in-the-Hat. The *Gazette* acknowledged how much these names "irritated the old man. If any one spoke to him on the street and addressed him 'Mr. Thornton,' he would be all smiles, inquire about the health of the party and of the whole family. When he started to walk away a whistle would cause him to stop, turn around, and the invective he would hurl at the same party was something fearful."

Local lore has it that Thornton acquired his "dog in the well" nickname from a trick of his trade. Trying to create work where none existed, Thornton is said to have thrown a dog—one assumes a dead one—down the well in the yard of George Hanks, who had a thriving boat livery on the lake. He then went to Hanks to tell him that his well smelled and must need cleaning. Hanks hired Thornton, whereupon Thornton simply pulled the dog out.

He was called Butter-in-the-Hat because of another incident that is probably more folklore than fact.[1] It is said that Thornton once walked into a Geneva grocery store, picked up a roll of butter, put it under his top hat, and tried to walk out with it. The storekeeper, who had watched him steal the butter, stopped him and asked him to sit down and talk for a while. Thornton could not refuse, and as they talked, the story goes, the butter began to melt down his face, and as a parting gesture the storekeeper "gave the tall hat a hard slap in the crown and the melted butter splashed all over him." Thornton is said to have professed utter surprise at the fact that the butter was even concealed there.

He was thought to have been "rather feeble minded," "a comical fellow about two thirds what they call baked." White people found Thornton comical partly because of what he wore, the cast-off, unaltered clothes of the "South Main St. people and college boys and the professors" he worked for.

> They would give him their old clothing, beaver hats, straws and shoes of all sizes and he wore them as they were. If they gave him a straw hat in the winter, he wore it; if in summer it was silk, all

the same to him. If it was large or small he got it down in some way, as he had a big head. . . . Someone about 6 feet tall would give him a pair of pants. He would put them on twice his size. He would turn them up at the bottom and push them down, all full of wrinkles. He was a sight. I have seen him in the winter coming down Seneca St. Hill with a straw hat and linen duster on, that someone had given him.[2]

When the commentary is stripped away, the plainest details of Thornton's life establish him as more a tragic than a comic figure. He was probably crippled, perhaps born with physical defects. He was desperate for work. Even if the butter-in-the-hat story is apocryphal, it and other tales nonetheless demonstrate that Thornton was poor. Like other people in the same penurious historical circumstances, he probably relied at least some of the time on small crimes of property.[3] The well-to-do Genevans who hired Sam Thornton paid him partly in clothing. They gave him summer hats and coats in winter and then found it odd not only that he wore them but that he did not alter them to fit better. No one at the time paused to wonder whether Thornton had much choice but to wear the clothes he was given when he was given them, to wonder how he might possibly have managed their alteration. And even if he had been able to have his hand-me-downs fixed to fit, it is possible that he deliberately chose not to. He may willfully have worn oversized clothing out of season, an act that visibly stated his recognition that in every way, even in the clothes he wore, Sam Thornton was ill fitting. Disenfranchised politically, economically, and socially, he scraped a life together amid the patent and repeated embarrassments and actual pain he suffered at the hands of white Genevans. In his eyes, he might have been a living and persistent protest to the narrowness of local understanding and, consequently, of his life.

But white people pushed away the real dissonance of his "invective," of his hurling bricks, of his chasing boys who would not call him his real name. Only that part of Sam Thornton that fitted the persistent caricature seemed to register—his colorful masquerade, his petty offenses, the butter in the hat. Whites behaved as though they were insensible of the full range of meanings that his demeanor held, to the literally unsuitable garments of their charity. To them, Thornton was a character. He was local color, the "blackface farce" that, as Ralph Ellison later observed, whites used to convert the tragedy of the nation's "moral evasions."[4] Genevans used such farce repeatedly to distance themselves from the real situation of the village's African Americans. Three people who attended a "fancy dress party" on South Main Street in 1904 dressed as blacks, one woman apparently as a maid, one man possibly as a chauffeur, and another man as an African warrior in a skirt, a wild wig, large looped earrings, and a necklace of feathers. He stared with mock ferocity—his teeth bared, his eyes wide—at the man who photographed the costumed group. In 1931, the Geneva High School chorus performed the operetta "Ghost of Lollypop Bay," whose characters included "Dinah, a colored maid," and "Marcus Adam Johnson, a middle-aged negro." Both parts were played by whites in blackface. Eugene and Marian Linzy graduated from Geneva High School that year, the only two African Americans in a class of ninety-four seniors. The local Kiwanis Club staged blackface minstrel shows annually in the late 1930s and early 1940s (fig. 60). Decades later, the year that Beth Kenney and John Sales were the only two African-American graduates in a class of 178, the class play featured a crew of blackfaced white students in "Minstrels, 1961." Beth Kenney barely recalled it.

> As far as the minstrel—I never went to see it, but it didn't faze me. Now, if it were my brother Gary, he would have had a letter and everything else, cussing them out. But there's that six-year span. Gary wouldn't play that game with anybody. I didn't even give it a second thought. I used to be that easy-going. My mother always used to say, "Well, what do you think about so-and-so?" "Oh, they're fine; they're okay. Oh, I like them; no problem." Everybody was okay, everybody was just wonderful. And they said, "Do you think life is just, everything's okay and everything's just wonderful?" And I says, "Yeah." Now that's naive. And then finally, Jim and mother both would say, "How can you find everybody being so nice? You don't even look beyond—if they're stepping on your toes, you don't know if somebody's slapping you across the face, being sarcastic"—I didn't realize any of that. I honestly didn't.

Beth Kenney was brought up in the relatively comfortable but tightly controlled milieu of the old families, the African Americans whose kin had stayed in Geneva for generations and who accepted, or at least appeared to accept, the way they functioned within the community. They were, like Art Kenney and the postwar church choruses, visible but compliant, ostensibly happy with their situation. Or they were, like Sam Thornton, openly, demonstratively dysfunctional. But most were like John Kenney, industrious, uncomplaining, and relatively unknown (fig. 61). Kenney described how Castle Street whites seemed to view his family.

60. Kiwanis Minstrels, Geneva, about 1940. The one African American in the group is not identified. *Courtesy Geneva Historical Society.*

We did not have a car; no one did, then, and we'd walk to Sunday school, and Mrs. Burns always looked out the window [imitates Irish brogue]—"Isn't that a lovely sight, all those well-dressed Kenney kids"—we'd go by; there were various others that said that my mother did a good job for what she had. They never knew that she had a regular job, or what *he* did, even. There wasn't that much interest.

To avoid hostility and to live in some measure of security and comfort in a society controlled by whites, African Americans have had to learn the nature and mechanism of the stereotypes that whites have used to structure, simplify, and limit their knowledge of and contact with them—to develop, as Washington put it, a "double-consciousness, this sense of always looking at one's self through the eyes of others."[5] In 1937, John Dollard observed that African Americans in Southern Town usually adjusted to the local caste barrier in ways that whites preferred them to, that they "accept and cultivate" a set of behaviors that sometimes included a "whining, cajoling tone."[6] However, cultivating roles and accepting them are phenomenologically discrete acts that parallel the social psychological distinction between mask and identity. As one character advised the protagonist of *Invisible Man*, "Play the game, but don't believe in it."[7]

As Lawrence Levine has pointed out, the stories and songs of African-American culture illustrate their unwillingness to accept and believe in the roles white culture has consigned them to play. Like

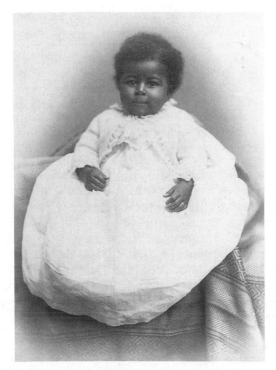

61. Portrait of a baby, unidentified, 1869–1880. Courtesy *Geneva Historical Society.*

Thornton's butter in the hat, another story with folkloric quality celebrates the pragmatic sagacity of blacks when confronted with the foibles and heedless malice of whites. At least since the 1850s, writers of both races have noted the odd tendency of whites to accept persons of color if they were foreign or somehow exotic. A porter on the train from New York City to Atlanta was about to ask James Weldon Johnson and a friend to move to the "Negro car" when the two men began speaking in Spanish. The conductor was silenced, and, Johnson observed, "In such situations, any kinds of Negro will do; provided he is not one who is an American citizen."[8] HenryEtta McDonald Hughes told an identical story about Genevan Pauline Ray.

> My mother's best friend was Pauline Ray. That was Charlie Moore's grandmother's daughter. Pauline went on and became a

professor, and then she had a daughter. They had one child, and that daughter graduated from college—I think she was thirteen, or something like that. Both of them were professors. She was a professor in a university, I think in Indianapolis. And she spoke languages; I remember my mother telling me she spoke languages fluently, and when she would go on a train, she would speak her languages, and they wouldn't touch her because they thought she was from some other country, you know, because they didn't bother you if you could speak a language. Hey—"you're not American."

Stories like this became canonized in the stock of knowledge African-American people used to fathom and navigate their anomalous situation in American life. They rest behind the silence that whites confront; they stand ready to provide moral solace, practical guidance, and pertinent critique. The vitality of these aspects of African-American life and of their political culture shows that their souls were not always, or perhaps even often, at risk because of the "double-consciousness" that characterized their lives. And the ways in which whites have historically described their contact with African Americans suggests the presence of a nagging, persistent anxiety that their accommodation may not have been genuine, that the social order was somehow not as orderly as it seemed. Like John Widner's admonition that Robert Rose's slaves be watched constantly lest they fall into theft and idleness, white legislators feared the consequences of arming American blacks during the Civil War, and plantation owners watched in alarmed wonder as the slaves they thought most faithful were the first to desert them afterward.[9] It was the same confusion of impulses that made it possible for Henry Clay to see African Americans as a plaintive danger at the same time that he spoke of them as useless.

A black physician whom James Weldon Johnson knew in the District of Columbia once complained bitterly that all blacks were judged by the few who were lazy because they were the ones "always in evidence on the street corners, while the rest of us are hard at work." But like Sam Thornton, they wore their marginality on their sleeves.[10] They were graphic testimony of how superfluity had been imposed upon them, of how they had been used when they were needed and cast aside when they were not. From their earliest disappointments as Americans, blacks have warned whites that such control carried inevitable moral consequences. David Walker wrote in 1830, "Can they get us any lower? Where can they get us?

They are afraid to treat us worse, for they know well, the day they do it they are gone." On the day the Emancipation Proclamation became law, one African-American minister in Philadelphia said, "Be not deceived; the black man under God holds largely the future destiny of this country in his hands. Your destiny as white men, and ours as black men, is one and the same; we are all marching on to the same goal; if you rise, we will rise in the scale of being. If you fall, we will fall, but you will have the worst of it."[11] From the fervid antislavery decades before the Civil War to the present, African Americans in Geneva and elsewhere endeavored continually to remind whites of the mutuality of their lives, to seek a fraternal society in place of the paternalistic order they had so long endured, to be taken for, in the words of their nineteenth-century leaders, a man and a brother.

Notes
Bibliography
Index

Notes

Prologue

1. *Ontario Debating Club Book, Geneva,* Jan.–Mar. 1871, Geneva Historical Society Archives; *Geneva Gazette,* 24 Mar. 1871.

2. Pamela Y. Mirabito, "History of Black Education: Nineteenth Century Geneva, New York" (M.A. thesis, State University of New York College at Cortland, 1989), provides information on both state education law and local school district meetings from 1837 forward. Minutes of these meetings, formerly on file at the office of the Ontario County Clerk, cannot now be located. See also "Fair Play" [pseud.], "A Few Words About Our Common Schools," *Geneva Courier,* 9 Nov. 1870. The great majority of nineteenth-century issues of the *Courier,* the local newspaper more sympathetic to local African Americans, have not survived; they are especially sparse in the important decades of the 1840s and 1870s. Many thanks to Steve O'Malley at the Geneva Historical Society for unearthing the two letters "Fair Play" wrote to the *Courier* in 1870 in an 1867 tax assessor's book, where they had been pasted over handwritten assessment records.

3. S. R. W. [Samuel R. Ward], "Editorial Correspondence," *Impartial Citizen,* 24 Oct. 1849. A microfilm of this newspaper, published first in Syracuse and later in Boston from 28 Feb. 1849 to 7 Dec. 1850, is in the collections of the Strong Museum, Rochester, N.Y.

4. Henry Bibb, "The Spirit of Anti-Slavery in Western New York," *Impartial Citizen,* 14 Mar. 1849.

5. Evidence that geographic mobility was quite high in the nineteenth century among both whites and blacks is abundant. See Stephan Thernstrom, *The Other Bostonians: Poverty and Progress in the American Metropolis, 1880–1970* (Cambridge: Harvard Univ. Press, 1973), 31, whose findings suggest that the tendency to migrate was strongly associated with lesser occupational skill. Thernstrom also suggests that ethnic minorities may have been more transient than white Anglo-Saxon Protestants in the same economic circumstances. See also Stephan Thernstrom and Peter R. Knights, "Men in Motion: Some Data and Speculations about Urban Population Mobility in Nineteenth-Century America," in Tamara K. Hareven, ed., *Anonymous Americans: Explorations in Nineteenth-Century Social History* (Englewood Cliffs, N.J.: Prentice-

Hall, 1971), 20, 25, 27, 29–30, 32–33. Thernstrom and Knights cite findings similar to their own in the work of Herbert Gutman and Laurence Glasco for Buffalo and Elizabeth Pleck for Boston; see 36n., 46. See also Faye Dudden, *Serving Women: Household Service in Nineteenth-Century America* (Middletown, Conn.: Wesleyan Univ. Press, 1983), 47–48, who suggests that young women were as likely to leave home for the city as were young men.

6. James Freeman Clarke, "Condition of the Free Colored People of the United States," *Christian Examiner* 66, 5 (Mar. 1859): 246–65. In an analysis of late eighteenth-century runaway slave advertisements, Jonathan Prude has suggested the presence of an "observational structure" that shaped interactions between genteel Americans and common people, and that in fact may have constrained how polite people actually *looked* at the "lower sort." Prude suggests that whites in effect may have seen blacks less clearly than they did their social peers and white indentured servants. See " 'To Look upon the Lower Sort': Runaway Ads and the Appearance of Unfree Laborers in America, 1750–1800," *Journal of American History* 78, 1 (June 1991): 130–31, 153.

7. J. W. Loguen, "Missionary Labors Amongst the Colored Population of Syracuse," *Impartial Citizen*, 28 Nov. 1849. See also Frederick Douglass's address in *Proceedings of the Colored National Convention, Held in Rochester, July 6th, 7th and 8th*, 1853 (Rochester, N.Y.: Frederick Douglass' Paper, 1853), 16, 13; and Mary Church Terrell, *A Colored Woman in a White World* (Washington, D.C.: Ransdell, 1940).

8. The suggestion that censuses undercounted racial and other minorities appears in Thernstrom, *The Other Bostonians*, 271. Nineteenth-century African-Americans certainly believed it to be true. The 1854 meeting of the New York State Council of Colored People—of which Geneva's James W. Duffin was a member—called for an independent count of the "Colored Population of the State of New York, with the number of Farmers, quantity of Land owned, the number of Mechanics, and amount of Capital invested" because the number recorded in the 1850 federal census, "a fraction less than 50,000," was believed to be "erroneous"—that is, too low. See Philip S. Foner and George E. Walker, *Proceedings of the Black State Conventions, 1840–1865*, vol. 1, *New York, Pennsylvania, Indiana, Michigan, Ohio* (Philadelphia: Temple Univ. Press, 1979), 81.

9. Charles Peyton Lucas took the name Charles Bentley in flight and was so listed in the 1850 Geneva census. His verbal account of his escape, eventual settlement in Geneva, and ultimate removal was recorded by Benjamin Drew in Toronto in the early 1850s and published in Drew, *The Refugee: A North-Side View of Slavery* (1855; reprint, Reading, Mass.: Addison-Wesley, 1969), 73–74. In his *Autobiography of a Fugitive Negro* (1855; reprint, New York: Arno and New York Times, 1968), 17–18, Samuel R. Ward identified Lucas as one of Toronto's most highly skilled blacksmiths. Lucas died in Toronto in about 1870 at the age of forty-eight. See issues of the *Geneva Gazette* from 1807 through 1826 for notices about runaways; in one announcement from the 16 July 1818 issue, Geneva merchant David Naglee warned would-be slavecatchers that his "Negro Boy named Philip Hardy" would probably "alter his name, and change or sell his clothes to prevent getting detected." For other accounts of fugitive aliases, see Prude, " 'To Look upon the Lower Sort,' " and William Still, *The Underground Railroad: A Record of Facts, Authentic Narratives, Letters, &c., Narrating the Hardships, Hair-breadth Escapes, and Death Struggles of the Slaves in Their Efforts for Freedom* . . . (1871; reprint, Chicago: Johnson, 1970).

10. In a record of slave manumissions in Albany between 1800 and 1828, only 15 percent of 340 names recorded had surnames, and these were almost never the

names of the masters who freed them. See Harry B. Yoshpe, "Record of Slave Manumissions in Albany, 1800–28," *The Journal of Negro History* 26, 4 (Oct. 1941): 499–522.
Gary B. Nash, in *Forging Freedom: The Formation of Philadelphia's Black Community,
1720–1840* (Cambridge and London: Harvard Univ. Press, 1988), 95, 85–86, and Herbert Gutman, in *The Black Family in Slavery and Freedom, 1750–1925* (New York: Vintage, 1976), 230–35, have discussed the tendency to take names dissimilar to those of
their former owners and the psychic meaning of taking new names among newly
freed people. In Philadelphia, only nineteen of 270 slaves manumitted between 1770
and 1790 chose names that could be found on the list of 197 slaveholders during that
time. Gutman found similar instances in his review of the marriage records of former
slaves kept by planters, the Union Army, and the Freedmen's Bureau in certain parts
of Virginia and Mississippi between 1864 and 1866. Gutman notes, in addition, the
tendency of some to take the names of masters far removed from the ones who manumitted them, as does Booker T. Washington in *Up From Slavery* (1901) in *Three Negro
Classics* (New York: Avon, 1865), 41. On naming patterns among free and enslaved
African Americans, see Newbell Niles Puckett, *Black Names in America: Origins and
Usage* (Boston: G. K. Hall, 1975), and J. L. Dillard, *Black Names*, vol. 13 in Joshua A.
Fishman, ed., *Contributions to the Sociology [of] Language* (The Hague: Mouton, 1976).
For accounts of particular name changes, see Frederick Douglass, *My Bondage and My
Freedom* (1855; reprint, Urbana: Univ. of Illinois Press, 1987), 209; William Wells
Brown, "Narrative of the Life and Escape of William Wells Brown," in Brown, *Clotel;
or, The President's Daughter: A Narrative of Slave Life in the United States* (1853; reprint,
New York: Carol, 1969), 322, 34–35; Joel Schor, *Henry Highland Garnet: A Voice of Black
Radicalism in the Nineteenth Century* (Westport, Conn: Greenwood, 1977), 4–5; [The
Rev. J. W. Loguen], *The Rev. J. W. Loguen, as a Slave and as a Freeman: A Narrative of
Real Life* (Syracuse, N.Y.: J. G. K. Truair, 1859); and, on Sojourner Truth, Emma
Brown Galvin, "The Lore of the Negro in Central New York" (Ph.D. diss., Cornell
Univ., May 1943), 53, 62.

11. Richard Wright, *Black Boy: A Record of Childhood and Youth* (1937; reprint, New
York: Harper and Row, 1966, 1989), 45.

12. Frederick Douglass, "Address of the Colored National Convention to the
People of the United States," *Proceedings of the Colored National Convention, Held in
Rochester, July 6th, 7th and 8th, 1853* (Rochester, N.Y.: Frederick Douglass' Paper,
1853), 16; Richard Wright, "Introduction: How 'Bigger' Was Born," in *Native Son*
(1940; reprint, New York: Harper and Row, 1989), xii.

13. Folklorist Lydia Parrish lived three years on St. Simon's Island before she
heard a slave spiritual and fifteen years before she discovered that her African-American cook could sing the slave songs Parrish was trying to collect. "When I periodically
ask why, in all those years, she never told me she could sing, she smiles quizzically,
but says nothing," Parrish wrote, adding, "I am convinced that the average Negro
enjoys intensely knowing something the white man does not." In William Wells
Brown's novel *Clotel*, the white plantation mistress warns a visitor not to let the slaves
see them as they walked along, "or they will stop singing." See Brown, *Clotel*, 154.
Parrish's account is cited in Lawrence W. Levine, *Black Culture and Black Consciousness:
Afro-American Folk Thought from Slavery to Freedom* (Oxford: Oxford Univ. Press, 1977),
101.

14. My point of view about knowledge and its manipulation by majority and
minority groups and about the function of typification in social life is largely influenced by the work of Peter L. Berger and Thomas Luckmann, *The Social Construction of*

Reality: A Treatise in the Sociology of Knowledge (Garden City, N.Y.: Doubleday, 1966); Erving Goffman, *Interaction Ritual: Essays on Face-to-Face Behavior* (New York: Doubleday, 1967); Alfred Schutz, *The Phenomenology of the Social World,* Northwestern University Studies in Phenomenology and Existential Philosophy, trans. George Walsh and Frederick Lehnert (Evanston, Ill.: Northwestern Univ. Press, 1967); Arthur Brittan, *Meanings and Situations* (London: Routledge and Kegan Paul, 1973), and Edmund R. Leach, "Anthropological Aspects of Language: Animal Categories and Verbal Abuse," in William A. Lessa and Evon Z. Vogt, eds., *Reader in Comparative Religion: An Anthropological Approach,* 3d ed. (New York: Harper and Row, 1972), 206–20.

15. The term "given reality" is coined and discussed in Berger and Luckmann, *Social Construction of Reality,* 60, 88–89; Richard Wright described how blacks view the world in his introduction to *Native Son,* xvii.

1. Arrivals and Departures

1. William Wyckoff, *The Developer's Frontier: The Making of the Western New York Landscape* (New Haven: Yale Univ. Press, 1988), 46, 115.

2. On the migration into western New York, see Wyckoff, *The Developer's Frontier,* esp. 104–6; Whitney Cross, *The Burned-Over District: The Social and Intellectual History of Enthusiastic Religion in Western New York, 1800–1850* (Ithaca, N.Y.: Cornell Univ. Press, 1950), 3–29; and O. [Orsamus] Turner, *History of the Pioneer Settlement of the Phelps and Gorham's Purchase, and Morris' Reserve* (Rochester, N.Y.: William Alling, 1851). On Williamson's plans for Geneva and its access to the Chesapeake Bay, see G. David Brumberg, *The Making of an Upstate Community: Geneva, New York* (Geneva, N.Y.: Geneva Bicentennial Commission, W. F. Humphrey Press, 1976), 32–42.

3. J. L. Dillard, *Black Names,* vol. 13 in Joshua Fishman, ed., *Contributions to the Sociology of Language,* 18. "Tryphena," a Genevan listed in the 1820 census, may derive from the female "Quasheba" or "Beneba"; the latter may also have been the source of Harriet Jupiter's middle name, Bethena. The first name Qualm (Qualm Demun, who lived in nearby Ovid in 1850) and the surname McQuon (James McQuon and his daughters lived in Geneva in the 1840s) may derive from day names as well.

4. Phyllis F. Field, *The Politics of Race in New York: The Struggle for Black Suffrage in the Civil War Era* (Ithaca: Cornell Univ. Press, 1982), 31–32; Leon F. Litwack, *North of Slavery: The Negro in the Free States, 1790–1860* (Chicago: Univ. of Chicago Press, 1961), 14, 3; Ward, *Autobiography,* 40.

5. Alexander Coventry, "Memoirs of an Emigrant: The Journal of Alexander Coventry, M.D., in Scotland, the United States, and Canada during the Period 1788–1831," typescript prepared by the Albany Institute of History and Art and the New York State Library, 1978. See esp. 532, 610, 630–33, 640, 645–47, 670, 688, 698–703, 727, 732–38, 744. Collections of the Albany Institute. A 4 Dec. 1883 letter to Arthur P. Rose from Geneva historian George S. Conover suggests that Coventry's laborers were largely white. Writing of Rose's ancestor Robert during settlement years, Conover stated, "At that time Rose Hill farm could not have been worked by white people as well as by the blacks—Dr. Coventry had tried and failed." Conover alleged that Coventry's failure was due to the fact that whites were susceptible to the air, "full of malaria," from swamps at the northeastern end of Rose's property bordering Seneca Lake. Conover claimed that the "blacks . . . were not affected" by the unhealthy air at Rose Hill and so could live along the shore and work in the swamps to "overcome the source of malaria." But Bett, like many whites, may have fallen victim to this ague,

popularly called "Genesee Fever." Conover's letter to Rose is in the collections of the Geneva Historical Society.

6. Conover's statement was cited in A.P. Rose, "Slavery in the Early Day" (Typescript of paper presented at the Geneva Historical Society, 3 Dec. 1883), collections of the Geneva Historical Society. Before 1800, one family in the township may have been composed of free blacks or mulattoes. Joshua Dunbar and eight others in his household were listed as "free persons other than Indians not taxed" in the 1800 township census; the minutes of an 1811 town meeting state that Dunbar appeared to declare himself a free man who had been born free. Typically, only blacks made such official declarations. In his certification of freedom, Dunbar was said to be "of a pretty dark Complexion," which suggests he may have been a mulatto. The fact that none of his descendants are listed as colored persons in censuses suggests that they had come to "pass for white" and probably intermarried with whites. See Turner, *History of the Pioneer Settlement*, 412, 426, 429, and Austin Steward, *Twenty-Two Years a Slave, and Forty Years a Freeman* (Rochester, N.Y.: William Alling, 1857), 12–55.

7. Gillam is listed in every census between 1820 and 1855, and his death is recorded in the *Geneva Gazette*, 28 Oct. 1859. The New Jersey Historical Society has a manuscript record of a five-page bill of sale of a "mulatto man slave" named Phillip Gillam, aged twenty-nine, from George Lee to James Rees of Charles County, Maryland, dated 21 July 1801. Although the document itself cannot be found, the record indicates that Rees agreed therein to manumit Gillam after ten years. The bill of sale also notes that Rees purchased Gillam's wife and children and freed all of them. Assuming this Gillam to be the same one who was associated with Rees in Geneva, it seems likely that Gillam had been hired out to Rees before the sale. In his last years he lived with his son Philip Jr. on High Street. The last Gillam in Geneva appears to have been Joseph C. ("Chris") Gillam, who may well have been living on the land Philip Gillam Jr. bought sometime before 1822. He died in 1931. His wife Mary Douglass Gillam, descended from two of John Nicholas's slaves, died in 1934.

8. Woods was married to a woman named Eliza, who may have been the sister of Alexander F. Rose of Hampstead, Virginia, and Robert Selden Rose of Geneva. In Alexander Rose's will, dated 29 October 1831, he left "the four negroes now in possession of Nathaniel Anderson Esquire of Memphis, Tennessee, by name Fanny, William, John and a little girl" to "my beloved sister, Eliza Woods," "with power to bequeath them to whom she pleases." As Woods's origins and whereabouts after 1824 are unknown, it is not possible to document any family relation to the Roses nor the possession of slaves after Alexander Rose's death.

9. According to descendant Arthur Patrick Rose, Robert S. Rose also owned extensive Wayne County acreage; the town of Rose is named for him. Some of the county's African Americans may have descended from Rose slaves, which may help explain the historically close ties between Wayne County and Geneva blacks. See [D. Willers], "Robert S. Rose," *Waterloo Observer*, undated clipping [about 1879] in the collections of Geneva Historical Society.

10. "An account of the emigration of the Rose and Nicholas families from Virginia to New York State as given by George W. Nicholas Esq. of Geneva N.Y.," Geneva Historical Society. On Peregrine Fitzhugh, see E. Anne Schaetzke, "Slavery in the Genesee Country, 1789 to 1827" (Empire State College, 1983), 11–18, Geneva Historical Society.

11. In his autobiography *Twenty-Two Years a Slave, and Forty Years a Freeman*, 12–55, Steward discusses Helm's cruelty and his ultimate dissolution in the Genesee

Country. Steward's mother was Helm's cook; he was Helm's errand boy and eventually parlayed the contacts he made into a successful retail operation in Rochester.

12. The Nicholas family papers at the Geneva Historical Society include two records of slave sales, one dated 31 May 1802 from Gerard B. Cousin to Nicholas Cousin in Maryland, the other dated the next day from Nicholas Cousin to John Nicholas. Presumably, these slaves were part of the migration to Geneva, though the names do not match those Nicholas gave the Ontario County Clerk in 1803.

13. Field, *Politics of Race*, 32; Alexander C. Flick, ed., *History of the State of New York*, vol. 6., *The Age of Reform* (New York: Columbia Univ. Press, 1934), 250–51; "Titles of acts passed the thirty-first session of the Legislature of the State of New-York," *Geneva Expositor*, 25 May 1808; *Geneva Expositor*, 13 July 1808; *Geneva Gazette*, 2 May 1810.

14. The manumission records for Ginna, John Duncan, and Mingo and Maria are dated 5 Dec. 1799, 6 Dec. 1808, and 13 Dec. 1809, respectively, and are preserved in a partial typescript of early Seneca township records in the collections of the Geneva Historical Society.

15. In his computer-assisted analysis of 1724 runaway notices appearing in northern and southern newspapers from 1750 to 1800, Jonathan Prude has suggested that the expectation that slaves would return, the cost of placing ads, and "transportation difficulties" combined to cause only comparatively prosperous slaveowners "located near newspaper offices" to advertise for the return of slaves. Prude's data is from the later eighteenth century, but conditions were probably similar in Geneva's early nineteenth-century settlement years. See " 'To Look upon the Lower Sort,' " 129. Van Gelder's advertisement appeared in the *Geneva Gazette*, 6 Sept. 1826.

16. The story of Rose's maltreatment of the slave Henry appeared in the *Geneva Gazette* of 5 Nov. 1828 and was part of a general attack on Rose mounted by the newspaper's publisher. The story of Peter Lincoln appears among "Family Sketches," in George S. Conover, ed., *History of Ontario County New York* (Syracuse, N.Y.: D. Mason, 1893), 107. Helm's ad for Steward appeared under the headline "40 Dollars Reward" in the *Geneva Gazette* of 20 Apr. 1814, and Steward presented his own account of his escape in *Twenty-Two Years a Slave*, 108–11.

17. "40 Dollars Reward," *Geneva Expositor*, 30 Sept. 1807; "Ten Dollars Reward!" *Geneva Gazette*, 16 July 1817; "Ten Dollars Reward!" *Geneva Gazette*, 7 May 1817.

18. See Prude, " 'To Look upon the Lower Sort,' " for an interpretation of the importance of slave clothing as a descriptor in such advertisements. Prude's analysis also considers the frequency with which other descriptors, such as precise age and height and facial expression, appeared in runaway ads.

19. "Stop the Villain!" *Geneva Expositor*, 5 Aug. 1807; "50 Dollars Reward," *Geneva Expositor*, 7 Oct. 1807; "40 Dollars Reward," *Geneva Gazette*, 20 Apr. 1814; "10 Dollars Reward," *Geneva Gazette*, 16 July 1816. Steward's account of his sister's treatment appears in Steward, *Twenty-Two Years a Slave*, 92. Four of the six female runaway slaves advertised in Geneva newspapers escaped without men, and two escaped with small children. The *Geneva Expositor* for 17 June 1807 described a "Negro wench named DINE," who ran away from Albany with her six-month-old child Jim; on 31 July 1811, Samuel Shekell, a Southerner who settled in Phelps, offered a reward of only six cents for the return of "a Black Woman, named ESTHER" who "took with her two children, one about 3 and the other about one year old." See *Geneva Gazette*, 31 July 1811. The fugitive rescuer Harriet Tubman, who grew up on a Maryland plantation, had fits of somnolence all her life after a planter threw an object at her with such

fury that it broke her skull. Her abuse is described in Sarah Elizabeth H. Bradford, *Harriet: The Moses of Her People* (New York: George R. Lockwood, 1897), 14–15.

20. Murray, probably Charles Condo, and at least one other slave—Ben, owned by Geneva banker Robert Scot—were all captured and returned to their owners. A Charles D. Condol appeared in the 1850 census, though he was too young to be the same person. Jacob Murray was returned to Bogert and manumitted in 1819. His name does not appear in censuses, although other African Americans with that surname do. Scot's notice of Ben's escape appeared in the 23 September 1812 *Geneva Gazette*. In 1814, Scot sold a "Ben" to Charles Pumpelly in Owego. A letter from Scot to Pumpelly recording the sale is in the collections of The Tioga County Historical Society, Owego, N.Y.

21. These Duncansens may have emigrated to Michigan by 1836 and may have been related to the African-American painter. James E. DeVries, in *Race and Kinship in a Midwestern Town: The Black Experience in Monroe, Michigan, 1900–1915* (Urbana: Univ. of Illinois Press, 1984), 9, 35, discusses a "New York emigrant" named John Duncanson (1771–1851), who came with Lucy Nickles Duncanson (1781–1854) and Robert S. Duncanson (1821–1872) to Monroe sometime after 1830. John Duncanson's birthdate tallies with the age range in which he was classed in the 1820 Geneva census, and, because he does not appear in the 1830 census, he may have migrated westward before the census enumeration. Robert S. Duncanson would appear to be a son or perhaps a nephew. DeVries notes that Robert S. Duncanson was a landscape artist recognized as one of the earliest American black artists "of importance." The possibility that these are the same Duncansons is heightened by Lucy's maiden name Nickles: in the 1820 Fayette census, where the Rose Hill estate was located, a Billie Nichols appears as a free black with twelve people in his household. Rose manumitted Billie "Nicholas" in 1815. DeVries also notes that William Wells Brown, who lived in Farmington, New York, near Geneva in 1847, lived in Monroe in 1835.

22. Williamson is cited in E. Thayles Emmons, *The Story of Geneva* (1931; reprint, Geneva, N.Y.: Finger Lakes Times, 1982), 85.

23. Much of the information about Geneva has been taken from my research for the exhibition *Geneva's Changing Waterfront, 1779–1989* and for the catalog of the same title published by the Geneva Historical Society in 1989. Among the accounts of transients in the waterfront area are "Great Conflagration!" *Geneva Gazette*, 10 Feb. 1871; "The Fire Fiend Again? The Seneca House and Knight's Canal Barn in Ruins!" *Geneva Gazette*, 2 June 1876; "Drowned in the Harbor," *Geneva Daily Times*, 13 Nov. 1903. See Brumberg, *Making of an Upstate Community*, 62–66, 79–83, for an account of the beginnings of Trinity Church and Hobart College.

24. An 1806 act of the Virginia legislature required all slaves manumitted after 1 May of that year to leave the state; Louisiana, in 1830, restricted the entry of free blacks into the state and curtailed the permissible activities of those already living there; Mississippi's Supreme Court maintained that "the laws of this state presume a negro *prima facie* to be a slave." See E. Franklin Frazier, *The Free Negro Family* (1932; reprint, New York: Arno and New York Times, 1968), 5–10. Gary B. Nash has pointed out that the black rebellion in Santo Domingo and the revolt of African-American Gabriel Prosser near Richmond about 1800 also unnerved southern white legislators and heightened the desire of freedmen there to move north. See Nash, *Forging Freedom*, 140–43.

25. Theodore Hershberg, "Free Blacks in Antebellum Philadelphia: A Study of Ex-Slaves, Freeborn, and Socioeconomic Decline," in Theodore Hershberg, ed., *Phila-*

delphia: Work, Space, and Family in the 19th Century (Oxford and New York: Oxford Univ. Press, 1981), 370.

26. In " 'The Seeming Counterfeit': Racial Politics and Early Blackface Minstrelsy," *American Quarterly* 43, 2 (June 1991): 241–42, Eric Lott suggests that the "commonplace" notion among antebellum labor historians that competition for work generated racial hostility between white and black laborers was "a cover story for white workers' precipitous descent in the class structure" brought about by a "diminished respect for labor."

27. On legal restrictions on blacks in the North, see Canter G. Woodson, *A Century of Negro Migration* (Washington, D.C.: The Association for the Study of Negro Life and History, 1918), 39–42; Litwack, *North of Slavery*, 35; Foner and Walker, eds., *Proceedings of the Black State Conventions*, xi; Daniel M. Johnson and Rex R. Campbell, *Black Migration in America: A Social Demographic History* (Durham, N.C.: Duke Univ. Press, 1981), 39–40; David Gerber, *Black Ohio and the Color Line, 1860–1915* (Urbana: Univ. of Illinois Press, 1978), 4; and James Forten, "Letters from a Man of Colour, On a Late Bill Before the Senate of Pennsylvania" (n.p., 1813).

28. On Pennsylvania in the 1830s, see Nash, *Forging Freedom*, 63, 274–76. "Legislature of New-York," *Geneva Gazette*, 17 Feb. 1813, related the Assembly action on black suffrage and certification. On racial trouble in other northern places, see Nash, *Forging Freedom*, 223–28, 274–79; Woodson, *Century of Negro Migration*, 43–48; Johnson and Campbell, *Black Migration in America*, 39–40, 43; and Litwack, *North of Slavery*, 39, 75–91. Tubman's statement is in Bradford, *Harriet: The Moses of Her People*, 38.

29. On 26 May 1807, Isaac Mitchell of Albany advertised in the *Geneva Gazette* for the return of his runaway Dine, who, he noted, spoke both English and Dutch because she had been owned by Dutch families.

30. Thernstrom and Knights, "Men in Motion," 19; Johnson and Campbell, *Black Migration in America*, 37. On the much earlier movement of blacks from the Pennsylvania countryside into Philadelphia, see Nash, *Forging Freedom*, 72–74, 135–37; on Ithaca, see Field Horne, "Ithaca's Black Community," in Cara A. Sutherland, ed., *A Heritage Uncovered: The Black Experience in Upstate New York, 1800–1925* (Elmira, N.Y.: Chemung County Historical Society, 1988), 18.

31. Sabbath School Register, Presbyterian Church of Geneva, 1829–1831, microfilm copy in the collections of the Geneva Historical Society; "Distribution of Lands to Colored Men Begun in 1846," volume 88, box 107, Gerrit Smith Papers, Arents Research Library, Syracuse University, Syracuse, N.Y.; James W. Duffin to Gerrit Smith, 9 Sept. 1846, Box 145, Gerrit Smith Papers.

32. Still's *Underground Railroad* is considered the most reliable source on the movement of fugitive slaves. See also Wilbur H. Siebert, *The Underground Railroad from Slavery to Freedom* (New York: The Macmillan Company, 1898). In *My Bondage*, 196, Douglass critized fugitive slave William Wells Brown for using the technique of fellow fugitives William and Ellen Craft as the means by which the heroine of his 1853 novel *Clotel; or, The President's Daughter* attempted to rescue her still-bound daughter.

33. In the multi-volume 1934 *History of New York State*, a map of underground routes in the state that purports to have been based on one published in Siebert, *Underground Railroad* (facing 113) shows a "known route" passing straight north from Elmira to Geneva, up the western shore of Seneca Lake. But the map in Siebert shows no such route. See Alexander C. Flick, ed., *Modern Party Battles*, vol. 7 of *History of the State of New York* (New York: Columbia Univ. Press, 1934), facing 68.

34. R. P. Bush, "The 'Underground' Railroad," *Penn Yan Democrat*, 3 May 1918;

Arch Merrill, *The Underground, Freedom's Road and Other Upstate Tales* (New York: American Book–Stratford Press, 1963), 72–73; Josephine M. Johnson, "From Corduroy to Black Top," Feb.–Oct. 1964, 68, 132, typescript in the collections of the Geneva Historical Society. Another fact seeming to suggest that Geneva's role was less than central in the Underground Railroad is that Sarah Bradford, a Genevan who wrote two biographies of Harriet Tubman while she was still living, does not mention Tubman or fugitive slaves in connection with Geneva. See Bradford, *Harriet: The Moses of Her People* and *Scenes in the Life of Harriet Tubman* (1886; reprint, New York: Corinth, 1961).

35. See *Geneva Palladium*, 26 Nov. 1827.

36. Edwin Barnard to Gerrit Smith, 30 July 1852, Gerrit Smith Papers.

37. Still, *Underground Railroad*, 98, 225, 291, 444. William Wyckoff has noted that cheap land attracted many settlers over the border; by the War of 1812, about 80 percent of the population of Upper Canada was of American origin. Surely some of these settlers were African American, perhaps including the Cleggett and Duffin families. See Wyckoff, *Developer's Frontier*, 117.

38. Lucas's narrative first appeared in Drew, *The Refugee*, 73–76; see also Ward, *Autobiography*, 192–93.

39. Jack Finzar, a volunteer at Geneva Historical Society, analyzed the 1850 census to compare the size of black and white families. Although kinship is not stated in the 1850 census, the analysis is based on probable kinship determined from surname and residence in the same household. This analysis found the average white family in Geneva to contain 5.2 persons; the average black household contained 4.4 persons. Data compiled by Gary Nash in Philadelphia and Stephan Thernstrom in Boston also suggest that black families were smaller, on average. See Nash, *Forging Freedom*, 76; Thernstrom, *The Other Bostonians*, 210.

40. Diary of Adelaide Cobleigh Prouty, 20 Oct. 1860–29 Dec. 1862; Geneva Historical Society. Thanks to Megan Ferrara for finding this entry.

41. Johnson and Campbell, *Black Migration in America*, 32–35; Fred Landon, "The Negro Migration to Canada after the Passing of the Fugitive Slave Act," *Journal of Negro History* 5, 1 (Jan. 1920): 22–27.

42. Ward, *Autobiography*, 109–10; *Proceedings of the Colored National Convention Held in Rochester*, 11; Douglass cited in Litwack, *North of Slavery*, 249. Samuel Ward went *"in some haste,"* he wrote, to Canada in November 1851 after aiding in the rescue of jailed fugitive Jerry McHenry in Syracuse. Garnet, who was Ward's cousin, left Geneva for England in August 1850. See Schor, *Henry Highland Garnet*, 111. Brown left for England before the law was passed, in 1849, having been invited to lecture there by English abolitionists. See Brown, "A Narrative of Slave Life," 45. Loguen, who with Gerrit Smith and Ward also aided in the Syracuse "Jerry Rescue," went to Skaneateles immediately afterward and then on to Canada, where he had lived in the mid–1830s. Alexander Crummel, an ordained Episcopalian priest, emigrated to Liberia in 1853. Bibb is Henry Bibb, and Remond is Charles Lenox Remond.

43. At the suffrage convention of colored citizens in Troy in September 1858, Duffin and other delegates proclaimed the Dred Scott decision "a foul and infamous lie, which neither black nor white men are bound to respect." See Foner and Walker, eds., *Proceedings of the Black State Conventions*, 99. In " 'An Examination of the Case of Dred Scott Against Sandford in the Supreme Court of the United States' prepared at request of and read before the Geneva Literary and Scientific Association, Geneva, N.Y., Dec. 28, 1858" (Geneva, N.Y.: W. C. Bryant, 1859), Geneva attorney Samuel

Alfred Foot publicly asserted that the country must decide "which is the greater evil"—to reorganize the Supreme Court (five of whose nine judges were from slave-holding states) in proportion to population, or to rewrite the United States Constitution—and that wholesale permission to bring slaves into free states would endanger the status of free labor. Foot's address is in the collections of Department of Rare Books and Special Collections, Rush Rhees Library, University of Rochester, Rochester, N.Y.

44. All of the manuscripts related to the VanTuyl kidnapping—including letters from Ohio station masters who tried to find Prue's lost carpet bag—passed from VerPlank to Waldo Hutchins, owner of Rose Hill in the mid-1900s, and then to Merrill Roenke, Rose Hill's administrator, who owns them now. I am grateful to Roenke for allowing me access to this collection. Prue's obituary appeared in the *Geneva Advertiser*, 23 July 1895.

45. On the postwar movement from the South, see Johnson and Campbell, *Black Migration in America*, 35, 46–47; on the tendency of single people to move, see Gutman, *Black Family*, 265, 9.

46. John Smith Duffin to Gerrit Smith, 11 Apr. 1873, Gerrit Smith Papers.

47. New York's African-American population increased 67 percent between 1870 and 1880. See Johnson and Campbell, *Black Migration in America*, 44–46, 58–63; Thernstrom, *The Other Bostonians*, 68, 181; Stanley Lieberson, "Generational Differences among Blacks in the North," *American Journal of Sociology* 79 (Nov. 1973): 552. On the movement to towns, see also W. E. B. Du Bois, *The Souls of Black Folk*, in *Writings* (New York: Library of America, 1986), 319; and Woodson, *Century of Negro Migration*, 121.

48. J. A. Miller, comp., *A Descriptive Review of the Fall Brook Coal Co.'s Route and the Principal Cities and Towns Along the Line of the Syracuse, Geneva and Corning RR* (Elmira, N.Y.: J. A. Miller, 1892), 63. For other information on Geneva's postwar growth, see Emmons, *The Story of Geneva*, Brumberg, *The Making of an Upstate Community*, and Grover, *Geneva's Changing Waterfront*.

49. Noble E. Whitford, *History of the Canal System of the State of New York*, vols. 1 and 2 (Albany, N.Y.: Brandow Printing, 1906), 1:477, 493–97, 2: 1064–65.

50. African Americans who moved to Philadelphia between 1870 and 1876 confronted virulent competition for industrial jobs, as well as housing shortages, tendencies that black historian Carter Woodson observed still prevailed generally in the North by 1918. See Woodson, *A Century of Negro Migration*, 190.

51. In his landmark study *Caste and Class in a Southern Town* (1937), sociologist John Dollard wrote, "Caste has replaced slavery as a means of maintaining the old status order of the South. By means of it racial animosity is held at a minimum." Dollard's analysis of the origins of this caste system in the South has relevance to the situation of blacks in the North. See Dollard, *Caste and Class*, 3d ed. (New York: Doubleday, 1957) pages 57–59, 62.

52. Dorothy Ethel Scott Cooke, interview with author, 26 Aug. 1989, Geneva, N.Y.

53. Theodore Hershberg noted a similar tendency in Philadelphia: for every 1,000 African-American males in 1838 there were 1,326 females, a ratio that climbed to 1,417 women per thousand men by 1860. In 1890, the proportion had grown more balanced, with 1,127 females for every 1,000 males, due to the increased number of men between the ages of twenty and forty. See Hershberg, "Free Blacks in Antebellum Philadelphia," 374.

54. In 1900, fully two-thirds of Geneva's African Americans had been born in New York State; in 1855, only 45 percent had been. See Johnson and Campbell, *Black Migration in America*, 63.

55. Carole Marks, *Farewell—We're Good and Gone: The Great Black Migration* (Bloomington: Indiana Univ. Press, 1989), 1, 11–15, 20–24, 36, 91–94; Johnson and Campbell, *Black Migration in America*, 67–68, 72; see also Elizabeth Clark- Lewis, "This Work Had A End: The Transition from Live-in to Day Work" (Working Paper 2 in "Southern Women: The Intersection of Race, Class and Gender," Center for Research of Women, Memphis State Univ. et al., 1985), 13.

56. Marks, *Farewell*, 1, 3, 21; Elizabeth Ross Haynes, "Negroes in Domestic Service in the United States," *Journal of Negro History* 8, 4 (Oct. 1923): 405; Johnson and Campbell, *Black Migration in America*, 81; see also Frank F. Lee, *Negro and White in Connecticut Town* (New York: Bookman, 1961), a sociological study of race relations in "Connecticut Town," where hiring practices at the local foundry caused a massive increase in the town's small black population between 1910 and 1930.

57. Marks, *Farewell*, 14, 36; see also Armstead L. Robinson, "The Difference Freedom Made: The Emancipation of Afro-Americans," in Darlene Clark Hine, ed., *The State of Afro-American History: Past, Present, and Future* (Baton Rouge: Louisiana State Univ. Press, 1986), 70–73. See also Johnson and Campbell, *Black Migration in America*, 77–78, and Thernstrom, *The Other Bostonians*, 180, for data on black population growth in large northern cities at this time.

58. U. S. Department of Commerce, *15th Census of the United States: 1930*, vol. 2, *Population: General Report, Statistics by Subjects* (Washington, D.C.: U.S. Government Printing Office, 1933), Table 21, 939–41, and Table 23, 67–73; *Sixteenth Census of the United States: 1940*, vol. 2, *Population: Characteristics of the Population*, part 5, *New York–Oregon* (Washington, D.C.: U.S. Government Printing Office, 1943); and Johnson and Campbell, *Black Migration in America*, 96–97.

59. Charles Kenney, interview with author, 26 Aug. 1989, Geneva, N.Y.

60. John Kenney, interview with author, 29 Oct. 1989, Brockport, N.Y.

61. Hilda R. Watrous, "Seneca Army Depot," *The County Between the Lakes: A Public History of Seneca County, New York, 1876–1982* (Waterloo, N.Y.: Seneca County Board of Supervisors / K-Mar Press, 1982), 1–35, 45–49; "Naval Training Station Presents Big Housing and Transportation Problem," *Geneva Daily Times*, 28 May 1942; Karl Drew Hartzell, *The Empire State at War: World War II* (n.p.: State of New York, 1949), 372; C. H. Freedman, "Report on Sampson Naval Base Area (Seneca County)," 31 Aug. 1942, Box 75, "Social and Economic Surveys," Sampson file, New York State War Council Records, New York State Archives, Albany. Hartzell cites four thousand African-American laborers "disappearing over Labor Day," but does not explain why.

62. Watrous, "Seneca Army Depot."

63. Hartzell, *Empire State at War*, 13, 67; Johnson and Campbell, *Black Migration in America*, 101–5, 116. After Franklin D. Roosevelt created the Committee on Fair Employment Practices in June 1941, the proportion of black employees in fifty-one defense areas, one Works Projects Administration study showed, rose from about 3 percent that October to more than 8 percent by mid-1944. On the use of southern African Americans in New York harvests, see Edward S. Godfrey Jr., New York Commissioner of Health, to Charles Poletti, State War Plans Coordinator, 15 October 1942, Box 152, State Health Department files, New York State War Council Records, New York State Archives; and Hartzell, *Empire State at War*, 148–66, 244–45.

64. New York had the greatest inmigration (282,000) of any state during the

1950s; Rochester's black population increased more than 600 percent between 1940 and 1960. See Thernstrom, *The Other Bostonians,* 180; Johnson and Campbell, *Black Migration in America,* 128–29; U.S. Department of Commerce, Bureau of the Census, *Sixteenth Census,* and *Eighteenth Decennial Census of the United States, Census of Population: 1960,* vol. 1, *Characteristics of the Population,* part 34, *New York* (Washington, D.C.: U.S. Government Printing Office, 1960), Table 21, 100–11; Table 77, 313–18.

65. Perry Carter Sr., interview with author, 29 Dec. 1989, Geneva, N.Y. Employment at Sampson stood at 150 on 3 June 1942 and at 6,000 by 21 July. See Watrous, *County Between the Lakes,* 48–49.

66. Cora Burke, interview with author, 30 Nov. 1989, Geneva, N.Y. African Americans from Sanford also settled in Rochester, where their numbers were large enough for a club to be created. Research on these former migrant workers appeared in a 1991 exhibition, "Going North: The Life and Times of Alice Mathis," at the Rochester Museum and Science Center, Rochester, N.Y.

67. Alvin Dion Robinson, interview with author, 23 Oct. 1989, Geneva, N.Y.

68. Olaf F. Larson and Emmit F. Sharp, *Migratory Farm Workers in the Atlantic Coast Stream: 1. Changes in New York,* 1953 and 1957 (Ithaca: New York State College of Agriculture, May 1960), 3–12.

69. Virginia Peek, interview with author, 25 Sep. 1989, Rochester, N.Y.

70. Essie Tucker, interview with author, 14 Dec. 1989, Geneva, N.Y.

2. Old Families and New Families

1. "Report of the Committee on Social Relations and Polity," *Proceedings of the Colored National Convention* (Rochester, 1853), 20–21.

2. Ibid., 23–24.

3. In Newburyport between 1850 and 1880, Thernstrom found the use that immigrants made of their savings to attest "their search for maximum security rather than for mobility out of the working class." See Thernstrom, *Poverty and Progress: Social Mobility in a Nineteenth Century City* (Cambridge, Mass.: Harvard Univ. Press, 1964), 68–69, 160–61. On ethnic property ownership elsewhere, see Gerber, *Black Ohio and the Color Line,* 88–89; John Bodnar, *Immigration and Industrialization: Ethnicity in an American Mill Town* (Pittsburgh: Univ. of Pittsburgh Press, 1977); Dean Esslinger, *Immigrants and the City: Ethnicity and Mobility in a Nineteenth-Century Midwestern Community* (Port Washington, N.Y.: Kennikat Press, 1978); Howard Chudacoff, *Mobile Americans: Residential and Social Mobility in Omaha, 1880–1920* (New York: Oxford Univ. Press, 1972); Clyde Griffen and Sally Griffen, *Natives and Newcomers: The Ordering of Opportunity in Mid–Nineteenth-Century Poughkeepsie* (Cambridge, Mass: Harvard Univ. Press, 1978); Thomas Kessner, *The Golden Door: Italian and Jewish Immigrant Mobility in New York City, 1800–1915* (New York: Oxford Univ. Press, 1977); and James Henretta, "The Study of Social Mobility: Ideological Assumptions and Conceptual Bias," *Labor History* 18 (Spring 1977): 164–78.

4. One study of twenty-five midwestern black and white families matched according to sex, socioeconomic position, and marital status found that black families tended to perceive their kin as more important than white families did, relied on them more often, and were much more apt to have kin other than children living in their households. Only parents were valued equally by white and black families. See William C. Hays and Charles H. Mindel, "Extended Kinship Relations in Black and White Families," *Journal of Marriage and the Family* 35 (Feb. 1973): 47–53.

5. Cited in Schor, *Henry Highland Garnet*, 97.

6. Tamara Hareven, *Family Time and Industrial Time* (Cambridge: Cambridge Univ. Press, 1982), 360; see also Thernstrom, *Poverty and Progress*, 117, 136–37.

7. Mrs. Clyde Mathis, letter to the editor, *Geneva Times*, undated clipping from Sept. 1965.

8. Douglass, *My Bondage*, 28–29, 36, 38, 209; Gutman, *Black Family*, 29. See also Woodson, *A Century of Negro Migration*, 118; and Ward, *Autobiography*, 3–4.

9. Douglass believed that "thousands would escape from slavery who now remain there" were they not bound to families and friends by "strong cords of affection." See *My Bondage*, 202. Gutman found that most who remained in slavery until the general emancipation had been members of two-parent families; see *Black Family*, 265, 9. Some families, such as Ward's and that of his cousin, Henry Highland Garnet, escaped as a body, but the work of some demographers and some contemporary sources, such as the letters that Underground Railroad operator William Still received from fugitives, document that many fugitives left family and friends behind. See Johnson and Campbell, *Black Migration in America*, 35; Steward, *Twenty-Two Years a Slave*, and, on Lucas, Drew, *The Refugee*, 74; Ward, *Autobiography*, 3–4.

10. See Nash, *Forging Freedom*, 76, 158, 163, for a discussion of African-American family formation in Philadelphia.

11. Gerry Munn McBroom, interview with author, 2 Jan. 1990, Seneca Castle, N.Y.

12. In Geneva in 1855 (the first census to record the names of all African Americans and their kinship), 12 percent of all African-American households were headed by females. Between 1875 and 1925, the proportion of female-headed households among all black households in Geneva was probably never higher than 19 percent, comparable to the proportion of such households in 1880 in Boston, where there were relatively more female-headed Irish households. See Thernstrom, *The Other Bostonians*, 212–13. See also Nash, *Forging Freedom*, 161–62; Paul J. Lammermeier, "The Urban Black Family of the Nineteenth Century: A Study of Black Family Structure in the Ohio Valley, 1850–1880," *Journal of Marriage and the Family* 35 (Aug. 1973): 439–40, 451; and Gerber, *Black Ohio*, 95, for similar findings for Philadelphia in 1790, 1800, and 1820, Pittsburgh, Cleveland, and Buffalo in 1850, and Ohio cities between 1850 and 1880.

13. The proportions of extended and nuclear households in Geneva remained roughly constant for the rest of the century and were comparable to those in other northeastern cities, with the exception of such places as Saratoga, whose race track and hotels drew many single African Americans. See Myra B. Young Armstead, "An Historical Profile of Black Saratoga, 1800–1925," in Sutherland, ed., *A Heritage Uncovered*, 34. See Gutman, *The Black Family*, xviii, for data on family configuration in Buffalo.

14. In 1925, households made up of unrelated black people were 20 percent of all black households in Geneva, down from 28 percent in 1900.

15. See Nash, *Forging Freedom*, 84, on this process of name formation.

16. Ida Foster died 21 Sept. 1942, less than three months after her husband died. Joseph A. Foster, born in 1893, enlisted in the army in 1917, but where he went after his 30 Sept. 1919 discharge from Company G of the 25th Infantry stationed at Fort Slocum, New York, is unknown; his parents' obituaries state his residence to be in New York (in June 1942) and in Boston (in September).

17. See Haynes, "Negroes in Domestic Service," 434; Clark-Lewis, " 'This Work

Had A End' "; and Gutman, *The Black Family*, 450–51, for data on nonkin households in Indianapolis in the 1920s and New York City in 1905, and on the prevalence of extended households among domestics in Washington from 1910 through the 1920s.

18. See Haynes, "Negroes in Domestic Service," 391–92, and Marks, *Farewell*, 128–29. In *Serving Women*, 207, Dudden notes that at the Anchorage, a home for unwed mothers in Elmira, staff cared for babies while their mothers did domestic work because few employers wanted servants with children.

19. James Henderson, interview with author, 18 Sept. 1989, Geneva, N.Y.

20. Douglass, *My Bondage*, 40, 48–49; Gutman, *The Black Family*, 185, 217–18; see also Robinson, "The Difference Freedom Made," 70.

21. In "Condition of the Free Colored People," 255, James Freeman Clarke had noted that the many benevolent societies among free blacks in the 1850s had kept many out of poor houses.

22. Thernstrom and Knights, "Urban Population Mobility," 36; Thernstrom, *Poverty and Progress*, 89–90; Esslinger, *Immigrants and the City*, 94–97; Bodnar, *Immigration and Industrialization*, 52. Foster's house was one of the oldest in Geneva, having been built on South Main Street in 1803 and moved to the site in 1836. See "Chapter 48: Old Houses in Geneva," undated newspaper clipping in anonymous scrapbook, collections of the Geneva Historical Society.

23. "Report of Committee upon Agriculture," *Minutes of the National Convention of Colored Citizens: Held at Buffalo, On the 15th, 16th, 17th, 18th and 19th of August, 1843* . . . (New York: Pierce and Reed, 1843), 30; Thernstrom, *Poverty and Progress*, 164.

24. On the tendency to buy and improve homes rather than to establish businesses, see Gerber, *Black Ohio*, 88, 113. In *Natives and Newcomers*, 77–79, Clyde and Sally Griffen found only two black workers in the city of Poughkeepsie who possessed real estate valued at $5,000 or more in 1870, and that "blacks owned a negligible share of the city's real estate." Concentrating on the value of holdings at the high end of the scale and at the proportion of the value of all real estate owned by blacks obscures an understanding of what property *meant* to blacks and conceals how many blacks probably owned some real estate in Poughkeepsie. The simple capacity to own land, however much, however valuable, was probably more significant than how their property compared with properties whites owned; as Gerber has argued, a "secure domesticity" may have been the predominant value among blacks.

25. John Nicholas Norton, *Allerton Parish: A Tale of the Early Days of Western New York* (New York, 1863), 86–87. Norton was John Nicholas's nephew. His father had joined the 1803 Rose-Nicholas migration and had settled in Richmond (Allerton Parish), a village to the west. It seems doubtful that Norton, born in 1820, himself saw slave cabins, but *Allerton Parish* may present his father's recollections. See also George S. Conover to A. P. Rose, Esq., 4 Dec. 1883, collections of the Geneva Historical Society. Conover did not cite the source of his assertion; born in Brooklyn, he did not move to Geneva until after the Civil War.

26. J. W. Loguen, "Missionary Labors." Martha M. Wright advertised a colored boarding house in Geneva in several issues of the *Impartial Citizen* in 1849, but it was not listed in the 1850 village census.

27. A note on the back of Katy Gillam's manumission paper from James Rees indicates Rees's intention to free Moses Lee at the same time. Gillam's and Lee's papers must have been folded together, Lee's inside Gillam's. Only Gillam's survives in the archives of Hobart College.

28. William Wyckoff has noted that rural lands near Canandaigua, the jumping-off place for lands in western New York's Holland Patent, were at a "premium" of

five to six dollars an acre in 1800. Land prices throughout the region rose after 1808, reaching as high as $4.50 an acre by 1811 in Holland Patent's less desirable northern townships. See Wyckoff, *Developer's Frontier*, 70–71. In 1883, Arthur P. Rose stated that Willis Lee, one of the "original stock" of slaves whom Rose and Nicholas brought north, "lived and died about three miles west of Geneva." Lee might have been the "Willis" whom Nicholas registered as one of his slaves with the Ontario County clerk, and he may be the same person whom John Nicholas Norton identified as "Uncle Willis" in *Allerton Parish*. Norton recalled driving "two or three miles" from White Springs Farm to see the elderly and infirm "Uncle Willis, an old family servant of Colonel Ashley's [Nicholas], who lived on a little farm of his own." See Norton, *Allerton Parish*, 25–29, 30, 32, 82–87.

29. Local historian G. M. B. Hawley presented evidence of the sale, not donation, of Woods's land in "Chronicles of Geneva: No. 9: Slavery in Ontario County," *Geneva Daily Times*, 15 June 1921, 10:2–4. Where Woods came from and where he went are unknown, though James H. Woods, probably their son, continued to sell land in the area to African Americans through at least 1845.

30. Field, *Politics of Race*, 37. Convention proceedings also reveal considerable lingering concern about earlier gradual emancipation legislation. Robert Rose was among the delegates, but any contribution he made to the debates is not recorded, nor is his vote on the question whether to shorten the time that the state's remaining slaves "should continue to serve masters." See Nathaniel H. Carter, William L. Stone, and Marcus T. C. Gould, *Reports of the Proceedings and Debates of the Convention of 1821, Assembled for the Purpose of Amending the Constitution of the State of New-York . . .* (Albany: E. E. Hosford, 1821), New York State Archives.

31. Samuel Ward had identified a "policy of coloured people settling themselves together, in a particular part of a town or village" among African Americans in Canada in the 1850s, which suggests his belief, however well founded, that such segregation was voluntary. Ward, *Autobiography*, 205.

32. Jeffrey's name appears on the *North Star* masthead in 1848, and that newspaper lists him among the executive committee of the Western New York Anti-Slavery Society in the same year. Cleggett's biography appeared in "Family Sketches" in Conover, ed., *History of Ontario County, New York* (Syracuse, N.Y.: D. Mason, 1893), 274. On Garnet's assignment to Geneva, see Schor, *Henry Highland Garnet*, 44–45n. 6.

33. In 1875, 72 percent of Syracuse's 551 African-Americans lived in the seventh and eighth wards; Auburn, Rochester, and Elmira also had heavy concentrations of blacks in certain neighborhoods. In Boston, residential segregation became steadily more pronounced between 1880 and 1960. See C. W. Seaton, comp., *Census of the State of New York for 1875 Compiled from the Original Returns* (Albany, N.Y.: Weed, Parsons, 1877), Table 14, 22; Sutherland, ed., *A Heritage Uncovered*, 21, 31–32; and Thernstrom, *The Other Bostonians*, 209–10. Carole Marks has observed that while educational and occupational advances had occurred among blacks by the 1950s, they were no less segregated residentially. See Marks, *Farewell*, 157.

34. "This is Queer," *Geneva Advertiser*, 23 July 1895.

35. Theodore Hershberg's work in Philadelphia tends to support the notion that these postwar African-American migrants were "not typical at all, but instead were representative of the 'Talented Tenth,' " a term coined by African-American historian Carter Woodson to describe an enterprising group that was not nearly so representative of most southern blacks as post–1915 migrants were. See Hershberg, "Free Blacks in Antebellum Philadelphia," 390n. 27.

36. Leona Hardy James, interview with author, 20 Nov. 1989, Geneva, N.Y.

37. "Race Discrimination End Aim of New York Plan," *Geneva Daily Times*, 2 Mar. 1939.

38. Memorandum from Thelma S. Ellis, 10 Aug. 1942, Box 75, "Social and Economic Surveys, M-Sampson," New York State War Council Records, New York State Archives.

39. C. H. Freeman, "Report on Sampson Naval Base Area," 31 Aug. 1942; memorandum from C. H. Freeman after visit to Geneva, 12 Aug. 1942, Box 75, "Social and Economic Surveys, M-Sampson," New York State War Council Records, New York State Archives.

40. "Twenty Flee House Swept by Night Fire," *Geneva Daily Times*, 2 Jan. 1945; "Exchange St. Block Gutted by Fire That Does $30,000 Damage," *Geneva Daily Times*, 8 Jan. 1945; "Two Genevans Burned in Two Blazes Here; Both are Recovering," *Geneva Daily Times*, 31 May 1946; "Shop, Apartment Damaged by Fire on Tillman St.," *Geneva Daily Times*, 21 Apr. 1948.

41. "Reminiscence No. 20," *Geneva Advertiser-Gazette*, 31 Mar. 1910; see also "Tons of Coal Washed Ashore," *Geneva Daily Times*, 30 Dec. 1908; *Geneva Advertiser-Gazette*, 31 Dec. 1908.

42. In 1943, Congress ruled that all 940,000 units built to house defense workers and the military across the country were to be removed "with the exception," the *Geneva Daily Times* reported, "of such housing as the administrator, after consultation with local communities, finds is still needed in the interest of orderly demobilization of the war effort." "Temporary Housing Must Be Demolished After War," *Geneva Daily Times*, 15 July 1943; "Fifty Victory Home Units Are Opened for Occupancy," *Geneva Daily Times*, 10 Mar. 1944; "Dixon Victory Homes Buildings to Be Made Adaptable for Prisoners," *Geneva Daily Times*, 8 May 1944; "German Prisoners Of War Begin Work at Comstock Canning Co.," *Geneva Daily Times*, 27 June 1944.

43. Archer E. Church Jr. "Sampson: A Study of the Growth and Impact of a Military Facility" (M.S. thesis, Princeton Univ., 1962), 85–86.

44. "Council to Discuss Water, Sewage Surveys, Parking Lot," *Geneva Daily Times*, 7 July 1955; Rev. John C. Laske, "Our Sub-Standard Housing," *Geneva Daily Times*, 9 July 1955.

45. "Complaints Heard About Conditions At Dixon Tract," *Geneva Times*, 21 Oct. 1955; "Letters to the Editor: Council Candidate on Dixon Tract," *Geneva Times*, 26 Oct. 1955.

46. On living conditions in the camp, see Dorothy Nelkin, "A Response to Marginality: The Case of Migrant Farm Workers," *British Journal of Sociology* 20 (1969): 375–89.

47. Edward S. Godfrey Jr., Commissioner of Health, to Charles Poletti, State War Plans Coordinator, 15 Oct. 1942, and Charles A. Winding to Mrs. Winthrop Pennock, 19 May 1943, Box 152, "DP State / Health, Department of," New York State War Council Records, New York State Archives; Hartzell, *Empire State at War*, 244–45; "RFK, Javits: One Difference" and "Farm Labor Camps 'Deplorable,' Kennedy, Javits Say after Tour," *Rochester Democrat and Chronicle*, 9 Sept. 1967, 1, 1B. The Wayne County Farm Bureau registered a protest against "Harvest of Shame" in the 16 January 1961 *Congressional Record*. Thanks to Wayne County historian Margery Perez for her help in tracking down the date of Kennedy's visit to Wayne County.

48. The number of dwelling units in Geneva rose by 704 between 1940 and 1950, but the growth was entirely due to the conversion of single-family homes into multiple-family units. There were in fact 112 fewer single-family homes in Geneva by 1950,

and the city was claimed to be "considerably above the average, in cities of comparable size, in two-or-more family dwellings." Moreover, the number of vacant units rose from 164 in 1940 to 256 in 1950, which may reflect the deteriorating condition of rental property. See Church, "Sampson," 50–51, 85.

49. Jean Brell, "Genevans Map War on Discrimination," *Geneva Times*, 2 Mar. 1964; "Housing Problem Nears Acute Stage at Geneva," *Syracuse Herald-American*, 23, 25 May 1965; "Urban Renewal—What's Happened So Far in Geneva," *Geneva Times*, 1 Apr. 1966; Everett Jennings, "Cost of Buying Urban Renewal Property: $585,277," *Geneva Times*, 6 Feb. 1967; Chris Lavin, "Good Home Life Still Starts with Good Homes," *Finger Lakes Times*, 24 Aug. 1978.

50. Ward, *Autobiography*, 205.

51. See Dollard, *Caste and Class in Southern Town*, 212, and Lee, *Negro and White in Connecticut Town*, 30.

52. James W. Duffin to Gerrit Smith, 9 Sept. 1846, Box 145, Gerrit Smith Papers.

53. By 1855, two of three African-American barbers and the only butcher did not own land. However, the whitewashers Edward Johnson and John Bland, whose work may not have required paying rent or purchasing many tools, did own property. The black community's only chairmaker, Albert Arnold, also owned a home, as did barber James W. Duffin. The hackman William T. Brown and the blacksmith Henry N. Baker both owned property, but they both may have been hired tradesmen who did not own their own equipment.

54. Tompkins's will and letters of administration are in Ontario County probate records, Ontario County Records and Archives Center.

55. Bland had mortgaged several of his village parcels. After his property was sold, his wife eventually received $154.33 after his debts were paid. The bill from Covert to Bland is dated 1 Oct. 1881 and is among the Baldwin Papers at the Geneva Historical Society. Bland's will and probate are on file at the Ontario County Records Center and Archive.

3. Just What They Could Get to Do

1. On the alienation of African-American labor both under slavery and in the northern commercial and industrial economy, see Douglass, *My Bondage*, 155, 188; Du Bois, *The Souls of Black Folk*, 249; Du Bois, "The Revelation of Saint Orgne the Damned," in W. E. B. Du Bois, *Writings* (New York: Library of America, 1986), 1055; Charles Denby, *Indignant Heart: A Black Worker's Journal* (Detroit: Wayne State Univ. Press, 1989), 97, 120–21, 283; and Levine, *Black Culture and Black Consciousness*, 124, 249.

2. Cited in John Blassingame, ed., *The Frederick Douglass Papers*, vol. 3 of *Series One: Speeches, Debates, and Interviews* (New Haven: Yale Univ. Press, 1989), 71.

3. For information of black tradespeople in other northern cities, see Frazier, *The Free Negro Family*, 18; Lindsay, "Economic Conditions of Negroes in New York," 198; and Clarke, "Condition of the Free Colored People," 252.

4. "Ethiopian Serenaders," *Geneva Gazette*, 29 Nov. 1850. Gillam advertised himself as a barber in the *Geneva Courier*, 19 Oct. 1841; his obituary appeared in the *Geneva Gazette*, 17 Dec. 1852. Thanks to Jim Kimball, professor of music at the State University of New York at Geneseo, who shared his knowledge about the connection between barbering and musical talent. See Levine, *Black Culture and Black Consciousness*, 16, for ex-slave Solomon Northup's description of how his musical talent changed his

working life. For a twentieth-century example of the same phenomenon, see James Weldon Johnson, *Autobiography of an Ex-Colored Man*, in *Three Negro Classics*, 393–511.

5. For African-American occupational profiles in other northern cities, see Litwack, *North of Slavery*, 155; Frazier, *The Free Negro Family*, 18; Nash, *Forging Freedom*, 251; Clarke, "Condition of the Free Colored People," 251–53; Arnett G. Lindsay, "Economic Conditions of the Negroes of New York Prior to 1861," *Journal of Negro History* 6, 2 (Apr. 1921): 198; and Gutman, *The Black Family*, xviii.

6. *Proceedings of the National Convention of Colored People* (Troy, N.Y., 1847), 27.

7. M. A. Shadd, letter to the editor, *North Star*, 23 Mar. 1849; *Minutes of the National Convention of Colored Citizens* (New York, 1843), 30, 32, 34.

8. Steward, *Twenty-Two Years a Slave*, 167; Ward, *Autobiography*, 27; Washington, *Up from Slavery*, 149. That the point was controversial is attested by the "considerable debate" about it at the 1853 colored national convention in Rochester, in which several delegates insisted that the report on social relations and polity be amended so that it did not imply that "the colored people of this country are not producers." See *Proceedings of the Colored National Convention* (Rochester, 1853), 25, 27.

9. *Proceedings of the Colored National Convention* (Rochester, 1853), 35; *Minutes of the National Convention of Colored Citizens* (New York, 1843), 33.

10. These lots, most of them in the Adirondacks, were marginal farm land at best. See Lindsay, "Economic Conditions of the Negroes of New York," 192–95.

11. Alexander Graham, John Graham, John Bland, and Salaby Hardy were probably farming in the village. In his 1835 will, John Graham left his "old horse" to Willis Lee and his cow to John Duffin, and empowered Charles Kinney and Duffin to "improve cultivate or rent" his three-acre village lot for his beneficiary.

12. Rosetta Brown Handy, interview with author, 5 Feb. 1990, Spencerport, N.Y.

13. See Nelkin, "A Response to Marginality," 379.

14. W. E. B. Du Bois, "The Damnation of Women" (1920), reprinted in Du Bois, *Writings*, 963–64; Larson and Sharp, *Migratory Farm Workers*, 4.

15. *Minutes of the National Convention of Colored Citizens Held at Buffalo* (New York, 1843), 34; Steward, *Twenty-Two Years a Slave*, 167.

16. In New York State in 1850, laborers and servants predominated among the fifty thousand free blacks fifteen years old or older; even Harriet Tubman and Sojourner Truth worked as domestics. In 1910, six hundred thousand African-American women and girls worked as servants and washerwomen. See Lindsay, "Economic Conditions of the Negroes of New York," 198; Du Bois, "Damnation of Women," 964.

17. Thernstrom, *Poverty and Progress*, 17–18, 20.

18. Seventeen of more than two hundred men listed as laborers in the 1862 directory were black; most others had Irish surnames.

19. Du Bois, "The Damnation of Women," 963–64; Lindsay, "Economic Conditions of the Negroes of New York," 198; Ruth Schwartz Cowan, *More Work for Mother: The Ironies of Household Technology from the Open Hearth to the Microwave* (New York: Basic Books, 1983), 120. The 1940 workforce statistics are derived from *Sixteenth Census of the United States*, vol. 2, *Characteristics of the Population*, table 33.

20. Nineteenth-century advice books such as Catharine E. Beecher, *Domestic Receipt Book: Designed as a Supplement to Her Treatise on Domestic Economy*, 3d ed. (New York: Harper, 1858), 240, included recommendations about hiring and using servants. On the prevalence of servants in middle-class households, see William J. Rorabaugh, "Beer, Lemonade, and Propriety in the Gilded Age," in Kathryn Grover, ed., *Dining*

in America (Amherst: The Univ. of Massachusetts Press / The Strong Museum, 1987), 26; Cowan, *More Work for Mother*, 121–22; and Dudden, *Serving Women*, 63.

21. Cowan, *More Work for Mother*, 120; Haynes, "Negroes in Domestic Service," 390, 404, 430; Clark-Lewis, " 'This Work Had A End,' " 1.

22. Only Gideon Van Horn, relatively well remembered but listed only in the 1857 Geneva directory, is known to have worked as a boatman, although blacks were often found in maritime trades in northern coastal cities. Free blacks might have been able to secure a foothold in coastal trade before the Irish immigration, but Erie Canal trade was dominated by Irish labor.

23. On the black "dandy," see Lott, " 'The Seeming Counterfeit,' " 246–47, 254n. 67. Many thanks to Merri Ferrell, curator of transportation artifacts at the Museums at Stony Brook on Long Island, for her help with transportation terms.

24. Thomas M. Johnson, "The Most Unforgettable Character I've Met," *Reader's Digest*, Sept. 1961, 168D–F; Arch Merrill, *Our Goodly Heritage* (New York: American Book–Stratford Press, 1957), 188; "Herm Kenney," *The Echo of the Seneca* (Geneva, N.Y.: Hobart College, 1901), 146.

25. The origin of the term "smash" in this sense is unknown, but it has been used before in Geneva. Henry Douglass, a former Rose family slave, was known locally as Pompey Smash. Douglass drove oxen and a trotter for his employer, Joseph Wright of Waterloo.

26. For statistics on middle-class use of laundresses and of the electric appliances that replaced them, see Marks, *Farewell, We're Good and Gone*, 130; Cowan, *More Work for Mother*, 29–30, 98, 154–58, 166; Dudden, *Serving Women*, 107, 143.

27. On the roles and status of laundresses in African-American communities, see Gerber, *Black Ohio and the Color Line*, 19; Brown, *Clotel*, 63–64; Clark-Lewis, " 'This Work Had A End,' " 19–20; and Dudden, *Serving Women*, 224–25.

28. See Dudden, *Serving Women*, 49, on domestic advice about hiring whitewashers.

29. *Geneva Gazette*, 12 Nov. 1874, 24 Oct. and 21 Nov. 1879.

30. For information on barbering among African Americans in other cities, see Clarke, "Condition of the Free Colored People," 252; Steward, *Twenty-Two Years a Slave*, 167; Gerber, *Black Ohio and the Color Line*, 80–81; Griffen and Griffen, *Natives and Newcomers*, 212–13; Sutherland, ed., *A Heritage Uncovered*, 5, 12, 30; see also Denby, *Indignant Heart*, 25, and Marks, *Farewell*, 64, on barbers in the South.

31. Brown, "Narrative of the Life and Escape," 21, 39–40.

32. *Geneva Gazette*, 19 Oct. 1841, 20 Oct. 1865, 3 Nov. 1865.

33. Octavius Brooks Frothingham, *Gerrit Smith: A Biography* (New York: G. P. Putnam's Sons, 1878), 358; Warren Hunting Smith, interview with author, 29 Nov. 1989.

34. Wright's advertisement appeared in the 24 Oct. 1849 *Impartial Citizen* and in several subsequent issues.

35. See, for example, Blassingame, ed., *Frederick Douglass Papers*, vol. 3 of *Series One*, 64–68; *Proceedings of the Colored National Convention* (Rochester, 1853), 39; Sutherland, ed., *A Heritage Uncovered*, 14. In view of the lack of solid evidence that whites would not patronize black-run businesses, Stephan Thernstrom has argued that there may be "cultural" reasons why "Negroes have been even less prone to mount business ventures of their own than even the least entrepreneurially oriented of the immigrants." See Thernstrom, *The Other Bostonians*, 217–18, and Gerber, *Black Ohio and the Color Line*, 87–89, for a different position.

36. Eric Lott has argued that the black male body and its postures, specifically as they were commercially produced in the minstrel show, in capitalist societies is a "potentially subversive site because to recognize it fully is to recognize the exploitative organization of labor that structures their economies." See Lott, " 'The Seeming Counterfeit,' " 230–32.

37. In 1854, Suzey was killed after having been struck in the head by a paint mill at Bennett and Bulkly's. See "Melancholy Accident," *American Budget* (Geneva, N.Y.), 23 Mar. 1854.

38. Warren Hunting Smith, *Hobart and William Smith: The History of Two Colleges* (Geneva, N.Y.: Hobart and William Smith Colleges, 1972), 112–14. Smith notes that Isaiah G. DeGrasse entered Hobart in 1832 but left in 1835 before he received his degree; he was later ordained an Episcopal deacon and died in Jamaica in 1840. No other African American is known to have attended Hobart until the mid–twentieth century.

39. The National Council proceedings are reprinted in Blassingame, ed., *Frederick Douglass Papers*, vol. 3 of *Series One*, 64–74.

40. On antebellum labor competition, see Douglass, *My Bondage*, 188–89; Nash, *Forging Freedom*, 223, 274; Steward, *Twenty-Two Years a Slave*, 131; Litwack, *North of Slavery*, 101, 165–66; Gerber, *Black Ohio and the Color Line*, 28.

41. The term "industrial opportunity" is from Woodson, *A Century of Negro Migration*, 190.

42. In 1919, Whitaker was killed instantly by a train at the East Washington Street crossing adjacent to the Herendeen foundry. A contemporary newspaper article stated that he somehow was caught on the train and drawn under its wheels, but one 1950s account maintained that Whitaker had been pushing a wheelbarrow loaded with pig iron across the tracks when he was fatally struck.

43. "The Colored Brother. Grand Emancipation Celebration in Geneva," *Geneva Gazette*, 5 Aug. 1881.

44. Gerber, *Black Ohio and the Color Line*, 65; Robert S. Lynd and Helen Morrell Lynd, *Middletown: A Study in Modern American Culture* (New York: Harcourt, Brace and World, 1956), 479; Lee, *Negro and White in Connecticut Town*, 26–30. On foundry work, see Denby, *Indignant Heart*, 29–31.

45. See notes 36 and 40 in this chapter.

46. M. B. Faithful, "Geneva Business Review of 1944," *Geneva Daily Times*, 30 Dec. 1944.

47. Widner's "Echoes of Seneca Lake; or, Reminiscences of a Centenarian" was published originally in the *Geneva Courier* in 1879 and reprinted as part of "The Address of George S. Conover before the Waterloo Library and Historical Society" in Conover, *Kanadesaga and Geneva* (Geneva, N.Y.: Courier Steam Press, 1880). Norton, *Allerton Parish*, 87.

48. Carter, Stone, et al., *Reports of . . . the Convention of 1821*, 485. Eric Lott has argued, "If in an age of industry men were supposed to be frugal and productive, black men came to represent laziness and license, the determining factor in white men's dread of miscegenation." See Lott, " 'The Seeming Counterfeit,' " 235.

49. Brown, *Clotel*, 98.

50. Dollard, *Caste and Class in Southern Town*, 304, 392; Levine, *Black Culture and Black Consciousness*, 253.

51. Douglass, *My Bondage*, 155–57; Dollard, *Caste and Class in Southern Town*, 392, 406, 408; Levine, *Black Culture and Black Consciousness*, 318.

52. Levine, *Black Culture and Black Consciousness*, 421–24.

53. Douglass, *My Bondage*, 160–61.

54. See Robert Ladner, "Folk Music, Pholk Music and the Angry Children of Malcolm X," *Southern Folklore Quarterly* 34 (1970): 140–41. Both Ladner's and other theories on this point are cited in Levine, *Black Culture and Black Consciousness*, 212–15, 477n. 47.

4. Inclusion and Exclusion

1. Douglass, *My Bondage*, 92–93, 98; Steward, *Twenty-Two Years a Slave*, 83; Brown, "Narrative of the Life and Escape," 35–38.

2. Sydney A. Ahlstrom, *A Religious History of the American People* (Garden City, N.Y.: Image Books, 1975), 2: 93, 102; Cross, *Burned-Over District*, 217–21; Lott, " 'The Seeming Counterfeit,' " 254n. 61.

3. Nash, *Forging Freedom*, 95, 130; Douglass, *My Bondage*, 104; Schor, *Henry Highland Garnet*, 10–11; Ward, *Autobiography*, 79–87; [Loguen], *Rev. J. W. Loguen*, 340–41.

4. Records of the Presbyterian Church, Geneva, New York, reel 1; *Records of Trinity Church, Geneva*, vol. 1 of vestry records; Geneva Historical Society.

5. "Early Sunday Schools in Geneva," *Geneva Courier*, 19 July 1876.

6. *Doings of the Third Annual Convention of the Sunday School Teachers of the State of New York, Held in Brooklyn, October 5th, 6th and 7th, 1858* (New York: Biglow and Bleecker, 1858), 21–22, collections of the New York State Library, Albany.

7. Jupiter Hammon, *An Address to the Negroes, in the State of New-York* (Philadelphia: Daniel Humphreys, 1787), 10–11.

8. See Nash, *Forging Freedom*, 210, about Philadelphia's black preachers in the 1810s; Hammon, *An Address*, 5.

9. Lucas quoted in Drew, *The Refugee*, 73.

10. Brown, *Clotel*, 103–4; Douglass, *My Bondage*, 101, 98.

11. In the 1850s, the African-American Methodist exhorter Samuel Greene was sentenced to ten years in the Maryland Penitentiary for having a copy of Harriet Beecher Stowe's *Uncle Tom's Cabin* in his home; in Mississippi, a free black named John Dubarry was imprisoned for reading and circulating the speeches of anti-slavery Senators Charles Sumner and William B. Seward. See Clarke, "Condition of the Free Colored People," 247, 257. See also the account of North Carolina slave Lunsford Lane, quoted in Frazier, *Free Negro Family*, 41; Richard Wright's description of how he managed to borrow library books, in Wright, *Black Boy*, 268–70; and Johnson, *Autobiography*, 415, for an account of how *Uncle Tom's Cabin* affected him.

12. Ward, *Autobiography*, 61, 67.

13. Mirabito, "History of Black Education," had access to Geneva school district meeting records that cannot now be located. Her observations (p. 33) about the change from female to male teachers is confirmed in the *Gazette*'s coverage of the colored people's Sunday school exhibition. See "Remarks on the S. School Exhibition," *Geneva Gazette*, 13 July 1836.

14. "The Abolitionists," *Geneva Gazette*, 16 July 1834.

15. "Remarks on the S. School Exhibition."

16. Letter to the editor, *Geneva Gazette*, 24 Aug. 1836.

17. "Education," *Geneva Gazette*, 21 Nov. 1838. On legislation affecting New York schools, see Carlton Mabee, *Black Education in New York State: From Colonial to*

Modern Times (Syracuse: Syracuse Univ. Press, 1979). See also Mirabito, "History of Black Education."

18. Litwack, *North of Slavery*, 118–19, 123–24, 129–31. The *Impartial Citizen* of 1 May 1850 reprinted a chronology of these and other instances of discrimination in New England and New York, taken from a speech presented to the United States Senate by New Hampshire antislavery congressman John Parker Hale on 19 Mar. 1850.

19. David Walker's 1829 assessment of northern churches is cited in Litwack, *North of Slavery*, 233. See also Garnet, "Self-Help.—The Wants of Western New York"; Shadd, letter to the editor, *North Star*, 23 Mar. 1849; *Minutes of the National Convention of Colored Citizens* (Buffalo, 1843), 11; Ward, *Autobiography*, 30.

20. Litwack, *North of Slavery*, 197; Douglass, *My Bondage*, 215; Steward, "Address of the New York State Convention of Colored Citizens, to the People of the State" (New York, 1840), in Foner and Walker, eds., *Proceedings of the Black State Conventions*, 19.

21. *Records of the Baptist Church in Geneva, Constituted February* 8th 1826, collections of the First Baptist Church, Geneva. African-Americans Judith Gaten, Edward and Eliza Tompkins, Flora Lucas, Hannah and Emeline McQuon, John and Thomas Lee, Thomas Freeman, Garrett Kenney, and Peter Lincoln became members in 1837. But Lincoln, Freeman, and nine others—Anthony Freeman, Mary and John Bland, George and Phillis Bowley (or Bowles), Hannah Gaten, Charles Kenney, Reuben (possibly Roswell) Jeffrey, and Betsey Freeman—were dismissed from the church between 1837 and 1840. Robert Bland had been dismissed in 1832; Samuel Jeffrey, Almira Gaten, Catherine Lee, Eunice Nobles, and Betsey Graham had been excluded from membership for various offenses, including adultery and intemperance, before 1836. Other African-American Baptists listed in the meeting minutes included Nancy Jupiter, Mary Lee, Mary and Jane Kenney, Mary Gaten, Amy Tompkins, Amarrillus Bland, Mary Dixon, Jane Thompson, and Harriet Douglass. Many thanks to Rev. Daniel Benedict for allowing me access to this record book.

22. Ward's lecture was announced in *Geneva Courier*, 2 Nov. 1841.

23. Ahlstrom, *Religious History*, vol. 2, 106–11; Myra C. Glenn, "Going His Own Way: The Proslavery Views of Rev. Thomas K. Beecher" (Paper presented at "A Heritage Uncovered: The Black Experience in New York State," Elmira College, Elmira, N.Y., 21 Apr. 1989).

24. "Auburn Resolutions," *Impartial Citizen*, 8 Aug. 1849.

25. Myers's statement is in Blassingame, ed., *Frederick Douglass Papers*, Series one, vol. 3, 71–72. See Dana Nelson Salvino, "The Word in Black and White: Ideologies of Race and Literacy in Antebellum America," in Cathy N. Davidson, ed., *Reading in America: Literature & Social History* (Baltimore: Johns Hopkins Univ. Press, 1989), 140–58, for a discussion of the ideology and empirical reality of acquiring literacy skills among African Americans.

26. *Proceedings of the Colored National Convention . . . 1853*, 22–23.

27. Schor, *Henry Highland Garnet*, 4–5, 7–8, 13–15; on Oneida, see Cross, *Burned-Over District*, 234–35; 263. Garnet wrote a letter to the *North Star* from Peterboro dated 5 Dec. 1849; another in the 3 Feb. 1850 issue was written from Geneva. When Garnet actually settled in the village is not known, though he and his wife were recorded in the 1850 census.

28. Schor, *Henry Highland Garnet*, 44–45, 54–55.

29. Schor, *Henry Highland Garnet*, 29, 44–45, 102; W. C. N., "Progress in Geneva," *North Star*, 13 Apr. 1849.

30. W. C. N., "Progress in Geneva"; Catherine Hanchett, "New York Central College and Its Three Black Professors, 1849–1857" (Paper presented at "A Heritage Uncovered: The Black Experience in New York State," Elmira College, Elmira, New York, 20–22 Apr. 1989); Cross, *Burned-Over District*, 234–35.

31. Mirabito, "History of Black Education," 65.

32. In 1860, Jeffrey had fifty-seven students in his charge, and it is probable that he and his predecessors taught these large classes by themselves. In 1854, the total salary figure for instruction at High Street School was $95.43. Ten years later, Condol reported that he earned thirty-two dollars a month teaching at the school, so the 1854 salary figure probably represents the earnings of only one teacher.

33. "Shall All Our Public Schools Be Opened to Colored Citizens?" *Geneva Gazette*, 5 Jan. 1872; "Mr. Squigden Goes to the School Meeting, and Ventures His Say," *Geneva Gazette*, 9 Feb. 1872.

34. Fair Play, "A Few Words About Our Common Schools," *Geneva Courier*, 9 Nov. 1870.

35. Mirabito, "History of Black Education," 86; Conover, ed., *History of Ontario County*, 300–1; Brumberg, *Making of an Upstate Community*, 86; Litwack, *North of Slavery*, 132–33, 136; Field, *Politics of Race*, 29. Squigden's *Gazette* article intimated that school commissioners in Geneva, as in Rochester, had tried to amass Irish voters to help defeat the motion to integrate the schools. George J. Bland also made this charge at the African-American civil rights celebration in Geneva in August 1873, where he asserted that "a brigade of three hundred and fifty Irishmen" had forced the tabling of the African-American request for integrated schools. Douglass's comment about the Irish faction of the Rochester school board is cited in Litwack, *North of Slavery*, 133. See also "Equal School Privileges," *Impartial Citizen*, 21 Nov. 1849, whose "Colorphobia" column reprinted Douglass's account of the formal protest registered in Rochester.

36. Born in 1843, Condol must have been one of Garnet's students, and, like Garnet, he worked for the American Missionary Association. In 1862, when he taught at High Street School, he was also a subscription agent for the association's periodical *American Missionary*. Condol was one of only five African Americans from Upstate New York to be sent to teach in the freedmen's schools. He taught in Mississippi until 1878, when he died in the yellow fever epidemic. His correspondence with AMA officials in search of a teaching position is preserved in the American Missionary Association Archives, Amistad Research Center, Tulane University, New Orleans, La. See especially Nathan Tappan Condol to George Whipple, 1 Oct. 1864; Condol to Whipple, 13 Sept. 1864; W. H. Goodwin and M. Wheeler to American Missionary Association, 12 Sept. 1864; Thomas K. Beecher to AMA, 24 Oct. 1865; Condol to Whipple, 10 Oct. 1865; Beecher to AMA, 24 Oct. and 12 Dec. 1865.

37. Fair Play, "A Few Words," 5 Nov. 1870.

38. Mirabito, "History of Black Education," 87; "Shall All Our Public Schools Be Opened to Colored Citizens?" *Geneva Gazette*, 5 Jan. 1872; Mabley quoted in Levine, *Black Culture and Consciousness*, 365.

39. "Mr. Squigden Goes to the School Meeting."

40. Mirabito, "History of Black Education," 84–85; Fair Play, "A Few Words About Our Common Schools," *Geneva Courier*, 5 Nov. 1870. Many thanks to Steve O'Malley at the Geneva Historical Society for unearthing the two letters Fair Play

wrote to the *Courier*. Unfortunately, the great majority of the nineteenth-century issues of the *Courier* have not survived; they are particularly sparse in the important decades of the 1840s and 1870s. O'Malley found these clippings in an 1867 tax assessor's book in which they had been pasted over handwritten assessment records, along with other articles about Geneva schools, poetry, and funeral eulogies.

41. "Mr. Squigden Goes to the School Meeting"; " 'Civil Rights Triumphant,' " *Geneva Gazette*, 15 Aug. 1873; "Colored Pupils at the Union School," *Geneva Gazette*, 9 May 1873.

42. "Colored Pupils at the Union School," *Geneva Gazette*, 9 May 1873; "Colored Children in the Schools," *Geneva Gazette*, 2 Feb. 1872; "The Negroes in our Public Schools," *Geneva Gazette*, 25 Apr. 1873.

43. Mirabito, "History of Black Education," 90.

44. On integration, see Ward, *Autobiography*, 205; *Douglass' Monthly*, Mar. 1859, cited in Litwack, *North of Slavery*, 143; and Terrell, *Colored Woman in a White World*, 33. On the resistance to school integration elsewhere in the North, see Griffen and Griffen, *Natives and Newcomers*, 30, and Litwack, *North of Slavery*, 151.

45. A structure stood at the corner of High and Grove in 1856, but the lot was vacant in later maps until the 1890s. The Union Religious Society might have constituted itself originally at High Street Sabbath school when Garnet, a Presbyterian, preached there. See "Ladies' Fair," *Impartial Citizen*, 3 Oct. 1849. The "Ladies' Sewing Society" announced its plan to hold a fair in Penn Yan courthouse "for the benefit of H. H. Garnet." Julia W. Condol was the group's president, Nancy P. Lucas its secretary.

46. In an 1852 issue of the *Geneva Gazette*, Charles J. Folger advertised "for sale the building and lot, on Castle St., lately occupied by the colored people as a church." *Geneva Gazette*, 9 Apr. 1852; "Christian Convention at Geneva," *Impartial Citizen*, 24 Oct. 1849.

47. The Baptists might have moved their services to the High Street Chapel, where Garnet preached and the district school held its classes until 1853. Garnet was a professed Presbyterian, but whether the High Street church was Presbyterian or nondenominational is unclear.

48. See Emmons, *Story of Geneva*; "Donation Party," *Geneva Gazette* 42 (1859).

49. "Departed," *Geneva Gazette*, 15 May 1868.

50. "Celebration of the Twenty-First Anniversary of the West Indian Emancipation at Geneva," *Frederick Douglass Paper*, 5 Aug. 1859. See the Caleb Swan Diary, 19 Aug. 1866, for a description of "bigotry" in the Baptist Church; collections of Rose Hill, Geneva Historical Society.

51. Ahlstrom, *Religious History*, 156. For contemporary accounts of the allegorical understanding of spirituals and hymns, see Bradford, *Harriet: The Moses of Her People*, 33; Douglass, *My Bondage*, 117, 170, 170n; Washington, *Up from Slavery*, 39; Du Bois, *Souls of Black Folk*, 345; Denby, *Indignant Heart*, 4; Wright, *Black Boy*, 150, 92–93.

52. "Report of the Committee on Education," *Proceedings of the National Convention of Colored People* (Troy, 1847), 34.

53. *Proceedings of the Colored National Convention* (Rochester, 1853), 30; see also Foner and Walker, eds., *Proceedings of the Black State Conventions*, xiv, 81; Blassingame, ed., *Frederick Douglass Papers*, 64–73, for similar recommendations at other colored people's meetings.

54. Lindsay, "Economic Condition of the Negroes," 194; *Geneva Gazette*, 4 Dec. 1868; Washington, *Up from Slavery*, 37–38, 77, 92–94, 112, 135, 138.

55. Terrell, *Colored Woman in a White World*, 191; Du Bois, *Souls of Black Folk*, 247–48, 251.

56. See Du Bois, *Souls of Black Folk*, 338, for a description of the differences between northern and southern churches.

57. Levine, *Black Culture and Black Consciousness*, 164, 188; Wright, *Black Boy*, 165–66; Dollard, *Caste and Class in Southern Town*, 88.

58. Stella Cecere, "Story jogs memories; black church recalled," *Geneva Times*, undated clipping after 2 Jan. 1976; Cecere, "Empty church full of history" and "When did congregation move?," *Geneva Times*, 2 Jan. 1976; "Old Colored Chapel: High Street Edifice Figures Before Surrogate Judge Ditmars," *Geneva Tri-Weekly Gazette*, 16 Dec. 1901; "Father Brown Leaving St. Simon's," unpublished press release, about 1945.

59. For accounts of nineteenth-century conversion experiences, see "Trial of William Lincoln for the Murder of George Davie," *Geneva Gazette*, 25 Feb. 1870; Bradford, *Harriet Tubman*, 26; Levine, *Black Culture and Black Consciousness*, 18.

60. Levine, *Black Culture and Black Consciousness*, 244, 240.

61. Ahlstrom, *Religious History*, 162–63.

5. Accommodation and Action

1. Thornton is quoted in Nash, *Forging Freedom*, 101.

2. See in particular Levine, *Black Culture and Black Consciousness*, and Litwack, "Free at Last."

3. Jason Jeffrey to Henry Bush, 25 Jan. 1848, Post Family Papers, Department of Rare Books and Special Collections, Rush Rhees Library, University of Rochester.

4. In different censuses, Duffin listed his birthdate at different years between 1814 and 1820 and his birthplace variously as Canada, New York State generally, Wayne County, and Geneva.

5. Foner and Walker, eds., *Proceedings of the Black State Conventions*, 5, reprints the *Colored American*'s account of the Albany convention. In *Black Abolitionists* (New York: DaCapo, 1969), 75, Benjamin Quarles has cited an article from the 2 February 1839 issue of *Colored American* reporting on the 1839 annual meeting of this antislavery group. The newspaper noted that members had been asked "to ponder the question whether they can innocently or consistently use the products of slave labor." No mention of this organization appears in any local record, however.

6. Blassingame, *Frederick Douglass*, 54–55; Foner and Walker, eds., *Proceedings of the Black State Conventions*, 37–41.

7. Blassingame, *Frederick Douglass*, 55n; Foner and Walker, eds., *Proceedings of the Black State Conventions*, 79–83, 88–96; "Liberty Party Nominations," *Impartial Citizen*, 26 Sept. 1849.

8. In 1849, Douglass reported having argued with "a recreant *black man*, by the name of *Duffin*" in a speech he made near Geneva. See Blassingame, ed., *Frederick Douglass Papers*, vol. 3, 55n, 65–72; Field, *Politics of Race*, 232–33, 237.

9. Foner and Walker, eds., *Proceedings of the Black State Conventions*, 99–101.

10. Frothingham, *Gerrit Smith*, 102–3.

11. Ibid., 103–7; James W. Duffin to Gerrit Smith, 7 Sept. 1846, 18 Nov. 1846, Gerrit Smith Papers.

12. J. W. Duffin to Gerrit Smith, 9 Sept. 1846, Gerrit Smith Papers.

13. "Distribution of Lands to Colored Men Begun in 1846," vol. 88, box 107, Gerrit Smith Papers.

14. J. W. Duffin to Gerrit Smith, 18 Nov. 1846, 15 Feb. 1847, 17 Mar. 1847, 6 and 19 Apr. 1848, 24 Nov. 1849, Gerrit Smith Papers.

15. J. W. Duffin to Gerrit Smith, 1 and 19 Nov. 1849, Gerrit Smith Papers.

16. "Aid for the Impartial Citizen," *Impartial Citizen*, 25 July 1849; "Fair in Aid of the Impartial Citizen," *Impartial Citizen*, 5 Sept. 1849.

17. The story about Polk appears in Smith, *Hobart and William Smith Colleges*, 117–18. Frederick Douglass to Gerrit Smith, 15 July 1853, Gerrit Smith Papers; in an undated letter to Smith, Condol reported that *North Star* subscription income was declining and that he planned to publish a column, "a Salamagundi Department for Fred's paper." William Condol to Gerrit Smith, n.d., Gerrit Smith Papers. Jeffrey was listed as one of eight agets in New York State for the *North Star* beginning with the 28 Jan. 1848 issue, the eighth number in the first volume; he was listed on the executive committee of the Western New York Anti-Slavery Society in the *North Star*, 7 Jan. 1848; on Bland, see Conover, "Family Sketches," 273.

18. Foner and Walker, eds., *Proceedings of the Black State Conventions*, 14.

19. Nash, *Forging Freedom*, 100–2, 184–85; Ahlstrom, *Religious History*, 94.

20. Schor, *Henry Highland Garnet*, 120–21.

21. *Minutes of the National Convention of Colored Citizens* (Buffalo, 1843), 19–20; Village of Geneva minutes book, vol. 2, 9 July 1845; Geneva Historical Society.

22. David Walker's anti-colonizationist views are cited in Litwack, *North of Slavery*, 233. See also Foner and Walker, eds., *Proceedings of the Black State Conventions*, 14; Nash, *Forging Freedom*, 238; Douglass, *My Bondage and My Freedom*, 227–29; Steward, *Twenty-Two Years a Slave*, 327; Ann King to Julia Griffiths, *Frederick Douglass' Paper*, 1 Apr. 1852; and *Proceedings of the Colored National Convention* (Rochester, 1853), 39.

23. Nash, *Forging Freedom*, 243–45.

24. Ibid., 126; Conover, "Family Sketches," *History of Ontario County*, 275; Schor, *Henry Highland Garnet*, 127.

25. Douglass, *My Bondage*, 227–29.

26. Woodson, *Century of Negro Migration*, 79–80; Benjamin Quarles, *The Negro in the Civil War* (1953; reprint, New York: Russell and Russell, 1968), 152.

27. Schor, *Henry Highland Garnet*, 139–41, 159, 176, 177.

28. Mrs. S. H. Bradford, "History of Geneva," in Brigham, comp., *Brigham's Geneva . . . Directory . . . for 1862 and 1863* (Geneva, N.Y.: Geneva Gazette, 1862), 22.

29. Quarles, *Negro in the Civil War*, 156; Woodson, *Century of Negro Migration*, 80; Schor, *Henry Highland Garnet*, 182.

30. J. W. Duffin to W. H. Seward, 16 June 1863, Department of Rare Books and Special Collections, Rush Rhees Library, University of Rochester.

31. Quarles, *Negro in the Civil War*, 146–49.

32. Ibid., 8–9; 157; 184–85; William Seraile, "The Struggle to Raise Black Regiments in New York State, 1861–1864," *New York Historical Society Quarterly* (July 1974): 220–21; *Rochester Union-Advertiser*, 4 Apr. 1863; "Negro Enlistments—How the Project Works," *Geneva Gazette*, 3 Apr. 1963. Adjutant General of Massachusetts, comp., *Massachusetts Soldiers, Sailors, and Marines in the Civil War*, vol. 4 (Norwood, Mass.: Norwood Press, 1932), which lists residences of all those mustered into the 54th and 55th Colored Regiments, shows no troops from Geneva.

33. Of about nine thousand African-American men in New York State eligible to serve in 1864, 4,125 ultimately enlisted. In Geneva, twenty of forty-one eligible African-American men were recorded or known to have served in either the Union Army or Navy. See Quarles, *Negro in the Civil War*, 188–91; William Seraile, "The Struggle to

Raise Black Regiments in New York State, 1861–1864," *New York Historical Society Quarterly* (July 1974): 221–31; Frederick Phisterer, comp., *New York in the War of the Rebellion, 1861 to 1865,* 3d ed. (Albany, N.Y.: J. B. Lyon, 1912), 22, 91; "A Negro Regiment," *Geneva Gazette,* 15 Aug. 1862; "The Colored Troops," *Geneva Gazette,* 22 Jan. 1864.

34. As early as 1805, Philadelphia's African Americans had been hounded away from Fourth of July festivities at Independence Hall. See Nash, *Forging Freedom,* 177; Forten, "Letters from a Man of Colour," 8. On the deliberate rejection of the Fourth of July among African Americans in New York City in the 1820s, see Schor, *Henry Highland Garnet,* 5. Canadian and American blacks still commemorate West Indian emancipation in early August at Toronto's annual "Caribana" parade and celebration. See Robert Fulford, "Into the Heart of the Matter," *Rotunda* 24, 1 (Summer 1991): 22.

35. *Ithaca Chronicle,* cited in Horne, "Ithaca's Black Community," 19.

36. "Celebration of the Twenty-First Anniversary of the West Indian Emancipation at Geneva," *Frederick Douglass Paper,* 5 Aug. 1859.

37. Achilles, "The First of August," *Impartial Citizen,* 13 Mar. 1850.

38. "The Emancipation Jubilee," *Geneva Gazette,* 28 Aug. 1868.

39. Ibid.; "The Colored Brother," *Geneva Gazette,* 5 Aug. 1881.

40. *Geneva Gazette,* 5 Aug. 1864. The title of this article is illegible.

41. *The Geneva Ledger,* 30 July 1859.

42. Blassingame, ed., *Frederick Douglass Papers,* vol. 3, 366–69, 386–87.

43. Village of Geneva records, book 4, 417.

44. Condol to Whipple, 21 Apr. 1866, AMA Archives.

45. "The Celebration," *Geneva Gazette,* 5 July 1881; "The Colored Brother," *Geneva Gazette,* 5 Aug. 1881; *Geneva Advertiser,* 9 Aug. 1881.

46. *Geneva Gazette,* 15 Mar. 1871; " 'Civil Rights Triumphant.' Celebration of the People of Color at Geneva," *Geneva Gazette,* 15 Aug. 1873; "Keeping to the Question," *Brother Jonathan,* 2 October 1858. See also G. M. M. Mundy, "Geneva Reminiscences," *Geneva Gazette,* 15 Mar. 1872, for a recollection of the 1850s debating club. Smith, *Hobart and William Smith Colleges,* 117, also mentions the 1850s debates.

47. "Fred Douglass," *Geneva Gazette,* 4 Oct. 1872.

48. "Diabolical Outrage. . ." and "Suffrage to Negroes," *Geneva Gazette,* 11 Aug. 1865.

49. B. F. Cleggett to Gerrit Smith, 1 Apr. 1870, Gerrit Smith Papers; Geneva village records, book 4, 128, Geneva Historical Society.

50. *Geneva Gazette,* 13 May 1870. Dolores Hayden, "The Power of Place: Exploring the Partnership of Public History and Public Art" (Paper presented at the New England Museum Association annual meeting, Lowell, Mass., 8 Oct. 1991) helped clarify my thinking about the significance of territory in studying how different groups occupy and use a city.

51. Folger family papers, Geneva Historical Society; Frothingham, *Gerrit Smith,* 358. Cleggett's employment questionnaire and resignation are in the National Archives; many thanks to Matt Mulcahy of the Smithsonian Institution's National Museum of American History for his help in locating them.

52. See the *Geneva Gazette,* 4 Dec. 1868; "Colored Jubilee Singers," *Geneva Gazette,* 6 Oct. 1872; *Geneva Gazette,* 3, 10, and 17 Mar. 1876.

53. "The First Colored Chautauqua," *Geneva Gazette,* 10 Aug. 1894; *Geneva Gazette,* 24 Aug. 1894.

54. See the comments of Chesnut and others in Litwack, "Free at Last," 141–49;

Brown in cited in Dorothy Sterling, ed., *We Are Your Sisters: Black Women in the Nineteenth Century* (New York: Norton, 1984), 288.

55. The Monrovia Society of 1894 may have been a lodge of the Knights of Pythias. The formation of this African-American chapter was disputed by local whites, who claimed that neither the Masons nor the Knights permitted, much less recognized, colored lodges. Local African Americans denied this claim in the newspaper and asserted the lodge had been legitimately incorporated. See *Geneva Advertiser*, 12 June 1894. On the school pageant, see "Pageant is Presented Depicting Growth of Local School System," *Geneva Daily Times*, 19 May 1939.

56. *Geneva Gazette*, 14 Dec. 1911; see also Minor Myers Jr., and Dorothy Ebersole, "Baseball in Geneva: Notes to Accompany an Exhibition at the Prouty Chew Museum" (typed pamphlet, 1988), collections of Geneva Historical Society.

57. Arch Merrill, "In Geneva Art Kenney Looks After the Memories," *Rochester Democrat and Chronicle*, 2 Aug. 1959. See also Thomas M. Johnson, "The Most Unforgettable Character I've Met," *Reader's Digest*, Sept. 1961, 168D–F; Arch Merrill, "A Living Hobart Legend," *Rochester Democrat and Chronicle*, 3 June 1856; Merrill, "Hobart's Living Legend," in Merrill, *Our Goodly Heritage* (New York: American Book–Stratford Press, 1957), 186–94; Al Laney, "Hobart in Salute to 'Old Art' Kenney," *New York Herald Tribune*, 29 Dec. 1955.

58. On Henry McDonald, see Norm Jollow, "Henry," in "Press Box Patter," *Geneva Daily Times*, 3 July 1976; Elizabeth Voisin, "1st Black in Pro Football Dies," clipping from unidentified newspaper, 14 June 1976; "First Black Pro Gridder Dies at 85," *Syracuse Post-Standard*, 14 June 1976; Scott Pitoniak, "First Black Pro-Football Player Ran His Way into Hall of Fame," *Rochester Democrat and Chronicle*, n.d. (about 1967); "Henry McDonald, Famed Athlete, Dies," *Geneva Times*, 14 June 1976; Dave Rosenbloom, "Henry McDonald Reminisces," *Rochester Democrat and Chronicle*, undated (about 1960); see also Edna Rust and Art Rust Jr., *Art Rust's Illustrated History of the Black Athlete* (Garden City, N.Y.: Doubleday, 1985), 227–30.

59. "Ku Klux Klan to Meet Here Tomorrow," *Geneva Daily Times*, 9 Oct. 1925; "Knights of the Burning Cross Put to Rout by Elements," *Geneva Daily Times*, 10 Oct. 1925; "Geneva's Klan Assembly Spoiled by the Weather," *Geneva Daily Times*, 12 Oct. 1925.

Epilogue

1. The story of a young black girl or boy named Epaminondas who steals butter and is apprehended in the same way that Sam Thornton is alleged to have been is part of the folklore whites growing up in the 1920s and 1930s were told about blacks. Moreover, the well-known Geneva puppeteer Paula McKay performed a play called "Epaminondas and her Mammy" in Geneva homes and clubs in the middle decades of this century. Epaminondas was a theban military leader known as a great tactician. See unidentified correspondent to "My Dear Niece," 22 Mar. 1913, Hollywood, Ill. box 83, folder 1:10, Geneva Historical Society; *Geneva Gazette*, 22 Dec. 1910.

2. "My Dear Niece"; *Geneva Gazette*, 22 Dec. 1910. Gideon Mundy wrote about Thornton in local newspapers in the 1870s, 1880s, and 1890s; these articles were cited in Smith, *Hobart and William Smith Colleges*, 127. Smith states that "Sammy Dog-in-the-Well" had a contract with the state prison, probably at Auburn, to dispose of cadavers.

3. Douglass, *My Bondage*, 118–19; see also Wright, *Black Boy*, 283–84.

4. Ralph Ellison, *Invisible Man* (1947; reprint, New York: Vintage, 1989), xvi. Lott, " 'The Seeming Counterfeit,' " 225–27, suggests how whites understood antebellum blackface minstrelsy: "when . . . Northern white men 'blacked up' and imitated what they supposed was black dialect, music, and dance, some people, without derision, heard Negroes singing." Lott's argument that minstrel shows demonstrated "a complex dialectic: an unsteady but continual oscillation between fascination with blackness and fearful ridicule of it" seems to apply equally to these twentieth-century events.

5. Washington, *Up from Slavery*, 215.

6. Dollard, *Caste and Class in Southern Town*, 65, 257.

7. Ibid.

8. Levine has suggested that the popularity of trickster tales in African-American folklore endures because they "emphasize the necessity of comprehending the ways of the powerful, for only through such understanding could the weak endure." See *Black Culture and Black Consciousness*, 101–15. On blacks as exotics, see Clarke, "Condition of the Free Colored People," 247; Terrell, *Colored Woman in a White World*, 383–84; and Johnson, quoted in Franklin, "Introduction," in *Three Negro Classics*, xv.

9. Leon F. Litwack, "Free at Last," in Hareven, ed., *Anonymous Americans*, 141–45. See also Dollard, *Caste and Class in Southern Town*, 308, and Brown, *Clotel*, 154.

10. Johnson, *Autobiography of an Ex-Colored Man*, 479. Prude, in " 'To Look Upon the Lower Sort,' " 154–55, discusses the significance of clothing, particularly of "dressing up," as one of the "visual strategies laboring Americans used to announce their own priorities and purposes" in the eighteenth century; like the garments fugitive slaves wore or carried with them, Thornton's clothing elicited similar attention in nineteenth-century Geneva. While Prude sees dressing up as a possible "quiet bid for equality and autonomy," I see this form of display as protest in a situation where equality and autonomy are not perceived to be possible.

11. Walker quoted in Litwack, *North of Slavery*, 232–33; Litwack, "Free at Last," 167.

Bibliography

Blassingame, John, ed. *The Frederick Douglass Papers*. Vol. 3 of *Series One: Speeches, Debates, and Interviews*. New Haven and London: Yale Univ. Press, 1989.

Brown, William Wells. "Narrative of the Life and Escape of William Wells Brown." In William Wells Brown, *Clotel; or, The President's Daughter: A Narrative of Slave Life in the United States*. 1853. Reprint. New York: Carol, 1969.

Clarke, James Freeman. "Condition of the Free Colored People of the United States." *Christian Examiner* 66, no. 5 (Mar. 1859): 246–65.

Clark-Lewis, Elizabeth. "This Work Had A End: The Transition from Live-in to Day Work." Working Paper 2 in "Southern Women: The Intersection of Race, Class and Gender." Center for Research of Women, Memphis State Univ. et al., 1985.

Conover, George S. *Kanadesaga and Geneva*. Geneva, N.Y.: Courier Steam Press, 1880.

———, ed. *History of Ontario County, New York*. Syracuse, N.Y.: D. Mason, 1893.

Denby, Charles. *Indignant Heart: A Black Worker's Journal*. Detroit: Wayne State Univ. Press, 1989.

DeVries, James E. *Race and Kinship in a Midwestern Town: The Black Experience in Monroe, Michigan, 1900–1915*. Urbana: Univ. of Illinois Press, 1984.

Dillard, J. L. *Black Names*. Vol. 13 in *Contributions to the Sociology [of] Language*, edited by Joshua A. Fishman. The Hague: Mouton, 1976.

Douglass, Frederick. *My Bondage and My Freedom*. 1855. Reprint. Urbana: Univ. of Illinois Press, 1987.

Drew, Benjamin. *The Refugee: A North-Side View of Slavery*. 1855. Reprint. Reading, Mass.: Addison-Wesley, 1969.

Du Bois, W. E. B. *The Souls of Black Folk.* 1903. In W. E. B. Du Bois, *Writings.* New York: Library of America, 1986. 357–548.

Ellison, Ralph. *Invisible Man.* 1947. Reprint. New York: Vintage, 1989.

Field, Phyllis F. *The Politics of Race in New York: The Struggle for Black Suffrage in the Civil War Era.* Ithaca: Cornell Univ. Press, 1982.

Foner, Philip S., and George E. Walker. *New York, Pennsylvania, Indiana, Michigan, Ohio.* Vol. 1 of *Proceedings of the Black State Conventions, 1840–1865.* Philadelphia: Temple Univ. Press, 1979.

Forten, James. "Letters from a Man of Colour, On a Late Bill Before the Senate of Pennsylvania." N.p., 1813.

Frazier, E. Franklin. *The Free Negro Family.* 1932. Reprint. New York: Arno and New York Times, 1968.

Frothingham, Octavius Brooks. *Gerrit Smith: A Biography.* New York: G. P. Putnam's Sons, 1878.

Galvin, Emma Brown. "The Lore of the Negro in Central New York." Ph.D. diss., Cornell Univ., 1943.

Gerber, David. *Black Ohio and the Color Line, 1860–1915.* Urbana: Univ. of Illinois Press, 1978.

Gutman, Herbert. *The Black Family in Slavery and Freedom, 1750–1925.* New York: Vintage, 1976.

Hammon, Jupiter. *An Address to the Negroes in the State of New-York.* Philadelphia: Daniel Humphreys, 1787.

Hareven, Tamara K., ed. *Anonymous Americans: Explorations in Nineteenth-Century Social History.* Englewood Cliffs, N.J.: Prentice-Hall, 1971.

Haynes, Elizabeth Ross. "Negroes in Domestic Service in the United States." *Journal of Negro History* 8, no. 4 (Oct. 1923): 384–442.

Hays, William C., and Charles H. Mindel. "Extended Kinship Relations in Black and White Families." *Journal of Marriage and the Family* 35 (Feb. 1973): 47–53.

Hershberg, Theodore. "Free Blacks in Antebellum Philadelphia: A Study of Ex-Slaves, Freeborn, and Socioeconomic Decline." In *Philadelphia: Work, Space, and Family in the 19th Century,* edited by Theodore Hershberg. Oxford: Oxford Univ. Press, 1981.

Hine, Darlene Clark, ed. *The State of Afro-American History: Past, Present, and Future.* Baton Rouge: Louisiana State Univ. Press, 1986.

Horton, James Oliver, and Lois E. Horton. *Black Bostonians: Family Life and Community Struggle in the Antebellum North.* New York: Holmes and Meier, 1979.

Johnson, Daniel M., and Rex R. Campbell. *Black Migration in America: A Social Demographic History.* Durham, N.C.: Duke Univ. Press, 1981.

Lammermeier, Paul J. "The Urban Black Family of the Nineteenth Century: A Study of Black Family Structure in the Ohio Valley, 1850–1880." *Journal of Marriage and the Family* 35 (Aug. 1973): 439–51.

Landon, Fred. "The Negro Migration to Canada after the Passing of the Fugitive Slave Act." *Journal of Negro History* 5, no. 1 (Jan. 1920): 22–36.

Larson, Olaf F., and Emmit F. Sharp. *Migratory Farm Workers in the Atlantic Coast Stream: 1. Changes in New York, 1953 and 1957.* Ithaca: New York State College of Agriculture, 1960.

Levine, Lawrence W. *Black Culture and Black Consciousness: Afro-American Folk Thought from Slavery to Freedom.* Oxford: Oxford Univ. Press, 1977.

Lieberson, Stanley. "Generational Differences among Blacks in the North." *American Journal of Sociology* 79 (Nov. 1973): 550–65.

Lindsay, Arnett G. "Economic Conditions of the Negroes of New York Prior to 1861." *Journal of Negro History* 6, no. 2 (Apr. 1921): 190–200.

Litwack, Leon F. "Free at Last." In *Anonymous Americans: Explorations in Nineteenth-Century Social History,* edited by Tamara K. Hareven, 131–71. Englewood Cliffs, N.J.: Prentice-Hall, 1971.

———*North of Slavery: The Negro in the Free States, 1790–1860.* Chicago: Univ. of Chicago Press, 1961.

[Loguen, the Rev. J. W.]. *The Rev. J. W. Loguen, as a Slave and as a Freeman: A Narrative of Real Life.* Syracuse, N.Y.: J. G. K. Truair, 1859.

Lott, Eric. "'The Seeming Counterfeit': Racial Politics and Early Blackface Minstrelsy." *American Quarterly* 43, no. 2 (June 1991): 223–54.

Lynd, Robert S., and Helen Merrell Lynd. *Middletown: A Study in Modern American Culture.* New York: Harcourt, Brace and World, 1956.

Mabee, Carlton. *Black Education in New York State From Colonial to Modern Times.* Syracuse, N.Y.: Syracuse Univ. Press, 1979.

Marks, Carole. *Farewell—We're Good and Gone: The Great Black Migration.* Bloomington: Indiana Univ. Press, 1989.

Minutes of the National Convention of Colored Citizens: Held at Buffalo, On the 15th, 16th, 17th, 18th and 19th of August, 1843. . . . New York: Pierce and Reed, 1843.

Mirabito, Pamela Y. "History of Black Education: Nineteenth Century Geneva, New York." M.A. thesis, State Univ. of New York, College at Cortland, 1989.

Nash, Gary B. *Forging Freedom: The Formation of Philadelphia's Black Community, 1720–1840.* Cambridge: Harvard Univ. Press, 1988.

Nelkin, Dorothy. "A Response to Marginality: The Case of Migrant Farm Workers." *British Journal of Sociology* 20 (1969): 375–89.

Proceedings of the Colored National Convention, Held in Rochester, July 6th, 7th and 8th, 1853. Rochester, N.Y.: Frederick Douglass' Paper, 1853.

Proceedings of the National Convention of Colored People. Troy, N.Y., 1847.

Prude, Jonathan. "'To Look upon the Lower Sort': Runaway Ads and the Appearance of Unfree Laborers in America, 1750–1800." *Journal of American History* 78, no. 1 (June 1991): 124–59.

Puckett, Newbell Niles. *Black Names in America: Origins and Usage.* Boston: G. K. Hall, 1975.

Salvino, Dana Nelson. "The Word in Black and White: Ideologies of Race and Literacy in Antebellum America." In *Reading in America: Literature and Social History*, edited by Cathy N. Davidson, 140–56. Baltimore: The Johns Hopkins Univ. Press, 1989.

Schor, Joel. *Henry Highland Garnet: A Voice of Black Radicalism in the Nineteenth Century*. Westport, Conn.: Greenwood, 1977.

Seraile, William. "The Struggle to Raise Black Regiments in New York State, 1861–1864." *New York Historical Society Quarterly* (July 1974): 215–33.

Siebert, Wilbur H. *The Underground Railroad from Slavery to Freedom*. New York: Macmillan, 1898.

Steward, Austin. *Twenty-Two Years a Slave, and Forty Years a Freeman*. Rochester, N.Y.: William Alling, 1857.

Still, William. *The Underground Railroad: A Record of Facts, Authentic Narratives, Letters, & c., Narrating the Hardships, Hair-Breadth Escapes, and Death Struggles of the Slaves in Their Efforts for Freedom, as Told by Themselves and Others*. Philadelphia: Porter and Coates, 1872.

Sutherland, Cara A., ed. *A Heritage Uncovered: The Black Experience in Upstate New York, 1800–1925*. Elmira, N.Y.: Chemung County Historical Society, 1988.

Terrell, Mary Church. *A Colored Woman in a White World*. Washington, D.C.: Ransdell, 1940.

Thernstrom, Stephan. *The Other Bostonians: Poverty and Progress in the American Metropolis*. Cambridge, Mass.: Harvard Univ. Press, 1973.

———. *Poverty and Progress: Social Mobility in a Nineteenth-Century City*. Cambridge, Mass.: Harvard Univ. Press, 1964.

Ward, Samuel Ringgold. *Autobiography of a Fugitive Negro*. 1855. Reprint. New York: Arno and New York Times, 1968.

Woodson, Carter G. *A Century of Negro Migration*. Washington D.C.: The Association for the Study of Negro Life and History, 1918.

Wright, Richard. *Black Boy: A Record of Childhood and Youth*. 1937. Reprint. New York: Harper and Row, 1989.

———. "Introduction: How 'Bigger' Was Born." In Wright, Richard, *Native Son*. 1940. Reprint. New York: Harper and Row, 1989.

Yoshpe, Harry B. "Record of Slave Manumissions in Albany, 1800–28." *The Journal of Negro History* 26, no. 4 (Oct. 1941): 499–522.

Index

Italic page number denotes illustration.